Noyes. Lori

Organ Procurement and Transplantation

ASSESSING CURRENT POLICIES AND THE POTENTIAL IMPACT OF THE DHHS FINAL RULE

Committee on Organ Procurement and Transplantation Policy
Division of Health Sciences Policy
INSTITUTE OF MEDICINE

NATIONAL ACADEMY PRESS
Washington, D.C.

NATIONAL ACADEMY PRESS • 2101 Constitution Avenue, N.W. • Washington, D.C. 20418

NOTICE: The project that is the subject of this report was approved by the Governing Board of the National Research Council, whose members are drawn from the councils of the National Academy of Sciences, the National Academy of Engineering, and the Institute of Medicine. The members of the committee responsible for the report were chosen for their special competences and with regard for appropriate balance.

The Institute of Medicine was chartered in 1970 by the National Academy of Sciences to enlist distinguished members of the appropriate professions in the examination of policy matters pertaining to the health of the public. In this, the Institute acts under both the Academy's 1863 congressional charter responsibility to be an adviser to the federal government and its own initiative in identifying issues of medical care, research, and education. Dr. Kenneth I. Shine is president of the Institute of Medicine.

Support for this project was provided by the General Accounting Office (Contract No. N00014-98-1-0789) and the Greenwall Foundation (Award No. 3302). The views presented in this report are those of the Committee on Organ Procurement and Transplantation Policy and are not necessarily those of the funding organizations.

Library of Congress Cataloging-in-Publication Data

Institute of Medicine (U.S.). Committee on Organ Procurement and Transplantation Policy.
Organ procurement and transplantation : assessing current policies and the potential impact of the DHHS final rule / Committee on Organ Procurement and Transplantation Policy, Division of Health Sciences Policy, Institute of Medicine.
p. ; cm.
Includes bibliographical references and index.
ISBN 0-309-06578-X (casebound)
1. Procurement of organs, tissues, etc.--Law and legislation--United States. 2. Transplantation of organs, tissues, etc.--Law and legislation--United States. I. Title.
[DNLM: 1. Organ Procurement--legislation & jurisprudence--United States. 2. Health Services Accessibility--United States. 3. Organ Transplantation--legislation & jurisprudence--United States. 4. Tissue Donors--legislation & jurisprudence--United States. WO 690 I59o 1999]
RD129.5 .I57 1999
362.1'783'0973--dc21

99-044515

The full text of this report is available on-line at **www.nap.edu/readingroom.** For more information about the Institute of Medicine, visit the IOM home page at **www.iom.edu.**

Printed in the United States of America

The serpent has been a symbol of long life, healing, and knowledge among almost all cultures and religions since the beginning of recorded history. The image adopted as a logotype by the Institute of Medicine is based on a relief carving from ancient Greece, now held by the Staatliche Museen in Berlin.

COMMITTEE ON ORGAN PROCUREMENT AND TRANSPLANTATION POLICY

EDWARD D. PENHOET (*Chair*), Dean, School of Public Health, University of California at Berkeley

NAIHUA DUAN, Statistics Group, RAND Corporation, Santa Monica (until May 6, 1999)

NANCY NEVELOFF DUBLER, Director, Division of Bioethics, Montefiore Medical Center, Professor of Bioethics, Albert Einstein College of Medicine, New York

CHARLES K. FRANCIS, President, Charles R. Drew University of Medicine and Science, Los Angeles

ROBERT D. GIBBONS, Professor of Biostatistics, Departments of Biostatistics and Psychiatry, University of Illinois at Chicago

BARBARA GILL, Clinical Nurse Specialist, Abilene Cardiothoracic and Vascular Surgery of Texas, Abilene

EVA GUINAN, Associate Professor of Pediatrics, Harvard Medical School, Boston

MAUREEN HENDERSON, Professor Emeritus of Epidemiology and Medicine, University of Washington, Seattle

SUZANNE T. ILDSTAD, Director, Institute for Cellular Therapeutics, University of Louisville

PATRICIA A. KING, Carmack Waterhouse Professor of Law, Medicine, Ethics, and Public Policy, Georgetown University, Washington, D.C.

MANUEL MARTINEZ-MALDONADO, Vice Provost for Research and Professor of Medicine, Oregon Health Sciences University, Portland

GEORGE E. MCLAIN, Assistant Chief of Anesthesiology, Martin Memorial Medical Center, Stuart, Florida

DAVID MELTZER, Assistant Professor, Section of General Internal Medicine, Department of Economics, and Harris School of Public Policy Studies, University of Chicago

JOSEPH E. MURRAY, Professor of Surgery, Emeritus, Harvard Medical School, Boston

DOROTHY NELKIN, University Professor, New York University Department of Sociology and School of Law, New York

MITCHELL W. SPELLMAN, Director of Academic Alliances and International Exchange Programs, Harvard Medical International, Harvard Medical School, Boston

IOM Project Staff

ANDREW POPE, Director, Division of Health Sciences Policy
CHRISTINE DOMZAL, Senior Program Officer (until 5/7/99)
SARAH PITLUCK, Research Assistant
ALDEN CHANG, Project Assistant
GLEN SHAPIRO, Research Assistant (until 6/4/99)
STEPHANIE SMITH, Research Associate (until 6/1/99)
THELMA COX, Senior Project Assistant
CARLOS GABRIEL, Financial Associate

IOM Auxiliary Staff

NICOLE AMADO, Project Assistant
JENNIFER COHEN, Research Assistant
JANE DURCH, Senior Editorial Associate
MICHAEL EDINGTON, Managing Editor
CHARLES EVANS, JR., Senior Advisor for Clinical and Biomedical Research
SUSAN FOURT, Librarian
FREDERICK J. MANNING, Senior Program Officer
VIVIAN NOLAN, Research Associate
PHILLIP RENZULLO, Staff Officer
MELVIN H. WORTH, Jr., Scholar-in-Residence

Consultant

KATHI HANNA

Copy Editors

FLORENCE POILLON
BETH GYORGY

REVIEWERS

This report has been reviewed in draft form by individuals chosen for their diverse perspectives and technical expertise, in accordance with procedures approved by the National Research Council's Report Review Committee. In particular, reviewers were sought to provide a broad spectrum of views and a wide variety of positions on relevant transplantation issues. The purpose of this independent review is to provide candid and critical comments that will assist the Institute of Medicine in making the published report as sound as possible and to ensure that the report meets institutional standards for objectivity, evidence, and responsiveness to the study charge. The review comments and draft manuscript remain confidential to protect the integrity of the deliberative process. The committee wishes to thank the following individuals for their participation in the review of this report:

NANCY L. ASCHER, School of Medicine, University of California at San Francisco
J. STEVENSON BYNON, Division of Transplantation, University of Alabama at Birmingham
CLIVE O. CALLENDER, Transplant Center, Howard University College of Medicine, Washington, D.C.
ANTHONY M. D'ALESSANDRO, Department of Surgery, Medical School, University of Wisconsin, Madison
CHARLES FISKE, National Transplant Action Committee, Brookline, Massachusetts
RICHARD D. HASZ, JR., Transplant Coordinator Services, Gift of Life Donor Program, Philadelphia
ROBERT S.D. HIGGINS, Thoracic Transplantation, Henry Ford Hospital, Detroit
LARRY G. HUNSICKER, Department of Internal Medicine, College of Medicine, University of Iowa
ALAN N. LANGNAS, Section of Transplantation, University of Nebraska Medical Center, Omaha
ELAINE L. LARSON, Columbia University School of Nursing, New York
BERNARD LO, Program in Medical Ethics, University of California at San Francisco
JOSHUA MILLER, Division of Transplantation, University of Miami School of Medicine, Miami
JAMES H. SOUTHARD, Department of Surgery, Medical School, University of Wisconsin, Madison
HAROLD C. SOX, Jr., School of Medicine, Dartmouth University, Lebanon, New Hampshire
MICHAEL A. STOTO, Department of Biostatistics and Epidemiology, George Washington University, Washington, D.C.
CHARLES THOMAS, Samaritan Transplant Services, Phoenix

KENNETH E. THORPE, Department of Health Systems Management, Tulane University

In addition to comments that the committee received from reviewers listed above, technical reviews of background material, and certain descriptive chapters, were also provided by representatives from Department of Health and Human Services and United Network for Organ Sharing. The committee also had access to and received input and technical assistance from transplant surgeons, experts on organ procurement, donor's families, and transplant recipients who served as expert liaisons. The 22 expert liaisons are listed in Appendix A.

Although the individuals listed above have provided constructive comments and suggestions, it must be emphasized that responsibility for the final content of this report rests entirely with the authoring committee and the Institute of Medicine.

Foreword

The procurement, allocation, and transplantation of human solid organs have undergone enormous change during the 15 years since enactment of the National Organ Transplant Act in 1984. The number and type of human organ transplants continue to increase rapidly. Although transplantation is increasingly effective and the quality of life of transplant recipients continues to improve, the total number of donor organs available falls significantly below the need for them. The resulting tension between supply and demand has raised many questions about organ procurement and transplantation policies.

In the fall of 1998, Congress requested that the Institute of Medicine (IOM) conduct a study to evaluate the potential impact of pending regulations developed by the Department of Health and Human Services on a set of important specific issues related to organ procurement and transplantation. The study was conducted by a committee of recognized experts who volunteered their time to provide an objective scientific analysis of the issues and the available relevant data. In assembling the Committee on Organ Procurement and Transplantation Policy, the Institute cast a broad net, asking for suggestions from all relevant parties. The committee that was appointed, and who authored this report, includes experts representing many areas of science, health, economics, ethics, and patient concerns. The committee does not include any currently practicing solid organ transplant surgeons. This was done to avoid direct conflicts of interest and out of a concern that the strong viewpoints publicly expressed by many transplant surgeons might adversely affect the objectivity of the committee's deliberations. The committee did, however, have access to and receive input and technical assistance from transplant surgeons, experts on organ procurement, donor's families, and transplant patients.

The committee conducted information-gathering sessions in two publicly announced open meetings. The organizations and individuals who made presentations are listed in Appendix A. In addition to these open meetings, the committee received a large amount of written material from a variety of sources, and conducted original research and analyses on an extensive data base provided by the United Network for Organ Sharing. The committee carefully and thoroughly evaluated the information available in making its assessment, reaching conclusions, and developing recommendations. During the course of the study, one committee member elected to resign when he learned that the organization that employed him was considering a letter of intent for the Organ Procurement and Transplantation Network contract, thus creating the possibility of a perceived conflict of interest.

As part of the normal process of developing an IOM report, an additional group of independent peer reviewers—who were not known to the committee during the report review process—then reviewed the committee's report to ensure that it met institutional standards for objectivity, evidence, and responsiveness to the study charge. This process involved review by individuals who had expressed strong opinions with regard to existing transplantation policies and procedures, as well as the pending Final Rule. The reviewers were selected to represent a broad range of quite different perspectives. The committee considered the reviewers' criticisms and suggestions in the course of finalizing its report as required by National Research Council procedures, but the report's conclusions and recommendations are solely those of the committee.

The committee worked under an extraordinarily tight deadline to provide its report to Congress during the current legislative session. Nonetheless, the report is thorough, comprehensive, and thoughtful, and reflects the unanimous view of the committee. We are deeply grateful to this hard-working group of volunteers who completed a difficult and challenging task in a timely and effective manner.

Kenneth I. Shine, M.D.
President, Institute of Medicine

Preface

The system of solid organ transplantation in the United States involves a wide and complex network of participants, including donor families, surgeons, physicians, nurses, hospitals, transplant centers, organ procurement organizations, and federal agencies and contractors. These individuals and organizations strive to optimize the health and survival of patients who have received or are waiting for transplanted solid organs. Under ideal circumstances, there would be a suitable donor organ for every person who needs one. Despite the best efforts of all involved, however, the availability of organs falls significantly short of current demand. Moreover, despite the best-intentioned efforts of those involved, many patients find the system confusing and difficult to understand—leading, in some cases, to distrust of the very system designed to help them.

In February 1999, the Institute of Medicine (IOM) formed the Committee on Organ Procurement and Transplantation Policy in response to a request from Congress to review proposed changes in the current system of organ procurement and transplantation. The so-called "Final Rule" of the Department of Health and Human Services would make several such changes as part of the stated purpose of achieving an organ allocation system that (a) functions as much as technologically feasible on a nationwide basis, (b) provides for effective oversight of the current network of operations, and (c) offers better information about transplantation to patients, families, and health care providers. The impetus behind parts of the Final Rule is a desire to correct apparent geographic disparities in the amount of time a given individual must wait for a transplant and to ensure that minorities and the economically disadvantaged receive equitable access to transplants.

Evaluating the potential impact of the Final Rule on organ procurement and transplantation was a difficult task for many reasons. Among these is the fact that the Final Rule does not specify what the new organ allocation rules should be, but instead establishes criteria and performance goals for the transplant community to meet through the development of appropriate policies. Conducting an evidence-based assessment was also difficult because of limitations both in the availability of data and, in some cases, in the data themselves. These data, the testimony provided to the committee, and the other information available to it, although quite voluminous in some areas, ranged in usefulness from helpful to contradictory or confusing. Moreover, as is often the case with complex data, its content and the way it is characterized by participants in the public discourse are often at odds.

A large part of the committee's work focused on a review and analysis of approximately 68,000 liver transplant waiting list records that describe every change in status made by every patient on the Organ Procurement and Transplantation Network (OPTN) waiting list for liver transplants from 1995 through the first quarter of 1999. In addition, the committee held two public meetings and solicited additional input from a broad range of interested individuals and organizations.

Based on its assessment of available data and other information, the committee finds that the current system is reasonably effective and equitable, but that it operates without effective supervision and oversight and could be more efficient in its allocation of livers to those with most urgent medical needs. Moreover, a lack of effective communication among the interested parties has polarized the discussions of various issues, such as those related to organ allocation, making them less productive than they could be and thus leaving significant room for improvement.

In the end, the committee emerged from its deliberations generally supporting the concepts presented in the Final Rule—for example, broader sharing of organs and enhanced oversight—tempered by the practicalities of the transplantation process. The committee's recommendations, if implemented, could go a long way toward facilitating the development of improved principles of allocation and improving what everyone agrees should be a patient-centered system.

The committee believes strongly that the federal government should provide effective oversight and review of the organ procurement and transplantation system, and that the system can be improved. This oversight and review should focus on assuring that the system is equitable, is grounded on sound medical sciences, and always places highest priority on the needs of the patients it serves. It is not the role of this oversight to micromanage day-to-day patient care.

Government oversight should also ensure that information about the system is available to the research community and the public. Although the United Network for Organ Sharing (UNOS) currently collects, analyzes, and disseminates a great deal of information about the OPTN—more data than are available for most other medical procedures—many people feel that these data should be more timely and more broadly available, and that independent review and analysis would be of added value. In this regard, as the committee tried to work quickly in reaching its assessment, it was struck by the paucity of readily available public information and the apparent lack of accountability and peer review of the data system. To answer questions properly about the adequacy of the organ procurement and transplantation system, data collection and dissemination must be improved, and information must be made widely available to the public and the research community, while respecting the confidentiality and privacy of both donors and recipients.

Finally, a perception of fairness is important to every aspect of this fragile system of procurement and transplantation. The system, therefore, not only has to be fair, but its fairness must be readily perceived by the public for many of the objectives to be accomplished, including increasing organ donations and improving minority access to transplantation.

As the committee was putting final touches on the report, the governing board of the OPTN announced a change in its liver allocation rules, designed to increase the number of organs going to the patients in greatest medical need. The change seems to be an incremental improvement over the prior policy with respect to status 1 patients, but still leaves room for improvement.

The short time frame of this study and the relative dearth of high-quality public information presented formidable challenges. The committee responded extremely well to these challenges and performed its task in a very professional manner. This would not have been possible without the help of many other people. I would especially like to thank the research staff at UNOS—Mary Ellison, Ann Harper, and Erick Edwards—who responded quickly and effectively to our numerous and complex data requests throughout the study. Their cooperation eased our task immeasurably. In addition, I would like to thank our colleagues at the General Accounting Office—Marcia Crosse, Roy Hogberg, and Donna Bulvin—who provided us with data on the costs of transplantation.

Last, the staff who supported this activity are in large part responsible for both its quality and its timeliness. In this regard, I wish to acknowledge in particular the efforts of the IOM project staff—Andrew Pope, Kathi Hanna, Mike Edington, Sarah Pitluck, and Thelma Cox—as well as the staff of the National Academy Press, Sally Stanfield, Estelle Miller, Jim Gormley, Dawn Eichenlaub, and Ron Weeks. Without their tireless assistance, we would not have been able to complete this project in the time frame requested by Congress or to the standards required by the Institute of Medicine.

Edward D. Penhoet, Ph.D.
Chair

Acronyms

AHA	American Hospital Association
AIDS	acquired immunodeficiency syndrome
ALUs	alternative local units
CFR	Code of Federal Regulations
CT	computerized tomography
CTP	Child-Turcotte-Pugh score
DHHS	Department of Health and Human Services
ESRD	end-stage renal disease
FDA	Food and Drug Administration
GAO	General Accounting Office
HCC	hepatocellular carcinoma
HCFA	Health Care Financing Administration
HEHS	Health Education and Human Services, GAO
HIV	human immunodeficiency virus
ICU	intensive care unit
INR	international normalized ratio
IOM	Institute of Medicine
MIXNO	mixed-effects nominal logistic regression
MMLE	maximum marginal likelihood estimates

MRI	magnetic resonance imaging
NHLBI	National Heart, Lung, and Blood Institute, NIH
NIH	National Institutes of Health
NMDP	National Marrow Donor Program
NOTA	National Organ Transplant Act
OAA	Organ Allocation Area
OPO	Organ Procurement Organization
OPTN	Organ Procurement and Transplantation Network
OTC	ornithinine transcarbamylase deficiency
TIPS	transjugular intrahepatic portosystemic shunt placement
TNM	tumor-node-metastasis
UNOS	United Network for Organ Sharing
USC	United States Code

Contents

List of Tables, Figures, and Boxes

TABLES

FIGURES

BOXES

Organ Procurement and Transplantation

Executive Summary

Abstract. This report provides an independent assessment of the current policies and potential impact of a pending new federal regulation (the "Final Rule") on the system of organ procurement and transplantation.

One of the most visible and contentious issues regarding the fairness of the current system of organ procurement and allocation is the argument that it results in great disparities in the total amount of time a patient waits for an organ (i.e., the time from registration at a transplantation center to transplant), depending on where he or she lives. Because much of the current debate has centered on the procurement and allocation of livers, the committee focused its examination on this organ.

In an analysis of approximately 68,000 liver patient records, the committee developed several conclusions and recommendations largely specific to liver transplantation policies. Included among these is the fact that, as previously calculated, the overall "median waiting time" that patients wait for organs—the issue that seems to have brought the committee to the table in the first place—is not a useful statistic for comparing access to or equity of the current system of liver transplantation, especially when aggregated across all categories of liver transplant patients. The committee also found that the current system is reasonably equitable within the category of the most severely ill (status 1) liver patients, since the likelihood of receiving a transplant is similar across organ procurement organizations (OPOs) for these patients. Similarly, pretransplantation mortality rates are also quite similar across OPOs, irrespective of the patient's status level. The committee also found, however, that the system can be improved by enlarging the current organ allocation areas to include larger populations. Doing so will likely increase the number of status 1 and 2 patients receiving liver transplants with a concomitant reduction in the number of transplants performed on status 3 patients, who are at much lower risk of imminent death. Such expansion of the geographic area of allocation would have to be done within the limits of cold ischemia time. Preliminary data on existing regional and statewide sharing seem to agree with this projection, indicating that status 1 transplantation rates will be increased, status 2B pretransplantation mortality will be decreased, and the transplantation of status 3 patients will be reduced as a result of broader sharing by smaller OPOs. In general, the committee finds broader sharing is likely to result in more of the most medically urgent patients receiving first attention when waiting for donated livers.

Since the enactment of the National Organ Transplant Act of 1984, the number of people receiving organs has increased annually. In 1998, more than 21,000 Americans—about 57 people a day—were transplanted with a kidney, liver, heart, lung, or other organ. On any given day, approximately 62,000 people are waiting for an organ and every 16 minutes a new name is added to the national waiting list (UNOS, 1999). These numbers represent only the indicated demand for organs. It is likely that there are many more people in need of transplantation who are not currently on a waiting list. Moreover, although the number of donors has increased steadily since 1988, donation rates are not growing as quickly as the demand for organs (GAO, 1997). As a result, approximately 4,000 Americans die each year (11 people per day) waiting for a solid organ transplant (UNOS, 1999).

The disparity between the supply of and demand for transplantable organs has focused attention on the policies and practices regarding the allocation of the scarce supply of organs. Concerns about need, supply, demand, access, and rationing have raised questions about the appropriate role of the federal government in regulating this important public health issue. The polemical nature of the debate has increased public skepticism about the integrity and fairness of the system. Such skepticism may serve to reduce donations and create more serious shortages (Dejong et al., 1995).

One of the most visible and contentious issues regarding the fairness of the current system of organ procurement and transplantation is the argument that it results in great disparities in the amount of time potential liver transplant patients wait for a transplant, depending on where the patient lives. (The term "waiting time" is used throughout this report to refer to the time from registration at a transplantation center to transplant, death, or removal from the waiting list for other reasons.) An additional concern is that minorities and the poor may have less access to organ transplants than do whites of higher socioeconomic status.

In response to concerns expressed about possible inequities in the existing system of organ procurement and transplantation, the U.S. Department of Health and Human Services (DHHS) published a new regulation in April 1998 (42 CFR Part 121, referred to in this report as the "Final Rule") to "assure that allocation of scarce organs will be based on common medical criteria, not accidents of geography" (DHHS, 1998b).

The Final Rule provides a framework within which the transplant system would operate. The stated principles underlying the Final Rule include the need for oversight in a system that permits variance in individual medical practice and the creation of a "level playing field" in organ allocation—that is, organs are allocated based on patients' medical need and less emphasis is placed on keeping organs in the local area where they are procured. A primary stated objective is to equalize waiting times among different areas of the country. To emphasize this, the Final Rule calls for standardized medical criteria to be used to determine the status of a person's illness and when that person can be placed on a waiting list. In addition, the rule aims to improve data collection and analysis so that patients, their physicians, and the public have timely, accurate, and user-friendly, center-specific data on the performance of transplant programs to help them to assess quality and make transplant decisions.

Issuance of the Final Rule generated considerable controversy in the transplant community. Concerns were expressed that its implementation would increase the cost of transplantation, force the closure of small transplant centers, adversely affect access to transplantation on the part of minorities and low-income patients, discourage organ donation, and result in fewer lives saved. Some opponents of the rule also argued that DHHS had exceeded its statutory authority by establishing a process for reviewing Organ Procurement and Transplantation Network (OPTN) policies and procedures.

In October 1998, the U.S. Congress suspended implementation of the Final Rule for 1 year to allow further study of its potential impact. During that time, Congress asked the Institute of Medicine (IOM) to conduct a study to review current OPTN policies and the potential impact of the Final Rule on:

- access to transplantation services for low-income populations and racial and ethnic minority groups, including the impact of state policies (under Title XIX of the Social Security Act) regarding payment for services for patients outside of the states in which the patients reside;
- organ donation rates, reasons for differences in donation rates, and the impact of broader sharing (i.e., based on medical criteria instead of geography), on donation rates;
- waiting times for organ transplants, including (a) determinations specific to the various geographic regions of the United States and, if practicable, waiting times for each transplant center by organ and medical status category, and (b) assessment of the impact of recent changes made by the OPTN in patient listing criteria and in measures of medical status;
- patient survival rates and organ failure rates leading to retransplantation, including variances by income status, ethnicity, gender, race, or blood type; and
- costs of organ transplantation services.

The legislation that called for this study included two additional areas for review: (1) confidentiality of information about the program, and (2) the possible legal liability of OPTN members arising from their peer review activities. As agreed, the U.S. General Accounting Office (GAO) addressed these two issues in a separate report (GAO, 1999). Also as agreed in response to the legislation, GAO assisted IOM by providing data to the committee regarding costs of organ transplantation services.

CURRENT POLICIES AND PRACTICES

The process of organ procurement and transplantation begins when a patient in need of an organ transplant is referred to one (or more) of the 272 organ transplant programs (125 of which perform liver transplants) currently in operation in the United States. If accepted for transplantation by a transplant program, the patient is placed on that program's waiting list until a donated organ that is determined to be medically appropriate is available. Patients in need of a liver transplant are assigned to one of several classifications—status 1, status 2A, status 2B, or status 3—depending on the nature and severity of the patient's illness (see Table ES-1).

The retrieval and preservation of donated organs, and their transportation (if necessary) from the site of donation to the site of transplantation, is the responsibility of organ procurement organizations (OPOs). There are 62 OPOs currently in operation in the United States. Each is responsible for the retrieval and allocation of organs within a defined geographical area, and in accordance with organ allocation policies (see Appendix C). These geographical service areas vary greatly in their size and population, as well as in the number of organs retrieved and the number of patients transplanted by the transplant centers in their service areas.

TABLE ES-1 UNOS Liver Status for Patients ≥ 18 Years of Age According to Disease Severity

Status 1	Fulminant liver failure with life expectancy < 7 days • Fulminant hepatic failure as traditionally defined • Primary graft nonfunction < 7 days of transplantation • Hepatic artery thrombosis < 7 days of transplantation • Acute decompensated Wilson's disease
Status 2A	Hospitalized in Intensive Care Unit for chronic liver failure with life expectancy < 7 days, with a Child-Pugh score ≥ 10, and one of the following: • Unresponsive active variceal hemorrhage • Hepatorenal syndrome • Refractory ascities or hepatic hydrothorax • Stage 3 or 4 hepatic encephalopathy
Status 2B	Requiring continuous medical care, with a Child-Pugh score ≥ 10, or a Child-Pugh score ≥ 7 and one of the following: • Unresponsive active variceal hemorrhage • Hepatorenal syndrome • Spontaneous bacterial peritonitis • Refractory ascites or hepatic hydrothorax
Status 3	Requiring continuous medical care, with a Child-Pugh score ≥ 7 but not meeting criteria for Status 2B
Status 7	Temporarily inactive

SOURCE: Keeffe, 1998; data obtained from UNOS website (http://unos.org) initially implemented July 1997, modified January 1998.

The process of identifying which patient on a waiting list should receive an available organ is facilitated by the OPTN. The OPTN, which was created by Congress as part of the National Organ Transplant Act of 1984, maintains a computerized listing of all patients, and certain vital data on such patients, on waiting lists for organ transplantation. When an OPO determines that an organ is available for transplant, it contacts the OPTN or more specifically, the United Network for Organ Sharing (UNOS), which has been the OPTN contractor since the system was created. UNOS then uses a complex, computerized algorithm to determine which patient is the most appropriate recipient of the available organ.

There is general agreement that status 1 liver patients should be given first priority for an available organ and, if no suitable status 1 patient is identified, the organ should be offered sequentially to status 2A, status 2B, and status 3 patients. At the present time, this set of priorities is exercised first (with some exceptions) within the geographical area served by the OPO that retrieved the organ. The organ is offered to a patient outside the OPO's service area (using a similar set of priorities) only if no suitable transplant recipient is identified within its service area. (See Appendix C for a description of current allocation policy.) Thus, despite the general consensus that status 1 patients should be given priority over other patients, the current allocation policies and practices may result in a status 2B or status 3 patient receiving an available organ because he or she is within the service area of the OPO that retrieved the organ, while a suitable status 1 patient in a different OPO service area continues to wait for an organ. This is the basis for much of the debate about the fairness and effectiveness of the current system and one of the major concerns that the DHHS Final Rule was designed to address.

CONCLUSIONS AND RECOMMENDATIONS

The committee developed conclusions regarding the potential impact of the Final Rule on each area listed in its charge, as well as recommendations as to how the Final Rule should be implemented. Because liver allocation was at the center of the debate leading to this study and there are several unique factors related to liver transplantation (e.g., the lack of medical alternatives to transplantation, such as dialysis for kidney patients), and because of the severe time constraints placed on this project by Congress, the committee focused its attention primarily on issues related to the policies, practices, and data concerning liver procurement and transplantation. Unless specified otherwise, the text, analysis, and conclusions and recommendations presented in this report relate to liver transplantation.

The committee views organ transplantation as a valuable, often lifesaving process that should be managed equitably across the nation. It also believes the federal government has a legitimate and appropriate oversight role to ensure that reasonable standards of equity and quality are met. Therefore, the committee offers conclusions and recommendations on several crosscutting issues that must be addressed to improve the overall system. These issues include the need for better data collection, analysis, and dissemination; the need for better scientific oversight of the entire transplant enterprise; and the need for more rigorous evaluation of the system's performance. The committee's conclusions and recommendations follow.

The Need for Larger Organ Allocation Areas

The committee concludes that the fairness of the organ procurement and transplantation system, and its effectiveness in meeting its stated goals, would be significantly enhanced if the allocation of scarce donated livers were done over larger populations than is now the case. This led to the following recommendation.

> **RECOMMENDATION 1:** ***Establish Organ Allocation Areas for Livers***
>
> **The committee recommends that the DHHS Final Rule be implemented by the establishment of Organ Allocation Areas (OAAs) for livers—each serving a population base of at least 9 million people (unless such an area would exceed the limits of acceptable cold ischemic time). OAAs should generally be established through sharing arrangements among organ procurement organizations to avoid disrupting effective current procurement activities.**

To arrive at this conclusion and recommendation, the committee reviewed all the literature and testimony submitted to it and conducted an independent analysis of 68,000 records for patients on liver transplant waiting lists. These data described every change in the waiting list status for every patient on a waiting list from 1995 through the first quarter of 1999. These patients were grouped by OPO as the unit of analysis for assessing allocation policies. A mixed-effects multinomial logistic regression model was used to examine the effects of various factors—including age, race, gender, blood type, waiting time, and size of OPO—on the likelihood of a patient either receiving a transplant or dying while on the waiting list. (See Chapter 5 and Appendix A for a complete description of this analysis.)

The committee's analysis revealed that OPO volume (the number of transplants performed within its service area) and OPO size (the population within its service area) are both statistically significant predictors of transplantation for status 2B and status 3 patients. OPOs with small and medium volumes (defined here as those with less than an average of 75 transplants in their service area per year over the 4 years for which data were available) were significantly more likely to provide organs to status 2B and status 3 patients than OPOs that averaged more than 75 transplants per year. In addition, patients served by small OPOs (those with fewer than 40 transplants in their service area per year) had a significantly increased risk of pretransplant mortality while on the waiting list.

The committee's analysis also provided strong statistical evidence that increasing the size of the population served in liver allocation will result in more opportunities to transplant sicker patients without adversely affecting less sick patients. For status 2B patients, the results of the statistical analysis reveal that both pretransplant mortality and the probability of transplantation falls as OPO size increases up to 9 million people—both desirable outcomes (see Figure ES-1). Results of the statistical analysis also reveal that status 3 patients are less likely to undergo transplantation as OPO size increases up to 9 million with no increase in pretransplant mortality (see Figure ES-2). Thus, the number of status 2B and 3 patients receiving transplants could be reduced to allow more status 1 and 2A patients to receive transplants without an increase in pretransplant mortality for the status 2B and 3 patients. The committee further observed a convergence of these two statistical findings in that all of the OPOs serving 9 million or more people performed a minimum of 75 transplants within their service areas per year. On the basis of this analysis, the committee reached the following conclusion:

> *Creation of organ allocation areas based on a minimum population of approximately 9 million persons would substantially increase the allocation of organs to patients with more urgent need of a transplant.*

The committee recognizes that achieving optimum results in procuring organs for transplantation is highly dependent on good working relationships at the local level among hospitals, OPOs, transplant centers, and others in the community interested in supporting organ transplantation. The OPOs currently in existence have been working diligently for some time to develop and maintain such relationships, and the committee does not want its recommendations to detract from or interfere with present operations where they are working effectively. The committee, therefore, is explicitly not recommending that these larger allocation areas be created by consolidating existing OPOs into fewer, larger organizations. Rather, it is recommending that allocation over larger populations be achieved through changes in policies and procedures and through sharing arrangements among OPOs.

Appropriate Consideration of Patient Waiting Times

Disparities in overall median waiting times for liver transplants have been cited as an indicator of the unfairness of the current system. However, for the reasons set forth below, the committee concluded that this is not an appropriate measure of the fairness of the system. Moreover, the committee also concluded that waiting time was not an appropriate consideration in determining priorities in the allocation of livers within certain classifications of less severely ill patients. This led to the following recommendation.

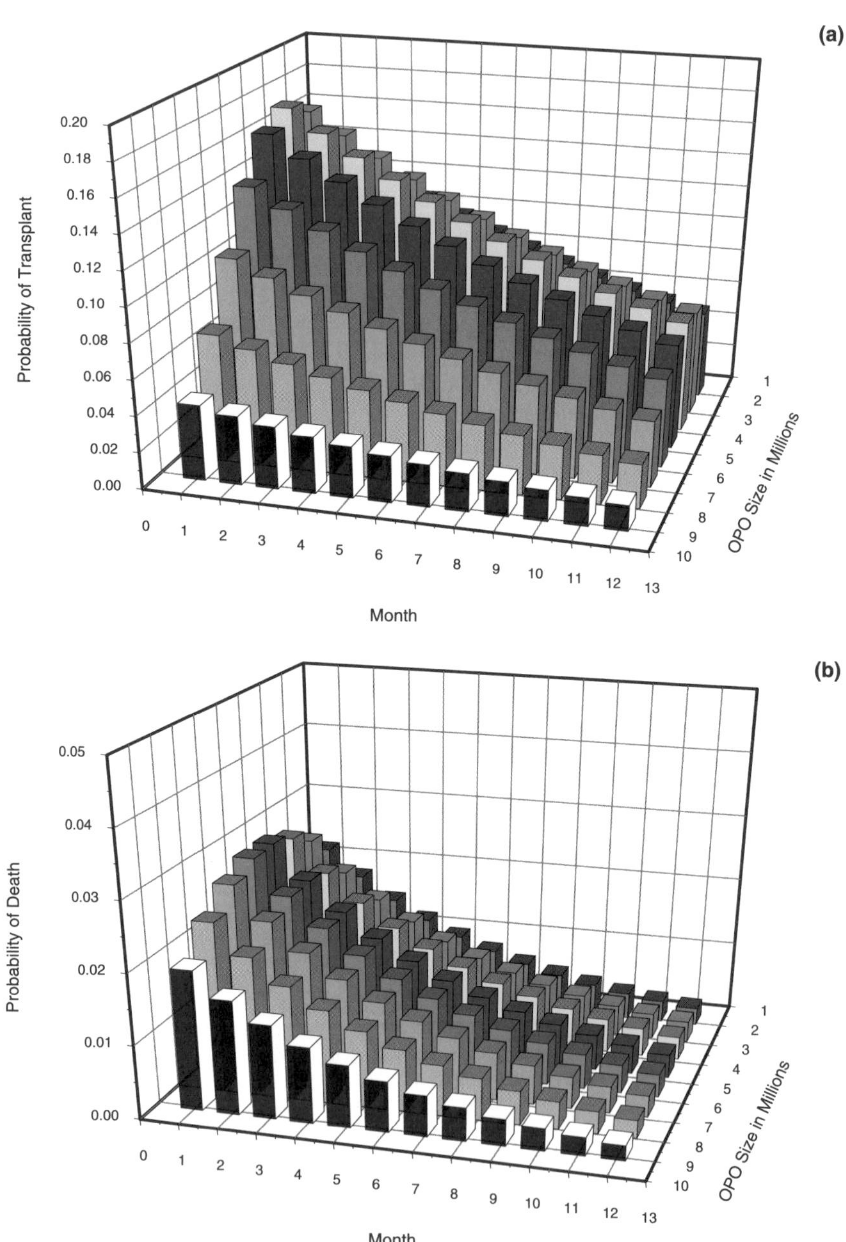

FIGURE ES-1 A three-dimensional view of the relationships among waiting-list time (measured in months), OPO population (in millions), and probability of transplant (a) and death (b) for status 2B patients.

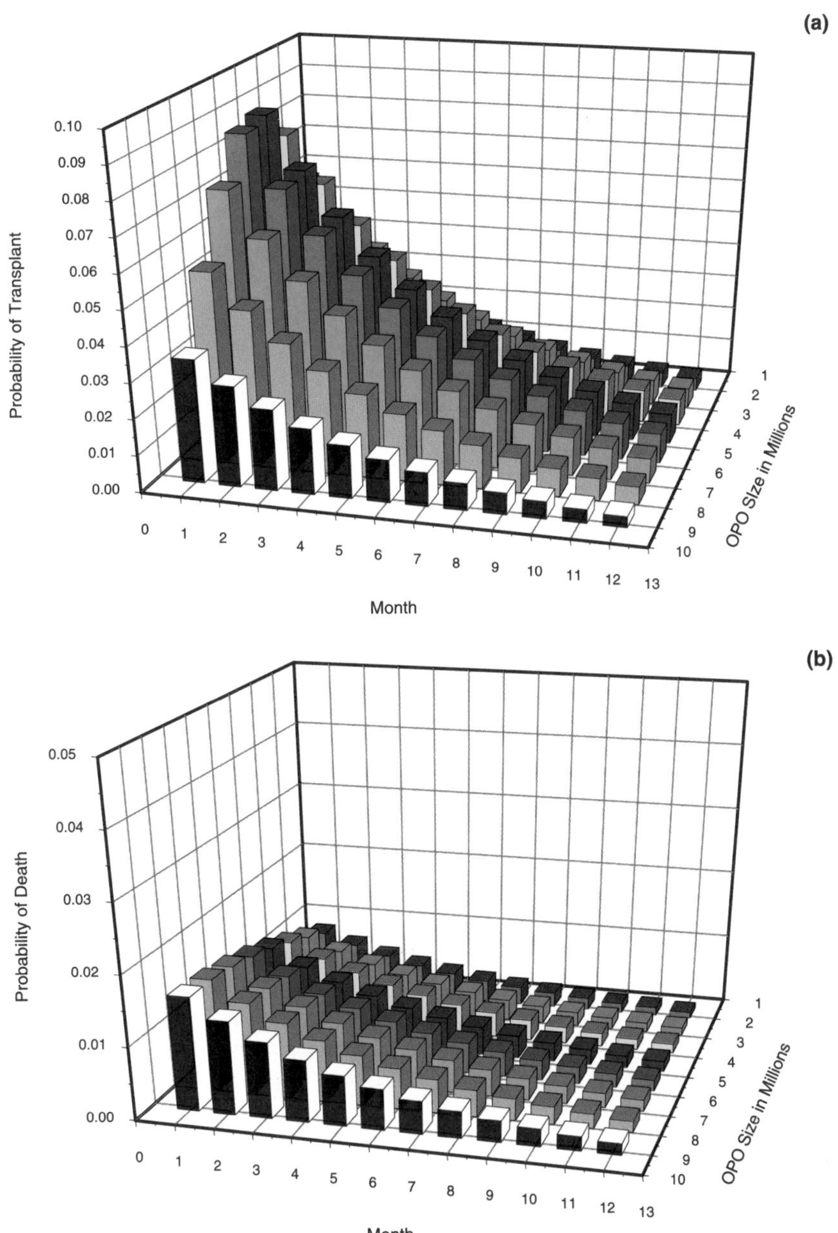

FIGURE ES-2 A three-dimensional view of the relationships among waiting-list time (measured in months), OPO population (in millions), and probability of transplant (a) and death (b) for status 3 patients.

RECOMMENDATION 2: *Discontinue Use of Waiting Time as an Allocation Criterion for Patients in Statuses 2B and 3*

The heterogeneity and wide range of severity of illness in statuses 2B and 3 make waiting time relatively misleading within these categories. For this reason, waiting time should be discontinued as an allocation criterion for status 2B and 3 patients. An appropriate medical triage system should be developed to ensure equitable allocation of organs to patients in these categories. Such a system may, for example, be based on a point system arising out of medical characteristics and disease prognoses rather than waiting times.

Because status 3 patients greatly outnumber those in other status groups, the overall median waiting time—for either an OPO or a transplant center—is primarily determined by the waiting times for these patients. However, these are the patients with the least urgent need of transplantation, as well as the patients, on average, with the longest periods of time on the waiting list. These facts led the committee to the following conclusion:

Overall median waiting time, which has dominated the policy debate, is a poor measure of differences in access to transplantation. Status-specific rates of pretransplantation mortality and transplantation are more meaningful indicators of equitable access.

The committee examined the 68,000 patient records described above to compare the waiting times and mortality rates across OPOs, for each of the patient status groups. Waiting times were typically only about 3–4 days for status 1 patients, 40–70 days for status 2 patients, and 100–400 days for status 3 patients. Moreover, there was far less variability in waiting times across OPO areas for status 1 patients than for status 2B and status 3 patients. Similarly, pretransplant mortality did not vary substantially across OPO areas for all three status levels. From this, the committee reached the following conclusion:

The current system appears to generate reasonably little variation in waiting times across OPOs for status 1 and 2A patients, indicating that waiting time is an appropriate criterion for organ allocation, along with necessary medical criteria, within these categories. Greater amounts of variation occur for status 2B and 3 patients across OPOs.

Further analysis of the waiting list data revealed that status 2B and status 3 patients have a decreased likelihood of either transplantation or death the longer they are on the list. This suggests that many of these patients, despite meeting the criteria for being placed on a waiting list, have little likelihood of receiving a transplant and little risk of dying. It may be that some patients are put on waiting lists at an early stage in their disease condition to accumulate waiting time and move up the priority list. If so, this is contributing to the appearance of an inequitable allocation system. Eliminating the use of waiting time in status 2B and status 3 patients as a component of the priority score would reduce the incentive to list patients who are in less urgent need of a transplant and would enhance the chances that patients more in need of a transplant would receive one.

> *Among the status 2B and status 3 patients, there appears to be a subgroup of patients who are more likely to require a transplant within a shorter period of time than the remainder of patients in that status. The remaining patients in that status will live a relatively long time with chronic liver disease, not become medically urgent, and not receive a transplant. Thus, the length of waiting time in status 2B and status 3 is not a good indicator of medical urgency or priority.*

Access to Organ Transplantation

The committee was charged to determine what, if any, impact the Final Rule would have on the access of low-income and minority populations to transplantation services. The available studies addressing this issue are limited in number and scope, making this a challenging assignment. Moreover, the data the committee received from the OPTN contained information on race, but not socioeconomic status or insurance coverage; our conclusion regarding low-income patients (below) is based on the limited available studies. Thus, the committee cautions that its findings (which follow) must be considered provisional rather than conclusive.

> *African American patients are less likely than white patients to be referred for evaluation and are placed on waiting lists at a slower rate, as are low-income patients of all racial and ethnic groups.*

> *African American kidney patients on waiting lists are transplanted at a lower rate than white patients, but similar disparities have not been shown for liver patients.*

> *The evidence is inconclusive that the Final Rule would result in the closure of smaller transplant centers located in areas that are more accessible to the residences of prospective transplant patients. Moreover, even if this were a result of the Final Rule, there is no evidence demonstrating that this would have an adverse impact on the access of minority and low-income patients to organ transplants.*

> *The most important predictors of equity in access to transplant services lie outside the transplantation system—that is, access to health insurance and high-quality health care services.*

Organ Donation

The committee was asked to assess whether implementation of the Final Rule, particularly efforts to achieve broader sharing, would affect organ donation rates. The committee found that many elements affect donation rates, most of which have little to do with local allocation policies. Thus, local preference seems not to be a significant factor in the decision to donate. The committee found little or no evidence to support the assertion that people would decline to donate, or that health professionals engaged in organ procurement would be less diligent in their efforts, if they knew a donated organ would be used outside the donor's immediate geographic area.

The committee heard testimony that the presence of a transplant center in a community enhances the community's awareness about organ transplantation and increases organ donation in that community. However, the fact that local transplant centers are important in stimulating organ donation does not lead to the conclusion that local use of donated organs is an important consideration of donors. Further, the committee notes that areas participating in broader sharing arrangements have experienced increased donation rates. It may be that the perception of fairness and effectiveness in distribution is as important as other factors in affecting donation rates beneficially.

The committee believes strongly that the effectiveness and productivity of organ procurement is highly dependent on good working relationships at the local level. However, it finds no evidence that broader organ sharing arrangements will lead to reduced rates of donation.

Organ Failure and Patient Survival

The committee was asked to determine the potential impact of the Final Rule on patient survival rates and organ failure rates leading to retransplantation. A number of biological factors influence short-term outcome as well as long-term function of transplanted organs. Not all organs are the same; for example, some organs are more sensitive to ischemic time than others, but ischemic times have not been rigorously evaluated in the past. The committee undertook a comprehensive assessment of the existing literature and made judgments based on this information that are in general agreement with current practices (see Table ES-2).

The committee's analysis of data on posttransplant mortality of recent liver transplant patients revealed that patients receiving transplants at centers served by lower-volume OPOs had higher mortality rates relative to larger-volume OPOs. In addition, the 1999 UNOS report on graft and patient survival rates showed that low-volume transplant centers had lower than expected 1-year graft survival rates. Although these findings may suggest a positive correlation between transplant volume and patient survival, the committee did not believe it had enough data to reach a conclusion regarding the impact of the Final Rule on survival.

TABLE ES-2 Summary of Literature on Cold Ischemic Time for Solid Organs

Organ	Medically Acceptable Cold Ischemic Time* (simple cold storage using appropriate preservation fluids) (hrs)
Liver	12
Pancreas	17
Kidney	24
Heart	4
Lung	6–8

*The committee defines medically acceptable cold ischemic time as the duration of cold ischemia that has been associated in clinical experience with an appropriate and acceptable percentage of acute and long-term graft function and survival. The times presented in this table are based on the committee's review of peer reviewed literature. Longer times are sometimes reported in clinical practice with acceptable outcomes. Outcomes vary as a function of many other factors, including age of donor and quality of organ.

Costs

The committee examined whether implementation of the Final Rule would increase transplantation costs because of the combined effects of sharing donated organs over a greater geographic area and using donated organs in patients who are more severely ill. Based on information obtained by the GAO about organ recovery practices from officials at six OPOs, the committee learned that costs vary considerably among transplant centers and OPOs. The cost of transporting an organ, for example, depends on the mode of transportation used (ground or air), the distance that the organ must travel, and whether the transplant team travels to the site of donation to retrieve the organ. The committee concluded that organ procurement costs would likely increase, but was not able to estimate by how much.

The committee also concluded that status 1 patients incur higher costs than status 2B or 3 patients, and this, too, would increase the cost of implementing the Final Rule. Again, the committee was unable to estimate the amount of the increase.

Expenditures for organ procurement and transplantation are likely to increase as a result of broader sharing. The committee is not, however, able to estimate with confidence how large the increase might be because it is not clear how the Final Rule will be implemented and how many patients in each status will be affected. Any increase in expenditures must, however, be weighed against the additional health benefits of broader sharing, which the committee believes will be substantial and could outweigh any net increase in expenditures.

Oversight and Review

During its deliberations, the committee came to the conclusion that the system of organ procurement and transplantation is not functioning as well as it could because responsibility is dispersed among many different participants without an effective means of holding them accountable to the patients that the system is designed to serve. The committee believes that the purposes of the National Organ Transplant Act would be better served if there were enhanced oversight and governance of the system, aided by improved efforts at assessing the performance of all key components. In addition, the committee concluded that, although a considerable volume of data is collected, some important data elements are missing, there is often a lengthy time lag in the data that are available, and these data are not readily accessible to patients, the health services research community, or the general public. These concerns led the committee to a series of important, related recommendations.

RECOMMENDATION 3: ***Exercise Federal Oversight***

The Department of Health and Human Services should exercise the legitimate oversight responsibilities assigned to it by the National Organ Transplant Act, and articulated in the Final Rule, to manage the system of organ procurement and transplantation in the public interest. This oversight should include greater use of patient-centered, outcome-oriented performance measures for OPOs, transplant centers, and the OPTN.

RECOMMENDATION 4: ***Establish Independent Scientific Review***

The Department of Health and Human Services should establish an external, independent, multidisciplinary scientific review board responsible for assisting the Secretary in ensuring that the system of organ procurement and transplantation is grounded on the best available medical science and is as effective and as equitable as possible.

RECOMMENDATION 5: ***Improve Data Collection and Dissemination***

Within the bounds of donor and recipient confidentiality and sound medical judgment, the OPTN contractor should improve its collection of standardized and useful data regarding the system of organ procurement and transplantation and make it widely available to independent investigators and scientific reviewers in a timely manner. The Department of Health and Human Services

should provide an independent, objective assessment of the quality and effectiveness of the data that are collected and how they are analyzed and disseminated by the OPTN.

The committee believes these measures will greatly enhance public confidence that the system is fulfilling its primary mission—serving the needs of transplant patients. The establishment of the scientific review board would make a particularly important contribution toward ensuring that there is a consistent and coherent view as to how the system should operate, that the policies and practices are based on the best scientific and medical knowledge currently available, and that the interests of transplant patients are given paramount importance.

1

Introduction

Advances in medical science and technology have made solid organ transplantation an increasingly successful and common medical procedure, a literal "second chance at life." Greater experience in performing transplantation and the development of better immunosuppressive regimens have increased the survival rates for transplant recipients. Since the enactment of the National Organ Transplant Act of 1984, the number of people receiving organs has increased annually. In 1998, nearly 21,000 Americans—about 57 people a day—were transplanted with a kidney, liver, heart, lung, or other organ (see Table 1-1).

More people are benefiting from organ transplants and their survival rates are steadily improving. Comparing data for transplantations performed in 1988 with data for transplantations performed in 1995, one-year patient survival rates increased from 81 to 87 percent for persons receiving a liver; from 83 to 85 percent for persons receiving a heart; and from 50 to 77 percent for persons receiving a lung (DHHS, 1998b). In addition, technological advances, such as the Belzer UW solution, have made it possible to preserve organs outside the body for longer periods of time.

A primary determinant of organ viability is "cold ischemic time," the time from when blood flow to the organ is stopped in the donor to the time that blood flow to the organ is restored in the recipient. The shorter the cold ischemic time, the more likely a transplant is to be successful. Ischemic injury results from prolonged lack of blood flow, and, at some point, affects organ function following transplantation. The amount of ischemia that compromises organ function differs by organ type and other factors, for example, donor age.

In the past 15 years, the national transplantation system has extended the lives of more than 200,000 individuals (Meier, 1999). Approximately 62,000 people wait for an organ on any given day and every 16 minutes a new name is added to the national waiting list (UNOS, 1999) (see Table 1-2). Each year the number of patients added to the waiting list grows (see Table 1-3). Also, although the number of donors has increased steadily since 1988, it is not growing as quickly as the demand for organs (GAO, 1997). Roughly 4,000 Americans die each year (11 people per day) waiting for organs (UNOS, 1999). Organs are obtained for transplantation from less than 1 percent of U.S. deaths.

In an effort to increase donation rates, the federal government announced the National Organ and Tissue Donation Initiative in December 1997. As a part of the initiative, the Department of Health and Human Services (DHHS) issued a regulation requiring all Medicare-participating hospitals to refer all deaths and imminent deaths to organ procurement organizations (OPOs). The regulation went into effect in August 1998. In April 1999, DHHS announced a 5.6 percent increase in donation in 1998 (DHHS, 1999a).

TABLE 1-1 Number of Transplants Performed in 1998

Kidney only (3,712 from living donors)	11,990
Liver	4,450
Heart	2,340
Lung	849
Kidney–pancreas	965
Pancreas only	253
Intestine	69
Heart–lung	45
Total	20,961

NOTE: Double kidney, double lung, and heart–lung transplants are counted as one transplant.

SOURCE: Based on UNOS Scientific Registry data as of April 14, 1999.

OPOs are subject to certification and recertification by the federal Health Care Financing Administration (HCFA), which issues performance standards. These standards are designed to promote the efficiency of OPOs. HCFA also approves waivers that permit a hospital to have an arrangement with a different OPO than the one assigned to its area.

EVOLUTION OF THE FEDERAL SYSTEM OF ORGAN TRANSPLANTATION

The current arrangement of 62 organ procurement organizations nationally evolved gradually, reflecting improvements in transplantation science, organ preservation, and other factors. Historically, the hospital in which the donor resided was responsible for locating a recipient. Thus the earliest days of solid organ transplantation, the donor and recipient were often in the same building. Gradually, a system of independent organizations, Organ Procurement Organizations (OPOs), developed to optimize matching of patients with donated organs. OPOs identified donors, retrieved organs, and found recipients within a reasonable time frame.

The designated geographic areas served by the various OPOs range in size from a few counties, to entire states, to multi-state areas covering parts or all of several states (see Figure 1-1).* The populations of these areas range from approximately 700,000 to 11,000,000 (DHHS, 1999b). In each area, only one OPO coordinates activities relating to organ procurement and allocation, and that OPO is required to have a working arrangement with all hospitals in its designated area. OPOs evaluate potential donors, discuss donation with family members, and arrange for the surgical removal of donated organs. OPOs also are responsible for preserving organs and arranging for their distribution according to nationally, regionally, or locally agreed upon organ-sharing policies.

TABLE 1-2 UNOS National Patient Waiting List for Organ Transplants

Type of Transplant	Registrations for Transplant[a]	Patients Waiting for Transplant[b]
Kidney	43,734	41,833
Liver	13,181	12,987
Heart	4,267	4,248
Lung	3,299	3,250
Kidney–pancreas	1,915	1,847
Pancreas	453	442
Heart–lung	248	244
Intestine	120	120
Pancreas islet cell	118	118
Total	67,335	63,219

[a]UNOS policies allow patients to be listed with more than one transplant center (multiple listing); thus, the number of registrations is greater than the actual number of patients.

[b]Some patients are waiting for more than one organ; therefore, the total number of patients is less than the sum of patients waiting for each organ.

SOURCE: Based on UNOS Scientific Registry data as of May 12, 1999.

*Figure 1-1 shows the 63 OPOS as they were in 1997. There are presently 62 OPOs, but the precise boundaries had not been determined at the time of publication of this report.

TABLE 1-3 Number of Registrations on the National Transplant Waiting List by Organ at Year End, 1988–1998

Organ	Year											10-Year Percentage Increase
	1988	1989	1990	1991	1992	1993	1994	1995	1996	1997	1998	
Kidney	13,943	16,294	17,883	19,352	22,376	24,973	27,498	31,045	34,550	38,236	42,364	204
Liver	616	827	1,237	1,676	2,323	2,997	4,059	5,691	7,467	9,637	12,056	1,857
Pancreas	163	320	473	600	126	183	222	285	323	361	455	179
Kidney–pancreas	0	0	0	0	778	923	1,067	1,234	1,463	1,591	1,841	N/A
Heart	1,030	1,320	1,788	2,267	2,690	2,834	2,933	3,468	3,698	3,897	4,185	306
Heart–lung	205	240	225	154	180	202	205	208	237	236	257	25
Intestine	0	0	0	0	0	42	75	83	83	94	100	100
Lung	69	94	308	670	942	1,240	1,625	1,923	2,309	2,664	3,165	447
Total	16,026	19,095	21,914	24,719	29,415	33,394	37,684	43,937	50,130	56,716	64,423	302

SOURCE: Based on United Network for Organ Sharing, and Organ Procurement and Transplantation Network waiting lists on the last day of each year (UNOS, 1999).

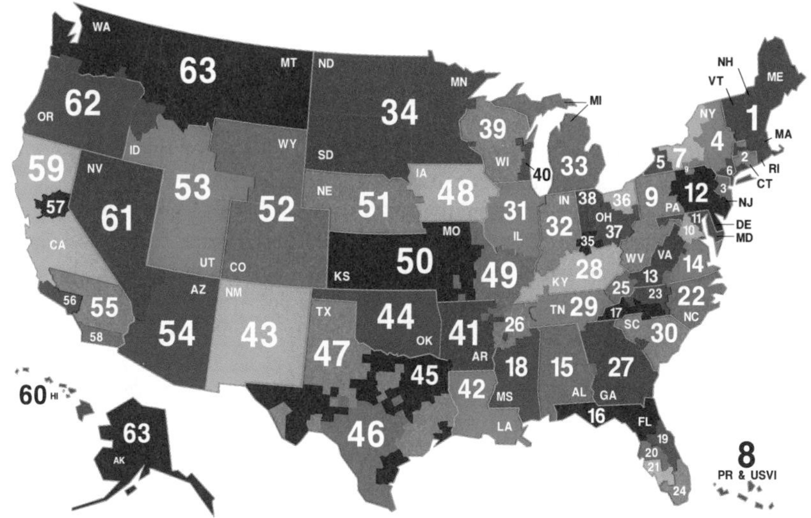

1. New England Organ Bank, Inc.
2. Northeast OPO and Tissue Bank
3. NJ Organ and Tissue Sharing Network
4. Center for Donation and Transplant
5. Upstate New York Transplant Services, Inc.
6. New York Organ Donor Network
7. Univ. of Rochester Organ Procurement Program
8. Lifelink of Puerto Rico
9. Center for Organ Recovery and Education
10. Washington Regional Transplant Consortium
11. Transplant Resource Center of Maryland
12. Delaware Valley Transplant Program
13. Virginia Organ Procurement Agency
14. Life Net
15. Alabama Organ Center
16. The OPO at University of Florida
17. Life Share of the Carolinas
18. Mississippi Organ Recovery Agency, Inc.
19. Translife
20. Lifelink of Florida
21. Lifelink of Southwest Florida
22. Carolina Organ Procurement Agency
23. Carolina Life Care
24. University of Miami OPO
25. Life Resources Donor Center
26. Mid-South Transplant Foundation
27. Lifelink of Georgia
28. Kentucky Organ Donor Affiliates
29. Tennessee Donor Services
30. SC Organ Procurement Agency
31. Regional Organ Bank of Illinois
32. Indiana OPO, Inc.
33. Organ Procurement Agency of MI
34. Upper Midwest OPO, Inc.
35. Ohio Valley Life Center
36. Lifebanc
37. Lifeline of Ohio
38. Life Connection of Ohio
39. University of Wisconsin OPO
40. Wisconsin Donor Network
41. Arkansas Regional Organ Recovery Agency
42. Louisiana Organ Procurement Agency
43. New Mexico Donor Program
44. Oklahoma Organ Sharing Network, Inc.
45. Southwest Transplant Alliance
46. South Texas Organ Bank
47. Life Gift Organ Donation Center
48. Iowa State Organ Procurement Organization
49. Mid-America Transplant Association
50. Midwest Organ Bank
51. Nebraska Organ Retrieval Systems, Inc.
52. Colorado Organ Recovery Systems, Inc.
53. Intermountain Organ Recovery Systems
54. Donor Network of Arizona
55. Southern California Organ Procurement Center
56. Regional Organ Procurement Agency of Southern CA
57. Golden State Transplant Services
58. Organ and Tissue Acquisition Center of Southern CA
59. California Transplant Donor Network
60. Organ Donor Center of Hawaii
61. Nevada Donor Network
62. Pacific Northwest Transplant Bank
63. LifeCenter Northwest

FIGURE 1-1 Organ procurement organization service areas, 1997. SOURCE: DHHS, Health Care Financing Administration and the Office of the Assistant Secretary for Planning and Evaluation, 1997, unpublished data.

Donated organs are transferred to one of 272 transplant centers in the United States (UNOS, 1998). Within these centers are 891 organ-specific transplantation programs (Hauboldt, 1996). The number of transplantation centers in the UNOS registry has increased by nearly 85 percent since 1988, an average increase of almost 10 percent per year (Hauboldt, 1996). For livers, the number of transplant center programs grew from 56 in 1988 to 125 in 1998.

In addition, the current system divides the country into 11 geographic regions, the second level of organization in the organ allocation system. The regions generally follow state boundaries: one region includes only a single state; the others consist of several states. The populations of these regions range from 9.6 million to more than 40 million (DHHS, 1999a). Very recently, UNOS' policies were modified to establish the 11 regions as a second tier for liver allocation.

The origin of the current system is the National Organ Transplant Act of 1984, which created a national transplant system to be operated by transplant professionals, with oversight by DHHS to ensure an equitable allocation system. The act created the Organ Procurement and Transplantation Network (OPTN), a nonprofit private-sector network to be operated by a contractor to DHHS. The United Network for Organ Sharing, or UNOS, has held this contract since 1984.

The statute did not impose a rigid system. Instead, each OPO was allowed to develop its own relationships with the local medical community, while maintaining considerable uniformity with other OPOs in the way they operate (see Chapter 2). Thus, although the system originated in federal statute and corresponding intent, it has over time accommodated local preferences and institutional variation in practice. Under the current system, local patients (i.e., within the OPO, or in some instances within agreed to areas of sharing) are given priority for organs that are procured in that local area. If a matching patient is not found, the search is broadened to the region.

Originally, OPTN membership and policies were voluntary, but with enactment of the Omnibus Budget Reconciliation Act of 1986, which added Section 1138 of the Social Security Act, all hospitals that perform transplants were required to abide by the rules and requirements of the OPTN to be eligible to participate in the Medicare and Medicaid programs.

This act has been amended twice to encourage the development of a fair, national system of organ allocation. The original statute (P.L. 98-507, Title II, Sec. 201, formerly codified at 42 U.S.C. 274(b)(2)(C)) required the OPTN to "assist organ procurement organizations in the distribution of organs, which cannot be placed within the service areas of the organizations." Congress changed the language in 1988 "so as to remove any statutory bias respecting the important question of criteria for the proper distribution of organs among patients" (P.L. 100-607, Title IV, Sec. 403, formerly codified at 42 U.S.C. 274(b)(2)(D)). In 1990, the language was again rewritten, this time to require that the OPTN "assist organ procurement organizations in the nationwide distribution of organs equitably among transplant patients" (P.L. 101-616, Title II, Sec. 202, now codified at 42 U.S.C. 274(b)(2)(D)). The language was also revised to redefine the definition of an OPO service area to be "of sufficient size to ensure the maximum effectiveness of organ procurement and equitable organ allocation."

In December 1989, DHHS issued a Federal Register notice indicating that all OPTN rules and requirements would remain voluntary until the secretary promulgated regulations to define the roles and policy making procedures of the OPTN and DHHS (HCFA, 1989). A Notice of Proposed Rule Making containing these definitions was published on September 8, 1994. The issue of appropriate federal oversight of the system—including procedures for joining the OPTN, the federal review processes, procedures and standards for information collection and dissemination, OPTN membership requirements and compliance procedures, and the criteria for allocation of each of the solid organs—has been a subject of debate since that time. The DHHS proposal, 42 CFR Part 121, "Organ Procurement and Transplantation Network; Final Rule" (DHHS, 1998b) was intended to bring closure to the Notice of Proposed Rule Making, but instead reactivated the debate.

THE LATEST CALL FOR CHANGE: THE "FINAL RULE"

Because human organs are a scarce medical resource, organ transplantation policies and practices have become the subject of controversy about supply, demand, access, rationing, and equity. A major concern expressed by DHHS is that the current system appears to have resulted in large disparities in the total amount of time a patient waits for an organ (i.e., the time from registration to transplant), depending on where he or she lives. For example, a patient with type O blood in need of a liver transplant in New York City may wait 511 days for a new organ, while the same category patient might wait only 56 days in Newark, New Jersey, just a short distance away (DHHS, 1998b).

These disparities have been attributed to a variety of factors. These include variability in the listing criteria; varying supply of and demand for organs among service areas; differences in criteria used in accepting a donated organ (e.g., age, medical factors); and limitations in the categorization schema used (i.e., the criteria used to determine the status of patients and their survivability pre- and posttransplant). Concerns have also been raised that minorities and the poor have less access to some organ transplants, specifically kidneys, than do whites of higher socioeconomic status (Alexander and Sehgal, 1998).

The Final Rule does not establish specific policies to guide transplantation. Rather, it requires that sharing areas be broadened, if necessary, to give priority to those whose needs are medically urgent, that listing criteria be standardized, and that policy and procedural reforms be enacted. The primary objectives are to address disparities in waiting times and in the allocation of organs to low-income and minority patients. A brief description of the major provisions follows.

Major Provisions of the Final Rule

The Final Rule provides a framework within which the OPTN, its members, and other participants in organ procurement and transplantation will operate. The stated principles underlying the final regulation include the need for oversight in a system that permits variance in individual medical practice. A major impetus is the creation of a "level playing field" in organ allocation, where organs are allocated based on patients' medical need and less emphasis is placed on keeping organs in the local area where they are procured. A primary focus is to equalize waiting times among patients similarly situated medically, regardless of residence or location of transplant program. In addition, the Final Rule calls for standardized medical criteria to be used to determine the status of a person's illness and when the person can be placed on a waiting list. Finally, the Final Rule aims to improve data collection and analysis so that patients, their physicians, and the public have timely, accurate, and user-friendly, center-specific data on the performance of transplantation programs to measure quality and make transplant decisions. In announcing the Final Rule, Secretary Shalala said,

> Patients who need an organ transplant should not have to gamble that an organ will become available in their local area, nor should they have to travel to transplant centers far from home simply to improve their chances of getting an organ. Instead, patients everywhere in the country should have an equal chance to receive an organ, based on their medical condition and the judgment of their physicians. (DHHS, 1998a)

DHHS charged that despite technological advances in preserving organs, the system for allocating scarce organs (especially livers) remains weighted to local organ allocation, instead of broader regional or national allocation according to medical need. Thus, a patient who is less ill in one geographic area with a short waiting list may get a matching organ before a patient whose condition is more medically urgent in another area with a longer waiting time. In the Final Rule, DHHS claims that by allocating organs primarily at the local level, current policies give some of the most medically urgent patients a substantially lower chance of being promptly matched to a suitable organ (and thereby receiving a potentially lifesaving transplant) than would be the case with broader geographic sharing.

In addition, DHHS maintains that medical criteria for listing patients and assessing their status vary from one transplantation center to another, making it difficult to objectively compare the medical need of patients awaiting organ transplantation in different centers and different areas of the country. Furthermore, although many data are available, DHHS asserts that there is still a need for more current and usable data collection and dissemination to help patients and doctors in measuring quality and making transplantation decisions.

In general, the Final Rule was developed to establish a framework within which both the OPTN and the DHHS will operate. It delineates the roles of each, providing a basis for the OPTN to act and the department to monitor and review these actions. Major provisions address policy development, allocation of organs, and procedural requirements. Appendix D of this report presents the complete text of the Final Rule; Appendix C presents the current liver allocation policies. The remainder of this section summarizes the following components of the Final Rule: procedural requirements, policy development, and performance goals.

Procedural Requirements

Procedural requirements contained in the Final Rule include:

Transition to New Policies—When the OPTN initially revises organ allocation policies, it must propose transition policies ensuring that people who are already on the national waiting list for transplantation do not receive less favorable treatment than they would have under previous policies.

Board Composition—The Final Rule modifies the composition of the OPTN Board of Directors. At least six public members must come from fields such as behavioral science, computer science, economics, ethics, heath care financing, law, policy analysis, sociology, statistics, or theology. Another eight members, at least 25 percent of the board, must represent transplant candidates, transplant recipients, organ donors, and family members. No more than 50 percent of the members are to be transplant surgeons or transplantation physicians.

Public Access to Data—The Final Rule pays special attention to public access to data. When the secretary determines that information will serve the public's interest, the secretary may release it. The Final Rule requires that the OPTN make performance data available to the public, and that such data be updated every 6 months and be available no more than 6 months later than the period to which they apply. The data are to include the characteristics of individual transplant programs as well as rates of nonacceptance of organs and waiting times, and other data useful to patients, their families, and physicians in making transplantation decisions.

Review and Evaluation—The secretary or her or his designee may review and evaluate member OPOs and transplant hospitals where there is evidence of noncompliance with the OPTN rule or actions that risk patients' health or compromise public safety. Sanctions may include removal of transplantation program designation, termination of the transplant hospital's participation in Medicare or Medicaid, or termination of an OPO's Medicare and Medicaid reimbursement.

Policy Development

The OPTN Board of Directors is responsible for developing organ allocation policies. The National Organ Transplant Act requires that members of the "general public" serve on the OPTN Board of Directors. The Final Rule, as described previously under procedural requirements, expands on this provision by requiring that "eight individuals representing transplant recipients, organ donors, and family members" be included on the board, as well as six members of the general public (42CFR 121.3(a)(1)(ii),(iv)). Proposed policies may be reviewed by the secretary and, if determined appropriate, published in the Federal Register for public comment.

In addition to policies for the equitable allocation of organs, the OPTN's policymaking role includes policies on the training and experience of transplant surgeons and physicians; policies for nominating OPTN board members; and other policies as directed by the secretary. Of particular note, given concerns regarding access to transplantation services for low-income populations and racial and ethnic minority groups, is the Final Rule's requirement that the OPTN board develop policies to reduce inequities resulting from socioeconomic status, including access to transplantation waiting lists (42 CFR 121.4(a)(3)).

Performance Goals

The OPTN Board of Directors is responsible for developing organ-specific policies for equitable organ allocation among potential recipients (including policies for combination transplants, e.g., heart–lung). The Final Rule sets three broad performance goals for organ allocation:

1. standardized listing criteria for placing patients on waiting lists, using to the extent possible objective and measurable medical criteria;
2. standardized criteria for determining medical status, also based, to the extent possible, on objective and measurable medical criteria, sufficient to differentiate patients from least to most medically urgent; and
3. organ allocation policies that give priority to those whose needs are most medically urgent, in accordance with sound medical judgment, with the result that differences in waiting times for patients of like medical status will be reduced.

Finally, the Final Rule requires the OPTN board to focus first on appropriate revisions to its current liver allocation policy and to propose a new liver allocation policy to the secretary within 60 days of the regulation's effective date. Other organ-specific policies must be provided to the secretary within 1 year of the regulation's effective date.

THE ENSUING CONTROVERSY

The issuance of the Final Rule raised a storm of controversy, with patient groups, transplant surgeons, OPOs, and UNOS bringing to the debate their reasons for either supporting or objecting to the proposed changes. Those who support the Final Rule argue that the current system is inequitable, that is, with allocation units that are too small for equitable organ sharing. Proponents argue that a system of broader sharing will alleviate the circumstances in which a very sick patient might die waiting for a liver transplant while a healthier patient just a few miles away (but outside the OPO territory) might receive a transplant (DHHS, 1998b). In addition, advocates for the Final Rule claim that a national system would hinder the ability of patients or physicians to take advantage of defects in the current rules in order to gain personal advantage, a practice often alleged but not substantiated with data.

Those opposed to the Final Rule claim that organ referral and retrieval will be hampered and organ donation rates will drop, if organs are not offered locally first. They argue that OPOs, donor hospitals (the hospital where the donation takes place), and transplant centers have developed working relationships that achieve good results and that disruption of these relationships will result in fewer organs being available for transplantation and, therefore, more deaths. They claim that current variations in waiting time are related to differing listing criteria (a problem being addressed in the current system), differing geographic demand, and differing levels of organ availability, not true inequities in the allocation system (DHHS, 1998b). In addition, they argue, a broader sharing system will result in the closure of some small transplantation centers.

Opponents of the Final Rule assert that "a sickest first policy would create a system that is wasteful and dangerous, resulting in fewer patients transplanted, increased death rates, increased retransplantation due to poor organ function, and increased overall cost of transplantation" (Benjamin, 1999). Some opponents of the Final Rule object in particular to the proposed ability of the DHHS Secretary to make OPTN allocation policies and direct the OPTN to implement them, claiming this will replace medical judgment with political judgment.

Opposition to broader organ sharing is exemplified by the efforts in several states in the last 18 months—Oklahoma, Louisiana, South Carolina, Tennessee, Texas, Arizona, Nevada, New Mexico, Ohio, and Wisconsin—to keep donated organs within their state borders. Some states enacted laws permitting an organ to be sent out of the state only on the condition that the state has entered into a reciprocal organ-sharing agreement with the receiving state. Others adopted resolutions urging Congress to oppose the Final Rule by pushing OPOs to use their best efforts to use organs within a state and by having potential donors stipulate that their organs be first offered to in-state recipients.

CHARGE TO THE COMMITTEE

In October 1998, Congress suspended implementation of the Final Rule for 1 year to allow further study of its potential impact (Omnibus Consolidated and Emergency Supplemental Appropriations Act, 1999, 11 USC, §213, 1999). The Institute of Medicine (IOM) was asked by Congress, through the General Accounting Office, to conduct a study to review the current policies of the OPTN and the potential impact of the Final Rule on:

• access to transplantation services for low-income populations and racial and ethnic minority groups, including the impact of state policies (under Title XIX of the Social Security Act) regarding payment for services for patients outside of the states in which the patients reside;

• organ donation rates, reasons for differences in organ donation rates, and impact of broader sharing (i.e., based on medical criteria instead of geography) on donation rates;

• waiting times for organ transplants, including: (a) determinations specific to the various geographic regions of the United States and, if practicable, waiting times for each transplant center by organ and medical status category, and (b) impact of recent changes made by the OPTN in patient listing criteria and in measures of medical status;

• patient survival rates and organ failure rates leading to retransplantation, including variances by income status, ethnicity, gender, race, or blood type; and

• costs of organ transplantation services.

The legislation that called for this study included two additional areas for review: (1) confidentiality of information about the program, and (2) the possible legal liability of OPTN members arising from their peer review activities. As agreed, the GAO addressed these two issues in a separate report (GAO, 1999). Also as agreed in response to the legislation, GAO assisted IOM by providing data to the committee regarding costs of organ transplantation services.

COMMITTEE METHODS AND FOCUS OF THE REPORT

The committee held three meetings between March and May 1999. At two meetings (March and April) time was devoted to invited public participants and presentations. Additional data were requested, as needed, from UNOS. To complete its work, the IOM committee conducted an independent assessment of the issues to prepare an evidence-based report. Appendix A describes in greater detail the data sources and methods used by the committee.

Focusing the Analysis on Livers

At the committee's first meeting, consideration of several factors suggested that the analysis would be most useful, and more practically conducted, if the committee were to focus on studying the policies, practices, and data concerning liver procurement and allocation. Although many concepts and principles that have to be addressed are not organ-specific (e.g., consistency in criteria for listing, donor motivation), there are some elements specific to livers that justify this focused effort. Among these are:

- Disparities in median waiting times for liver transplants was a primary factor in DHHS's rationale for developing the Final Rule;
- Liver allocation policies have been especially contentious, with the OPTN making several changes in policies in the recent past;
- Because the maximum desirable cold ischemic time for hearts and lungs is 3–4 hours, there is less opportunity to make significant changes in the current allocation rules for them than there is for livers, which have a longer ischemic time; and
- The medical urgency of transplanting livers differs from that for some of the other solid organs, e.g., kidneys (those waiting for livers are often terminally ill with no alternative therapy, while those waiting for kidneys have the potential backup of using dialysis).

The focus on policies and practices related to liver transplantation was also necessitated by the extremely limited amount of time that the committee had for conducting its assessment and preparing its report.

For these reasons, this report focuses on policies and practices related to liver transplantation, unless otherwise noted in the text. As noted above, however, some of the general principles (e.g., consistency in listing criteria) apply in general to all organs.

ORGANIZATION OF THE REPORT

Following this introductory chapter, Chapter 2 describes the current policies and practices in organ procurement and transplantation. The remainder of this report is organized around the five tasks that were received from Congress as follows: Chapter 3 discusses the issue of access to transplantation. Chapter 4 focuses on donation and the possible effects of the Final Rule on donation rates. Chapter 5 provides an analysis of data related to waiting times. Chapter 6 addresses patient survival rates and organ failure. Chapter 7 appraises the effect of the Final Rule on costs of transplantation. Chapter 8 addresses crosscutting issues related to government oversight and review. Several appendixes are included to assist the reader with additional information: Appendix A—Data Sources and Methods; Appendix B—Summary data tables from Chapter 5 regarding waiting time for liver transplantation; Appendix C—Current UNOS Liver Allocation Policies; Appendix D—DHHS Final Rule; and Appendix E—Committee and Staff Biographies.

2

Current Policies and Practices

The transplant community is joined under a nationwide umbrella: the OPTN, administered, since its inception, under contract by UNOS. UNOS, located in Richmond, Virginia, is a private, not-for-profit, membership corporation qualified as a charitable organization under Section 501(c)(3) of the Internal Revenue Code. UNOS also administers the U.S. Scientific Registry on Organ Transplantation under contract with the Department of Health and Human Services (DHHS). The U.S. Scientific Registry tracks all solid organ transplants since October 1, 1987.

UNOS members include every transplant program, OPO, and tissue-typing laboratory in the United States. Policies governing the transplant community are developed by UNOS membership through a series of regional meetings, deliberations at the national committee level, and final approval by a 40-member board of directors comprised of medical professionals, transplant recipients, and donor family members. All patients accepted onto a member transplant hospital's waiting list are registered with the UNOS Organ Center, where a centralized computer network links all organ procurement organizations and transplant centers (see Box 2-1 for definitions). Through the UNOS Organ Center, organ donors are matched to waiting recipients 24 hours a day, 365 days a year. UNOS uses a formula for matching based on medical criteria for each type of organ. Patients awaiting livers receive additional consideration based on the amount of time they have been on the waiting list. Those on the list for longer periods of time are situated higher on the list, Appendix C of this report contains the current UNOS Liver Allocation Policies.

As described in Chapter 1, there are currently 11 regions, comprised of 62 OPOs, with 891 organ-specific transplant programs (125 liver transplantation programs). This chapter summarizes the current policies and priorities related to organ procurement and transplantation. Since OPOs are a key component of the system, the discussion focuses on their operation and the organ allocation process. Particular attention is paid to liver allocation.

ORGAN PROCUREMENT ORGANIZATIONS

OPOs are nonprofit, private entities that facilitate the acquisition and distribution of organs. There are 62 nationally, all with similar responsibilities. As noted in Chapter 1, OPO service areas vary widely in geographic size and demographic composition, as well as in the number of hospitals, transplant centers, and patients served (GAO, 1997).

BOX 2-1 Definitions

OPO. An organ procurement organization is an organization that is accepted as a member of UNOS and authorized by the Health Care Financing Administration (HCFA) to procure organs for transplantation. For each OPO, HCFA defines a geographic procurement territory within which the OPO concentrates its efforts.

Transplant Center. A hospital that is a member of UNOS in which transplants are performed. A transplant center may also be called a transplant hospital.

Transplant Program. A transplant center, or hospital, may have one or more transplant programs. Each program oversees transplantation of one or more organ types.

UNOS Patient Waiting List. The computerized list of patients waiting to be matched with specific donor organs in hopes of receiving transplants. Patients are registered on the UNOS waiting list by UNOS member transplant centers, programs, or OPOs.

UNOS Match System. The computerized algorithm used to prioritize patients waiting for organs. It identifies potential recipients whose size or ABO type is compatible with that of a donor and then ranks these potential recipients according to the ranking system approved by the UNOS board.

Host OPO. The host OPO is the one that, having identified a potential organ donor, assumes responsibility for donor management and organ allocation.

Local and Alternative Local Unit. In most cases, the local unit is the OPO. Alternative local units, such as subdivisions of the OPO that function as distinct areas for organ procurement and distribution, entire states, UNOS regions, or other appropriate units, are acceptable if they can be demonstrated to the satisfaction of the UNOS Board of Directors to fulfill UNOS principles and adhere to applicable laws and regulations.

SOURCE: UNOS, 1999.

OPOs work with the medical community and the public through professional education and public awareness efforts to encourage cooperation in and acceptance of organ donation. They provide all the services necessary in a geographical region for coordinating the identification of potential donors, requests for donation, and recovery and transport of organs.

Federal regulations (42 CFR Part 486, Subpart G) require OPOs to meet service area and other performance requirements. Service areas must be "of sufficient size to ensure maximum effectiveness of organ procurement and equitable organ allocation." As of January 1, 1996, each OPO must meet at least one of the following service area requirements:

1. Include an entire state or official U.S. territory.
2. Procure organs from an average of at least 24 donors per calendar year in the 2 years before the year of redesignation, or request and receive an exception to this requirement.
3. If it operates exclusively in a noncontiguous U.S. state, territory, or commonwealth, achieve the rate of 50 percent of the national average of all OPOs for both kidneys procured and transplanted per million population.
4. If it is a new entity, demonstrate that it can procure organs from at least 50 potential donors per calendar year.

In addition, each OPO must have a board of directors or an advisory board with the authority to recommend policies on donating, procuring, and distributing organs. The board must have a transplant surgeon from each transplant center in the OPO's service area and representation from hospital administrations, tissue banks, voluntary health associations, and either intensive care or emergency room personnel, the public, and physicians or personnel skilled in human histocompatibility and neurology (§371(b)(1)(G) of the Public Health Service Act 42 U.S.C. 273(b)(1)(G)).

Demographic characteristics of a service area influence organ procurement. For example, the rate of donation among African American families is typically lower than among white families (Eckhoff et al., 1998; GAO, 1997). Further, most potential organ donors share certain characteristics, including causes of death, the absence of certain diseases such as AIDS, and being within a certain age range. However, OPO service area populations can differ greatly in these characteristics. Thus, the ratio of potential organ donors to the total population in the service area may vary greatly for OPOs (see Chapter 4).

Some OPOs have sharing arrangements between or among themselves. Two or more OPOs can agree to share organs, interregionally or intraregionally. OPOs distribute organs pursuant to a sharing arrangement with the prior approval by the OPTN Board of Directors. Organs must be distributed within the sharing area on the basis of a common patient waiting list unless an appropriate alternative local unit for the area is approved by the OPTN. With the exception of arrangements that are approved for a finite time period to test a stated hypothesis with defined parameters under controlled conditions, OPOs participating in a sharing arrangement must have geographically contiguous service areas.

OPO Performance Standards

The Health Care Financing Administration (HCFA) administers Section 1138 of the Social Security Act (42 U.S.C. 1320b-8), under which the agency sets performance standards for OPOs. The act requires the Secretary of DHHS to designate one OPO per service area and requires OPOs to meet DHHS-specified standards and qualifications to receive payment from Medicare and Medicaid.

Without HCFA certification, an OPO cannot continue to operate. Section 371(b)(3)(B) of the Public Health Service Act (42 U.S.C. 273(b)(3)(B)) provides that an OPO should "conduct and participate in systematic efforts, including professional education, to acquire all usable organs from potential donors." In addition, each OPO must meet HCFA performance standards in at least four of five categories to remain certified by HCFA and receive Medicare and Medicaid payment (45 CFR Part 486).

The performance standards include numerical goals in each of the five categories based on performance per million population in the OPO service area. The five categories include number of (1) organ donors; (2) kidneys recovered; (3) kidneys transplanted; (4) extrarenal organs (hearts, livers, pancreata, and lungs) recovered; and (5) extrarenal organs transplanted. HCFA assesses the performance standards and qualifications of OPOs every 4 years.

THE ORGAN ALLOCATION PROCESS

When organs are donated, a complex process begins that involves sequential matching efforts first within a local area and then outside. The procuring organization accesses a centralized computer operated by UNOS, enters information about the donor organs into the computer, runs the match program, and coordinates the procuring and transplanting surgical teams. The computer program generates a list of potential recipients ranked according to medical and other criteria (e.g., blood type, tissue type, size of the organ, medical urgency of the patient, as well as time already spent on the waiting list, and distance between donor and recipient). This list then reflects current allocation policies. Each type of organ has a specific matching algorithm because of differences among organs in their cold ischemic times and the requirements for improving the compatibility between the donor and the recipient. For livers, the list has three sections: (1) all medically suitable "local" patients in rank order by medical urgency status; (2) all medically suitable patients outside the local area but within the area's OPTN region in similar rank order; and (3) all medically suitable patients outside the region in rank order.

After obtaining the list of potential recipients, the transplant coordinator contacts the transplant surgeon caring for the top-ranked local patient to offer the organ. Laboratory tests designed to measure the compatibility between the donor organ and recipient are necessary for some transplants. A surgeon will not accept the organ if these tests show that the patient's immune system will reject it. Surgeons also turn away organs that they believe are less than optimal because of the age or health status of the donor (Hanto, 1999). Often, a "backup" patient is notified, because the organ may be declined by the transplant center, at least for the patient for whom it was initially accepted. If the organ is turned down, the OPO contacts the transplant surgeon caring for the next patient on the waiting list, and so on until a recipient is identified. Once the organ is accepted, transportation arrangements are made and surgery is scheduled.

Although potential transplant patients may select from among most transplant hospitals in the United States (subject to insurance coverage), under current OPTN policies the number of organs available to a hospital does not rise or fall as the number of patients on its waiting list increases or decreases. Rather, it is largely dependent on the number of donors in that hospital's OPO area. As a consequence of a "local-first" allocation policy, most organs leave the local OPO area only if there are no local patients who could use them.*

Once the appropriate donor information is provided, a transplant center is allowed 1 hour from the time of the organ offer in which to communicate its acceptance of the organ. After 1 hour, the offering entity may offer the organ to the transplant center for the patient listed next in priority by the UNOS Match System. After a transplant center indicates its initial acceptance of an organ, the transplant centers or OPOs involved must agree upon the time organ procurement will begin. If the procurement time cannot be agreed upon, the host OPO may withdraw the offer.

If an abdominal organ has been unsuccessfully offered to appropriate transplant centers for allocation to local patients (or unsuccessfully offered to transplant centers through an approved regional sharing arrangement), the UNOS Organ Center can be used to allocate the organ first regionally, and then nationally, based on a point system set forth in UNOS policies.

Listing Criteria, Patient Status

Because the current liver allocation policies give weight to waiting time, some people believe that some physicians list patients for transplants as early as possible, perhaps long before they are ready for transplant. For a variety of reasons some patients do not come to the attention of transplant professionals until later in the course of their illness. As a result, persons with a comparable medical need for a transplant may have substantially different waiting times.

---

*An exception is the policy of "no-mismatch" or "six-antigen match" kidneys, which are shared nationally.

Critics of the current system say that current liver allocation criteria fail to differentiate adequately among different degrees of medical urgency and express a desire for substantial improvements in the use of objective medical criteria for the classification of patients. In some cases, existing allocation criteria are based on situational factors, such as whether a person is hospitalized, which are neither medical criteria nor necessarily good proxies for an underlying medical condition or urgency (see Table 1-2). UNOS revised the listing criteria recently to address some of these issues, and some people argue that these changes, combined with advances in transplantation medicine and the OPTN's extensive investment in patient information systems, have resulted in substantial improvements in standardizing the medical urgency classifications of patients. Potential organ recipients may be placed on the waiting lists of more than one transplant center (UNOS, 1999). This UNOS policy was established in large part as a response to demands from the patient community. Each local listing will be added to the OPTN patient waiting list, so that the same patient may be on the OPTN waiting list multiple times. A patient may transfer his or her primary waiting time from one transplant center to another. Waiting time accrued by a patient for one type of organ may also be accrued for a second organ, if it is determined that the patient requires a multiple-organ transplant.

Changes in Liver Allocation Policies

In 1996, the OPTN board approved a new liver allocation policy. The policy gave higher priority to transplanting patients with acute hepatic failure and primary nonfunction over chronic patients. Advocates of this change believed that patients experiencing acute fulminant liver failure (and therefore with only a few days to live) have a high probability of survival and a low re-transplantation rate if transplanted quickly. In changing the policy, the OPTN Board believed that it would increase the total number of people nationwide benefiting from liver transplantation (Showstack et al., 1999).

Patients with chronic liver disease and their advocates asserted that their chance to receive a liver had been decreased significantly by the new policy. In addition, they asserted that there was no significant medical justification for favoring the "acute" group, arguing that the acute patients did not have a better posttransplant survival rate than chronic patients. They also criticized having all chronic patients being grouped together, rather than differentiating among chronic patients and their varying medical conditions. Opponents of the new policy requested the development of a system of classification based on objective and relevant medical criteria and for broader sharing of organs (DHHS, 1998b).

In June 1997, the UNOS Board of Directors voted to implement a new policy. The newer policy places very ill patients with chronic disease in a separate status subgroup and also assigns them a second priority (i.e., after acute patients). DHHS claims that this change reduces, but does not eliminate, the disadvantage that had been imposed on chronic patients in 1996. In 1998 further changes were made to improve consistency in listing (see Table 2-1).

Most recently, in June 1999, UNOS announced a revision to its liver allocation policy that aims to broaden access for the most urgent patients (UNOS, 1999). Under the revised policy, livers will be offered first to the most urgent category of patients (status 1) within the "local" area of the donor, usually defined as the designated service area of one of the 62 OPOs nationwide. If no match is found for a local status 1 patient, the liver would be offered to status 1 patients throughout the UNOS region where the donation occurred before being considered for any less urgent candidates (see Appendix C).

TABLE 2-1 UNOS Liver Status for Patients ≥ 18 Years of Age According to Disease Severity

Status 1	Fulminant liver failure with life expectancy <7 days • Fulminant hepatic failure as traditionally defined • Primary graft nonfunction <7 days of transplantation • Hepatic artery thrombosis <7 days of transplantation • Acute decompensated Wilson's disease
Status 2A	Hospitalized in Intensive Care Unit for chronic liver failure with life expectancy <7 days, with a Child-Pugh score of ≥10 and one of the following: • Unresponsive active vericeal hemorrhage • Hepatorenal syndrome • Refractory ascities or hepatic hydrothorax • Stage 3 or 4 hepatic encephalopathy
Status 2B	Requiring continuous medical care, with a Child-Pugh score of ≥10, or a Child-Pugh score of ≥7 and one of the following: • Unresponsive active variceal hemorrhage • Hepatrorenal syndrome • Spontaneous bacterial peritonitis • Refractory ascites or hepatic hydrothorax
Status 3	Requiring continuous medical care, with a Child-Pugh score of ≥7 but not meeting criteria for Status 2B
Status 7	Temporarily inactive

SOURCE: Keeffe, 1998; data obtained from UNOS website (http://unos.org) initially implemented July 1997, modified January 1998.

CRITICISMS OF THE CURRENT POLICIES

Partly as a result of the controversy surrounding the new UNOS liver allocation policies, some have questioned whether a private sector agency (i.e., the OPTN contractor) can or should set policy for a system that has such a profound effect on life-and-death decisions (DHHS, 1998b).

In comments provided on the Final Rule, a number of individuals and organizations argued that the approval of a flawed liver allocation policy in November 1996 and the failure to improve current policy in more fundamental ways illustrate systemic flaws in the current governance structure, specifically the structure of the UNOS Board of Directors. Some assert that the OPTN is dominated by hospitals (large and small) and transplant surgeons and physicians, and that the greater public interests—the altruistic motives of donors and their families and the health and survival of potential recipients—are not given adequate attention. Still others claim that hospitals, physicians, and payers can manipulate the current system of organ allocation and listing by excluding high-risk patients from the list, listing patients early to gain waiting time points, listing patients at more than one transplant hospital to increase the chance of getting an organ, and referring high-risk patients to other hospitals to avoid adverse performance outcomes.

Criticisms and concerns have also been raised about the role of the federal government in the oversight and regulation of decision making with respect to organ procurement and transplantation.

CONCLUSIONS

The discrepancy between the number of donated organs and the need for organ transplants has called into question current policies and practices regarding allocation and distribution of organs, particularly livers. There is ongoing controversy about the uniformity of listing criteria, referral practices, donation rates, access, and the effects of these factors on waiting times. The committee concludes that although controversy may continue regarding many of these issues, the objectives of uniform minimal listing criteria, better data collection, and greater accountability on the part of the organ transplant system, seem reasonable and should be pursued with vigor.

3

Access to Transplantation

***Task 1**: Assess current policies and the potential impact of the Final Rule on access to transplantation services for low-income populations and racial and ethnic minority groups, including the impact of state policies (under Title XIX of the Social Security Act) regarding payment for services for patients outside of the state in which the patients reside.*

***Abstract.* There is very little research describing or explaining differences in access to liver transplantation services across racial, ethnic, and income groups. Therefore, the committee's findings are based on a small number of studies, most pertaining to kidney transplants, that report differences between white and African American populations or income classes and on the committee's own analysis of patient waiting times on liver transplantation lists. The published evidence reveals that African American and low-income kidney patients of all racial and ethnic groups are slower to be placed on waiting lists and, once on a waiting list, African Americans do not receive kidney transplants as quickly as whites. Well-known biological and socioeconomic factors, and lack of access to health care in general, undoubtedly play large parts in this disparity. African Americans may also be referred for liver transplants more slowly than whites, but once patients are referred, there appears to be little or no racial disparity in transplantation. The committee found no unequivocal evidence one way or the other on whether broader organ sharing would result in either closure of small transplant centers or, in the event of some such closures, a reduction in minority access. The most important predictors of equity in access to transplant services lie outside the transplantation system in access to health insurance and high-quality health services.**

The committee was charged with determining what, if any, impact the Final Rule would have on access to transplantation services by low-income and minority populations. Although African Americans represent about 12 percent of the U.S. population, they comprise 27 percent of the patients diagnosed with end-stage renal disease. This is due to a variety of factors, including a higher incidence among them of hypertension and diabetes, but it underlines the need for analyzing all the possible effects of the Final Rule. Conducting this analysis required the committee to examine the determinants of access and how current policies affect access in order to draw conclusions about the potential impact of the changes proposed in the Final Rule. The very limited number of studies addressing these issues made this a challenging assignment, and the committee cautions that its findings must be considered provisional rather than conclusive.

The committee reviewed several articles that examine whether minorities have equal access to transplantation. Although almost all of these articles deal with kidney transplantation, the committee believes that some of the factors that bear on curtailed minority access to kidney transplants are also likely to bear on access to other solid organ transplants, although data on these issues are limited.

Lower access by African Americans to kidney transplantation is well documented (Alexander and Sehgal, 1998; Eggers, 1995). Much of the disparity appears to be due to the fact that African Americans are not placed on waiting lists as quickly, or in the same proportion, as their white counterparts. Moreover, once they are placed on a waiting list, African Americans do not receive kidney transplants as quickly as whites (Alexander and Sehgal, 1998; Eggers, 1995; DHHS, 1998c: Kasiske et al., 1991).

African Americans appear to fare somewhat better with respect to liver transplants than is the case with kidneys. Eckhoff and colleagues (1998) reviewed liver transplantation performed at the Alabama Organ Center and concluded that African Americans may experience a delay in referral to the center for evaluation or may not be referred at all, compared to the white population. However, they also concluded that once patients were referred, there were no racial disparities in being accepted onto the waiting list or in receiving a transplant. They suggested that access to health care, distrust of the medical community, lower socioeconomic status, and a lack of understanding about liver transplantation on the parts of both physicians and patients could be factors that influence the disparities in patient referrals. The DHHS Inspector General also found that the waiting times of African Americans for livers was quite similar to those of whites (DHHS, 1998c).

The committee's own analysis of waiting list data for 1995-1999 showed that for livers, African Americans comprised 8 percent of the list and received 9 percent of the transplants. These results indicate that the racial disparity in transplantation observed among patients on waiting lists for kidneys is not observed among patients waiting for livers. It does appear, however, that African Americans enter the list and receive liver transplants when they are sicker, relative to other racial groups. A greater percentage of African Americans are both listed and transplanted in status 1 (12 percent listed and 14 percent transplanted) relative to status 2 (10 percent listed and 8 percent transplanted) or status 3 (7 percent listed and 7 percent transplanted). The fact that African Americans are listed in disproportionately high numbers in status 1 reinforces the suggestion that initial access to health care and to referrals for transplant evaluation is an important impediment for African Americans with liver disease.

FACTORS AFFECTING ACCESS

Factors that might influence waiting list entry and account for differences in transplantation rates can be characterized broadly as: (1) socioeconomic factors; (2) severity of illness, general health status, and biological and medical suitability for transplantation; (3) characteristics of the transplant centers; and (4) in the case of kidney transplantation, patients' attitudes about dialysis versus transplantation.

Socioeconomic Factors

Ozminkowski and colleagues (1997), among others, have identified socioeconomic status as a major factor in determining whether kidney patients are able to get on a waiting list, accounting for one-third of the disparity between African Americans and whites. Patients with annual incomes greater than $40,000 were twice as likely to be added to a waiting list within 2 years of their first end-stage renal disease service as those with incomes less than $10,000 per year, and African Americans were disproportionately represented in the latter group. However, once a patient was placed on a waiting list, socioeconomic status seemed to have had little influence on whether the patient receives a transplant. A similar analysis by Alexander and Sehgal (1998) found black-white differences in transplantation even after controlling for income, but also found that the primary barrier for poor people as a group was gaining access to the waiting list.

The committee heard allegations that low-income patients were sometimes considered unsuitable candidates for kidney transplantation because of concerns about their ability to pay for immunosuppressive drugs. The committee could find only limited evidence to support this claim. For example, a telephone survey of four of the five renal transplant centers in Virginia found that 2 percent of all transplants performed over a 6.5 year period were lost to noncompliance due to inaffordability (Holman, 1999). On the other hand:

1. Medicare pays for these drugs, for virtually all kidney transplant patients, for 3 years post transplant.
2. Dosages, and therefore cost, are significantly reduced after three years.
3. Medicaid has no time limit for drug coverage.
4. There are a variety of state programs and private organizations (e.g., the American Kidney Foundation) that assist transplant patients in obtaining these medications.

The committee concluded that, although some patients might need additional help in maintaining immunosuppressive medication, implementation of the Final Rule is not likely to add to those numbers.

Biological Factors

Biological differences among racial and ethnic groups appear to be a factor in explaining the differential rates of transplantation. This is more important for kidney transplantation, which uses histocompatibility testing in matching organs and recipients, than it is for other solid organs, which rely on matching by blood type.

Histocompatibility testing works to the disadvantage of African Americans in two ways. First, the serological reagents currently used for such testing were developed primarily in whites and are not as reliable when used for African Americans. This problem may be alleviated in the future, however, by recent technological advances using molecular characterization of the genetic loci that give rise to histocompatibility antigens. Second, African Americans exhibit much greater heterogeneity in their histocompatibility antigens than whites, which makes it much more difficult to locate a fully matched organ in the pool of available donors. This problem could be alleviated to some degree by increasing organ donation among African Americans, although the high degree of heterogeneity within the African American populace means that successful matches will not necessarily increase in proportion to increased donation. De-emphasizing HLA matching would also result in more African Americans getting kidneys, though at the cost of a decrease in graft and host survival.

Another possible reason for the longer wait times for African American kidney patients is that nonwhite patients tend to survive longer on dialysis than do whites (Held et al., 1987). The reason for this is unknown, but adjustment for case mix, transplantation rates, withdrawal from dialysis rates, and initial treatment modality, although reducing the white-nonwhite disparity, did not eliminate the survival advantage for nonwhite dialysis patients (Mesler et al., 1999).

Other Factors

Ozminkowski et al. (1997) examined the influence of severity of renal disease, type of dialysis, contraindications for transplantation, and self-reported health and functional status, but found that none of these factors had a significant effect on racial disparities in terms of either access to a waiting list or receiving a kidney transplant. They did find that patient attitudes toward transplantation constituted a major factor in the racial disparities in both placement on a waiting list and receipt of a transplant. African Americans were less positive about the medical and health outcomes of kidney transplantation than whites and much more likely to express religious objections to transplantation, as well as uneasiness about having a dead person's organ in one's own body. However, a recent report by Ayanian and colleagues (1999) found black and white patients equally likely to report that they wanted a transplant, and similar in their expectations that transplantation would improve their quality of life.

POTENTIAL CLOSURE OF SMALL TRANSPLANT CENTERS

One of the arguments against the Final Rule is that it will cause some of the smaller liver transplant centers to close, forcing some patients to travel greater distances to be placed on a waiting list and receive a transplant. Some argue that this would be an insurmountable obstacle for poor patients and minorities.

The view that low-volume liver transplant centers would be forced to close if the Final Rule were implemented is apparently grounded on the assumption that since such centers currently have fewer status 1 or status 2A patients on their waiting lists, or have patients with shorter accumulated waiting times, a broader sharing arrangement that gave priority to status 1 and status 2A patients, and also took waiting time into account, would result in smaller centers' receiving fewer donated organs, with a corresponding decrease in the economic viability of these centers.

The committee was not persuaded by this argument. Even if the premise is a reasonably accurate characterization of the current situation for some of the low-volume transplant centers, the committee was not willing to assume it would remain unchanged after implementation of the Final Rule. The transplantation arena is dynamic and evolving. As policies and practices change, transplant centers and transplant patients will respond and adapt. Broader organ sharing may well increase the prospects that a patient listed at a low-volume transplant center will obtain a suitable matching organ. Thus, low-volume transplant centers may begin to increase the number of status 1 and status 2 patients on their waiting lists. In addition, the committee, later in this report (see Chapter 5), recommends that waiting times be discontinued as a factor in allocating organs among status 3 patients. These and other possible changes in the current allocation policies might dramatically alter the status quo. Moreover, the committee anticipates that the Department and the OPTN would fashion a transition process that would address these concerns. Given the paucity of evidence on this issue, this phase-in period should include close attention to impact on both access of minority and low-income populations, and the viability of small centers.

There is some preliminary information that counters the argument that broader sharing under the Final Rule would adversely affect small transplant centers. Beginning in January 1998, New York State began sharing donated livers statewide for patients of all statuses. This arrangement encompasses four OPOs, six liver transplant centers, a population of 18 million, and more than 300 liver transplants per year. Contrary to the argument put forward by opponents of the Final Rule, during the first year of statewide sharing the smallest transplant centers in New York State experienced an increase in organs allocated to them, and the largest center experienced a small decrease (Charles Miller, Recanati/Miller Transplantation Institute, The Mount Sinai Hospital, personal communication, April 23, 1999). Preliminary evidence for 1999 indicates that this trend is continuing. Although the committee does not consider this proof that the same will occur in other parts of the country under broader organ sharing, it does believe, in the absence of evidence to the contrary, that it is a plausible outcome.

The committee examined the proposition that access to transplantation on the part of minorities would be adversely affected if low-volume centers were to close. It did so by analyzing 1998 data supplied by UNOS (Mary Ellison, UNOS, personal communication, May 3, 1999) on the number of African Americans and the number of Hispanics who received transplants at each center, as well as the number in each group who were on the waiting list of each transplant center that year. Three separate analyses were conducted, using different criteria to identify transplant centers relevant to the argument.

First, the committee identified 12 transplant centers that did 25 or fewer liver transplants in 1998 and were the only transplant centers in their communities. Of the total of 181 transplants done by these 12 centers, 3 of the liver recipients were African Americans and 23 were Hispanics (which were predominantly performed in two centers).

In the second analysis, the committee identified 27 transplant centers that did 15 or fewer transplants in 1998 and were located in communities with at least two transplant centers. These 27 centers did a total of 193 liver transplants, of which 26 were African American and 38 were Hispanic.

Finally, the committee looked at the waiting lists at the seven smallest transplant centers, each of which was the only center in its community. A total of 239 patients were on the waiting lists of these seven centers in 1998. Of these, 15 were African Americans (all at one center) and 18 were Hispanics.

Although the committee was unwilling to draw definitive conclusions from this brief analysis, these figures do seem to suggest that small transplant centers do not differentially serve minorities' access to liver transplantation at this time. The committee had sought to do a similar analysis for low-income patients, but it was not able to obtain any data on the socioeconomic status of patients transplanted or on waiting lists.

The committee also approached this issue by looking for evidence that an increase in the distance from a transplant patient's home to the transplant center (which would result from the closure of a small transplant center closer to home) would be an impediment to access. No direct examination of this factor was found, but Ozminkowski and colleagues (1997) reported that neither the distance from the patient's home to the nearest kidney transplant center (more than 50 miles versus less than 50 miles) nor the volume of transplants done by the nearest center was associated with differences in access to either a waiting list or a transplant. To the contrary, they suggested that the consolidation of current waiting lists into larger regional lists might help reduce disparities in access by giving waiting list patients access to a wider range of donor organs.

Ozminkowski's conclusion that distance from the patient's residence to the transplant center did not affect access would appear to be contradicted by Tuttle-Newhall and colleagues (1997), who studied patients admitted to a North Carolina hospital with a diagnosis of liver disease. They found that the likelihood of such patients' receiving a liver transplant at one of the two transplant centers in

North Carolina was greater for those living closer to the centers. They also found that access was influenced by a variety of other factors, including age, gender, type of disease, and payer status. However, the committee notes an important limitation of this study, which would suggest caution in interpreting its results. The study included only patients who received their transplants at one of the two transplant centers in North Carolina; the researchers noted that more than half (136 of 261) of the North Carolina residents receiving liver transplants during the study period received their transplants at centers in other states. Moreover, the analysis included all patients admitted to a hospital with liver disease, rather than being limited to those whose condition indicated that a liver transplant was appropriate. The study did not report whether an analysis was done for the effects of race or socioeconomic status.

POTENTIAL IMPLICATIONS OF MEDICAID PAYMENT POLICIES

All third party payers have rules about when and where covered patients may get a transplant, including state Medicaid programs, which cover low-income patients. The committee reviewed current state Medicaid policies regarding payments for transplantation to determine whether potential transplant recipients who are eligible for Medicaid might be adversely affected by changes in the current transplantation system proposed under the Final Rule. Again, the major concern expressed by opponents of the Final Rule is that it would result in the closure of smaller transplant centers and would decrease access on the part of those who depend on Medicaid to pay for transplants.

Based on the information available to the committee, it appears that the most established solid organ transplants—kidney, heart, and liver—are a covered service in nearly any state (see paragraph 15,501ff of the CCH Medicare and Medicaid Guide). Coverage for pancreas and lung transplants is less consistent across states. Several states limit coverage of transplants to patients who are categorically eligible for Medicaid, but most include coverage for both categorically and medically needy eligible individuals.* Some states have set restrictions on the medical conditions for which transplants will be funded, and many require prior approval from the state Medicaid agency for some or all transplants. Some states do not specifically address organ transplants in their plan, presumably treating them as one of many unspecified, mandatory, inpatient hospital services, subject to the test of "medical necessity." There were no data available to the committee to assess the effectiveness of these policies in securing access to transplantation for those eligible for Medicaid.

Of interest to the committee is whether states will pay for transportation costs when a patient must travel from his or her residence to a distant transplant

*The reader is referred to Section 1902(a)(10) of the Social Security Act (42 USC 1396a(a)(10) for explanation of the varying types of Medicaid eligibility.

center. Under the federal regulations governing Medicaid, states must "ensure necessary transportation for [patients] to and from" the provider of care (42 CFR 431.53). "Transportation" is further defined to include related travel expenses, such as meals and lodging en route to and from medical care and while receiving care, both for the patient and, if necessary, for an attendant (42 CFR 440.170(a)). Payments for food and lodging are often marginal, however, and many states may restrict payment for transportation to the amount needed to reach the nearest available provider. Thus, if there is a transplant center located in a state, the state Medicaid plan may limit payments to transportation to this center. However, if there is no center in the state, payment will be made for transportation to and treatment in the nearest available transplant center. Thus, it appears that broader organ sharing resulting from implementation of the Final Rule is not likely to have a significant adverse effect on those who are dependent on Medicaid for their health care.

CONCLUSIONS

The committee did not find credible evidence that broader sharing or the Final Rule would result in the closure of smaller transplant centers. Moreover, even if smaller centers were to close, the committee was unable to conclude that it would have a significant adverse impact on access to organ transplantation on the part of minority and low-income patients. This does not mean, however, that the committee failed to recognize that there are serious concerns about equitable access that must be addressed. It only means that the committee believes that these problems will not be exacerbated if broader sharing is given a reasonable implementation. Broader sharing may even serve to alleviate some of these problems.

The committee notes that the Final Rule places responsibility on the Organ Procurement and Transplantation Network Board of Directors to develop:

> Policies that reduce inequities resulting from socioeconomic status, including, but not limited to:
>
> (i) Ensuring that patients in need of a transplant are listed without regard to ability to pay or source of payment;
>
> (ii) Procedures for transplant hospitals to make reasonable efforts to make available from their own resources, or obtain from other sources, financial resources for patients unable to pay such that these patients have an opportunity to obtain a transplant and necessary follow-up care;
>
> (iii) Recommendations to private and public payers and service providers on ways to improve coverage of organ transplantation and necessary follow-up care; and
>
> (iv) Reform of allocation policies based on assessment of their cumulative effect on socioeconomic inequities. (DHHS, 1998b, p.16334)

The larger problems of equitable access to transplantation occur prior to a patient being put on a waiting list for a transplant; they take the form of inadequate health insurance coverage and inadequate access to primary care, proper diagnosis and treatment, and referral for transplant evaluation.

4

Organ Donation

Task 2*: Assess current policies and the potential impact of the Final Rule on organ donation rates, the reasons for differences in organ donation rates and the impact of broader sharing (that is, based on medical criteria instead of geography), on donation rates.*

***Abstract.* Many factors unrelated to the size of organ allocation areas affect organ donation rates. Based on the limited data available, the committee found no convincing evidence to support the claim that broader sharing would adversely affect donation rates or that potential donors would decline to donate because an organ might be used outside the immediate geographic area. In fact, there is some evidence suggesting that broader sharing is associated with increased rates of donation, although the reasons for this are not clear. Regardless of the impact of the size of the allocation area on donation rates, current efforts to increase donation seem to be having a positive effect and should be encouraged to continue.**

The organ procurement and transplantation process begins at the hospital when a patient is identified as a potential organ donor. Most donated organs come from patients who are pronounced brain dead as a result of disease or injury, most notably, brain hemorrhage and injuries from motor vehicle crashes, gunshot or stab wounds, or asphyxiation (UNOS, 1999). Once a potential donor has been identified, someone from the hospital or an organ procurement organization (OPO) typically contacts the donor's family. If the family consents to donation, OPO staff coordinates the rest of the procurement activities, from organ recovery and preservation to transport to a transplant center for transplantation. The system by which organs are procured and transplanted includes many participants, including the family of the organ donor, the procuring surgeon, the OPO, the Organ Procurement and Transplantation Network (OPTN) operated by the United Network for Organ Sharing (UNOS), the transplant surgeon, the hospital staff, and the organ recipient.

The task of the committee with regard to organ donation was to determine what impact current allocation policies might have on organ donation rates and to assess the potential consequences of broader sharing of organs in larger geographic areas. The committee was not charged with solving the problem of the need for more donation, but instead, with determining the factors affecting donation that might be influenced by the Final Rule. This task is difficult because of the many elements that affect donation and the limited amount of published literature on this subject.

Among the many factors affecting donation are donor family motivation and OPO procurement practices, both having potentially significant influence on the number of organs actually recovered. Thus, for example, a highly motivated family might not be approached in a health care facility that does not actively pursue organ procurement. Conversely, ambivalent or unaware potential donor families could be persuaded to donate by health care providers trained in the appropriate procedures for actively pursuing organ procurement. Trying to parse out the relative contributions of donation versus procurement to organ availability rates is complex and few reliable data exist documenting the relative effects of either factor. To attribute any one factor—for example, local allocation policies—to potential changes in donation rates is overly simplistic.

Yet a central issue for opponents of broader sharing is that it will reduce organ donation because people will be less motivated to donate if the organs are not used locally. They also claim that health professionals will be less motivated to procure organs, knowing that they will not necessarily be used locally. Proponents of broader sharing argue that the changes in policy will not adversely affect donation rates because people are not motivated to donate for the purpose of local use.

CURRENT STATUS

Despite the increasing numbers of patients in need of organ transplantation, its potential to save lives is limited by the shortage of suitable organs for transplantation. National estimates of the number of potential organ donors vary widely, from 5,000 to 29,000 (Association of Organ Procurement Organizations, 1997; UNOS, 1998). In 1996 the number of medically suitable potential donors was estimated at 13,700 (Gortmaker et al., 1996), and in 1997 a review of medical records in hospitals in four regions of the United States estimated the pool to be between 12,000 and 15,000 annually (McNamara et al., 1997). Given that there were almost 5,800 cadaveric donors in 1998, these studies suggest that less than half of the nation's donor potential is currently being realized (McNamara and Beasley, 1997). Living donation is an additional option for centers that wish to increase the number of some solid organ transplant procedures (primarily kidney, although in some cases liver or lung).

In mid-April 1999, the U.S. Department of Health and Human Services (DHHS) and the United Network for Organ Sharing (UNOS) announced preliminary data showing that cadaveric donations increased 5.6 percent from 5,478 donors in 1997 to 5,794 donors in 1998, the first substantial increase since 1995 (DHHS, 1999a). Although donors increased in all age ranges, the greatest increase was among older donors. Donors age 60 or older increased by 10.8 percent; donors ages 40 to 59 increased by 9.6 percent; those ages 20 to 39 increased by 2.4 percent; and donors under age 19 increased by only 1.6 percent.

Rates of donation differed among racial and ethnic groups. There were substantial increases in the number of Caucasians (up 6.6 percent) and Hispanics (up 7.8 percent), but for this one year time period, the number of African American donors remained relatively unchanged and the number of Asian donors decreased by 8.4 percent (DHHS, 1999a). Interestingly, donation rates increased in areas of the country that participate in broader sharing of organs (UNOS Regions 10, 8, and 4) although the meaning of this is unclear (DHHS, 1999a).

Although some of these data show promising upward trends, the number of donations is still far short of what is needed to meet the growing demand. Moreover, it is not clear how much of the overall increase in donations is due to a liberalization of donor criteria, to better public education and understanding, or to increased procurement efforts by hospital and OPO personnel.

In the same period that overall donation rates increased, waiting list registrations climbed substantially, from 56,716 to 64,423 (DHHS, 1999a). Thus, even if donation rates continue to increase, the demand will likely continue to outstrip the supply, necessitating careful attention to the issues of donation, equitable access, and allocation.

Correlates of Donation

As mentioned above, organ donation rates vary, in part, as a function of sociodemographic factors. These include cultural attitudes, the age and race of the donor, the progression of illness in the donor, the attitudes of the donor's family, the manner in which individuals are approached, and the policies and practices of hospital staff and organ procurement organizations (OPOs). For example, it appears that higher donation rates are achieved when requests are made by the staff of the OPO working with the patient's physician or nurse, rather than by hospital staff alone (Gortmaker et al., 1998). Involving medical social workers and clergy also has a positive influence on rates of consent for donation (Siminoff et al., 1995).

Age and race are also associated with rates of donation. The families of potential donors who are less than 50 years old are five times more likely to agree to donate organs than families of potential donors over 60, although this difference may be due in large part to the way the families are approached and information is provided, rather than being a direct function of the age of the patient (Gortmaker et al., 1996).

Organ donation is not as common in the African American community as it is in others. In a study comparing African Americans and whites (see also Chapter 3), it was suggested that African Americans may be only half as likely to donate as whites, because they are less likely to be asked, and because health care professionals do not ask them for consent in an effective way (Ehrle et al., 1999; Gortmaker et al., 1996; Randall, 1996). Another reason for lower donation rates within the African American community may be distrust of the system that stems in part, from reports such as those that report African Americans with end-stage renal disease are more likely to wait longer, less likely to receive a transplant, and have less successful posttransplant outcomes than whites (Eggers, 1995; also see Gaylin et al., 1993; Held et al., 1988; Kallich et al., 1990; Kjellstrand, 1988; Sanfillippo et al., 1992). Knowledge and perceptions about these racial disparities affects the attitude towards organ donation in the African American community (Kasiske et al., 1991).

PUBLIC AND PROFESSIONAL ATTITUDES

There are few data available to determine with confidence the effects of organ allocation policies on donation rates. However, a July 1998 Gallup Poll conducted for the National Transplant Action Committee examined adults' attitudes toward organ allocation policies and their effects on organ donation (Gallup Organization, Inc., 1998). The study found that 75 percent of respondents reported it would make no difference in their decision to donate to know that the organ would go to a more seriously ill person elsewhere in the United States before being offered to a less sick person within the local region (see Box 4-1).

Another poll conducted by Southeastern Institute of Research (1994) reported similar findings. Respondents who were not donor card signers were asked which of two policies would have the strongest influence on their becoming an organ donor: one that keeps organs locally for local patients or one that ships organs nationally for all patients. Only 19 percent said that the local policy would have the strongest influence; 66 percent chose the national policy; and 13 percent said neither policy would influence them.

BOX 4-1 Excerpt from the 1998 Gallup Poll on Organ Donation

Question 4: "Thinking as if you were going to be an organ donor, if you learned that your organs would go to sick persons within your local region before they were offered to sicker persons elsewhere in the U.S. would you be more likely to want to donate, less likely to want to donate, or would it not matter in your decision."

In response, the report states: ". . . most adults say it would not affect their decision. However, 32% say if they knew the organ recipient was the sickest person, regardless of location, they would be more likely to donate an organ. In contrast, 10% would be more likely to donate if they knew their organ was going to a sick person in their local region. It may also be noted that those who have signed an organ donor card, are recipients or candidates for an organ, or have donated an organ or bone marrow are most inclined to say the location of a potential organ recipient would not affect their decision to donate."

SOURCE: Gallup Organization Inc., 1998.

As stated in the preamble to the Final Rule, "DHHS has seen no credible evidence that local preference encourages donation or that sharing organs regionally or nationally for the sickest patients will impact organ donation. Nor is there any evidence that transplant professionals perform differently when the retrieval is for a distant patient rather than a local patient" (DHHS, 1998b).

Testimony presented to the committee during the public meeting on April 16, 1999, by representatives from community hospitals supported this view, indicating that health professionals at the bedside are not aware of the destination of a procured organ and do not consider this in performing their duties. Others voiced opinions that some families of potential donors would not agree to donate if the organs were sent out of state. Most agreed, however, that families want organs to go to the patients most in need, preferably within the state, but within a broader region if this is where the most medically urgent patient is located.

Finally, preliminary data on organ donation rates seem to bear out the notion that local use does not necessarily improve donation rates. Although, as shown in Tables 4-1 and 4-2, the overall number of cadaveric donors rose in 1998 by approximately 6 percent, the largest increase (13 percent) occurred in UNOS Region 10 (Michigan, Indiana, and Ohio) (DHHS, 1999a; UNOS, 1999)—a region that recently instituted a voluntary regional sharing arrangement for livers. Other large increases occurred in Region 8 (Iowa, Missouri, Nebraska, Kansas, Wyoming, and Colorado)—11.3 percent—and in Region 4 (Oklahoma and Texas)—9.1 percent (DHHS, 1999a; UNOS, 1999). Each of these regions engages in broader sharing beyond the local OPO service area.

Need for Educational Interventions

While the consent rate for potential organ donors from African American families continues to be less than that of white families (Eckhoff et al., 1998), there are data demonstrating that a concerted effort to increase donation can be, and has been, quite successful. Between 1988 and 1996, organ donation among African Americans increased from 17 to 23 percent (Ehrle et al., 1999; UNOS, 1998), largely because of innovative programs that target the needs of minority populations with interventions such as race-specific requesters (Ehrle et al., 1999; First, 1997; Gentry et al., 1997; Kappel et al., 1993). Within this same time frame, the OPO for the University of Alabama at Birmingham was able to increase its organ donation rates from 6.1 percent to 21.9 percent (Eckhoff et al., 1998). This increase in donation was accomplished by improving the awareness by transplant coordinators about cultural differences and by hiring minorities for outreach and coordinator positions. Nevertheless, still more can be done on a national level to improve these statistics.

TABLE 4-1 Number of Cadaveric Donors by Donor Age from 1994 through October 31, 1998

	Year Donor Recovered											
	1994		1995		1996		1997		1998		Total	
Donor Age	No.	%	No.	%	No.	%	No.	%	No.	%	No.	%
Not reported	15		28		81		153		309		586	
<1	94	1.8	86	1.6	73	1.4	100	1.9	98	1.8	451	1.7
1–5	203	4.0	214	4.0	189	3.5	214	4.0	226	4.1	1,046	3.9
6–10	166	3.3	181	3.4	160	3.0	147	2.8	150	2.7	804	3.0
11–17	683	13.4	706	13.2	620	11.6	585	11.0	560	10.2	3,154	11.9
18–34	1,545	30.4	1,539	28.9	1,479	27.7	1,440	27.0	1,437	26.2	7,440	28.0
34–49	1,237	24.3	1,304	24.5	1,390	26.0	1,355	25.4	1,426	26.0	6,712	25.3
50–64	933	18.3	1,027	19.3	1,081	20.3	1,102	20.7	1,124	20.5	5,267	19.8
≥65	224	4.4	276	5.2	346	6.5	382	7.2	464	8.5	1,692	6.4
Total	5,100	100.0	5,361	100.0	5,419	100.0	5,478	100.0	5,794	100.0	27,152	100.0

SOURCE: Based on UNOS/OPTN (1999) Scientific Registry data as of May 22, 1999.

TABLE 4-2 Number of Cadaveric Donors by Donor Race from 1994 through October 31, 1998

	Year Donor Recovered											
	1994		1995		1996		1997		1998		Total	
Donor Race	No.	%	No.	%	No.	%	No.	%	No.	%	No.	%
Not reported	2		19		74		142		297		534	
White	3,972	77.9	4,129	77.3	4,096	76.6	4,030	75.5	4,198	76.4	20,425	76.7
African American	585	11.5	609	11.4	647	12.1	629	11.98	609	11.1	3,079	11.6
Hispanic	418	8.2	485	9.1	488	9.1	549	10.3	574	10.4	2,514	9.4
Asian	93	1.8	80	1.5	84	1.6	99	1.9	92	1.7	448	1.7
Other	30	0.6	39	0.7	30	0.6	29	0.5	24	0.4	152	0.6
Total	5,100	100.0	5,361	100.0	5,419	100.0	5,478	100.0	5,794	100.0	27,152	100.0

SOURCE: Based on UNOS/OPTN (1999) Scientific Registry data as of May 22, 1999.

In testimony to the IOM committee on April 16, 1999, it was stated that donor shortage is, in part, a result of perceived inequities in organ allocation (Callender, 1999). The shortage exists in all communities, but especially in the African American. To address this problem, it was suggested that there must be a focus on the impediments to donation, which include:

- the perception of inequitable organ allocation;
- suboptimal use of the community as a change agent for organ tissue donation and transplantation;
- lack of involvement of the community at all levels of problem resolution, research, and resource allocation;
- lack of transplantation awareness;
- religious myths and misperceptions;
- distrust of the health care system and health care professionals;
- fears that signing donor cards will lead to premature declaration of death;
- inadequate use of recipients, donors, and transplant candidates as community messengers; and
- inadequate allocation of funds for donation education efforts.

The example of lower rates of organ donation in the African American community helps illustrate that variability in organ donation rates is due to many causes. There is no evidence available to suggest that local allocation policies alone would significantly alter donation rates. It is more likely that enhanced educational interventions at the public and professional levels would significantly alter participation in the system, along with public policies that encourage donation. Some of these (i.e., "required request," "routine verification," and other approaches to improve donation) are described in the following section.

REQUIRED REQUEST AND ROUTINE NOTIFICATION

By the late 1980s, most states and the District of Columbia had enacted "required request" legislation in an effort to increase hospital referral rates. This legislation requires hospitals to consult with the potential donor's next of kin and specifically request organ donation should the patient be at, or near, death (American Hospital Association et al., 1988; Cate and Laudicina, 1991). In some instances, hospitals may be required to refrain from asking family members to consent if: the patient is medically unsuitable, there are contrary indications from the family, there are conflicting religious beliefs from either the family or potential donor, the family is too emotionally traumatized to be consulted for donation, or prior objections to organ donation have been made by the patient (American Hospital Association et al., 1988; Ehrle et al., 1999). However, several studies by the Partnership for Organ Donation and the Harvard School of Public Health have shown that more than one-quarter of the time, eligible families are not even offered the option to donate (Gortmaker et al., 1996).

The 1986 Omnibus Reconciliation Act (42 U.S.C. 1320b-8) required hospitals to have processes in place to ensure that all families of potential donors are identified and referred to the OPO and that all families are given the opportunity to consent or decline to donate the organs of their relative. The law authorizes Medicare and Medicaid funds to be withheld from hospitals that did not comply, but this authority has never been exercised.

"Required request" legislation, on both the state and national levels, did not appear to contribute to a substantial increase in donation. In continuing the effort to increase donation, several states, led by Pennsylvania, have passed "routine notification" legislation to address the problem of failure to determine which patients are potential donors (Ehrle et al., 1999). This legislation requires that all deaths or deaths that are imminent within a hospital be referred to the Medicare-certified OPO. In other areas of the United States, hospitals and OPOs have voluntarily adopted a policy of routine notification (Ehrle et al., 1999).

Reports from an OPO in Pennsylvania indicated substantial increases in organ as well as tissue and eye donations in the 3 years since implementation of routine notification (Ehrle et al., 1999). The Delaware Valley Transplant Program,* which serves Delaware, southern New Jersey, and the eastern half of Pennsylvania, reported a 49 percent increase in donations since 1994 when Pennsylvania passed its comprehensive law governing organ donation (Nathan, 1998).

An OPO in Texas, a state that does not have routine notification laws, worked with its hospitals to voluntarily implement routine notification and experienced a 12 percent increase in organ donation in the 2 years after implementation, an increase that was 352 percent greater than the national growth in organ donation (Ehrle et al., 1999; Shafer et al., 1998).

At the federal level, in June 1998 the Health Care Financing Administration (HCFA) issued an amendment to its *Hospital Conditions of Participation for Medicare and Medicaid*, which requires all acute care hospitals to notify their local OPO of all hospital deaths (Ehrle et al., 1999). The OPO could then request donation from families of potential donors. If followed consistently, it appears that this policy of routine notification would substantially increase the number of potential organ donors referred to OPOs (Ehrle et al., 1999).

Additional Approaches to Improve Donation

Health professionals and patient groups concerned with the low rate of organ donation have suggested additional approaches to increase donation. These have included development of standardized hospital practices; improvement of the consent process; better training of medical staff; refocusing public education to promote family discussion; and clearer guidance about brain death for fami-

---

* The Delaware Valley Transplant Program recently changed its name to Gift of Life Donor Program (Gift of Life Donor Program, 1999).

lies and health professionals (Dejong et al., 1995; Franz et al., 1997; Gortmaker et al., 1996; McNamara and Beasley, 1997). Other efforts to promote donation include public awareness campaigns, efforts by local OPOs nationwide to address donation at the community level, and projects conducted by national groups to educate health professionals and the public about donation and transplantation. In addition, donor criteria have been expanded to allow older and less healthy patients to donate organs.

A controversial method to encourage organ donation has been recently proposed in Pennsylvania. If adopted, this program will help defray the organ donor's family funeral expenses by providing $300 from a special state fund directly to the funeral home that handles the donor's burial arrangements (Nathan, 1999). Advocates of this law argue that this program is not established as a payment for organs because the law requires that any payment be made directly to the funeral home and not to the donor's family, next of kin, or estate (La Hay, 1999; Pennsylvania Act 1994-102, 1994). Rather, the intent of this pilot program is to increase awareness and participation in organ donation.

ASSESSING OPO PERFORMANCE

A major impediment to greater accountability and improved performance on the part of OPOs is the current lack of a reliable and valid method for assessing donor potential and OPO performance (Christiansen et al., 1998). HCFA currently evaluates OPO performance (on a per-million population basis) for the following performance measures: (1) organ donors; (2) kidneys recovered; (3) kidneys transplanted; (4) extrarenal organs recovered (heart, liver, pancreas, lungs); and (5) extrarenal organs transplanted. Each OPO must meet numerical goals in at least four of the five categories to be recertified by HCFA as the OPO for a particular area and to receive Medicare and Medicaid payment. Without HCFA certification, an OPO cannot continue to operate.

In 1997 the U.S. General Accounting Office (GAO) determined that the current performance measures do not accurately assess OPO performance because they are based on total population, not the number of potential donors (GAO, 1997). OPO service areas vary widely in the distribution of deaths by cause, underlying health conditions (e.g., HIV, liver disease), age, and race, which in turn affect the number of potential donors. The GAO identified four alternative performance measures that would better estimate the number of potential organ donors: organ procurement and transplantation compared with the number of deaths, deaths adjusted for cause of death and age, medical records reviews, and modeling (GAO, 1997). HCFA is currently evaluating the feasibility and usefulness of implementing revised measures.

Although efforts are under way to use a denominator that more accurately identifies potential donors, other performance criteria are needed for OPOs, (e.g., measures of the quality, function, and biological outcomes of the transplanted organs), rather than depending solely on donors per population or donors per hospital death.

CONCLUSIONS

Many variables affect organ donation rates, including cultural attitudes, the age and race of the donor, the progression of illness in the donor, the attitudes of the donor's family, the manner in which individuals are approached, and the policies and practices of hospital staff and organ procurement organizations. The most important way to increase donation is to ensure that all eligible families are approached about donation.

Based on a review of the literature and survey data, testimony received, and preliminary data on increased donation rates in UNOS regions that engage in broader sharing beyond the local OPO service areas, the committee concludes that organ donation rates are not likely to be affected adversely by broader sharing (i.e., allocation areas that exceed the geographic boundaries of the OPO). To address the continuing concerns about donation, the committee believes that concerted efforts among health professionals involved in organ procurement should continue—including development of standardized hospital practices; improvement of the consent process; better training of medical staff; refocusing public education to promote family discussion; and clearer guidance about brain death for families and health professionals. These activities and relationships of the OPO are necessary components of effective organ donation activities that should not be affected by broader allocation policies.

5

Analysis of Waiting Times

Task 3: *Assess current policies and the potential impact of the Final Rule on waiting times for organ transplants, including (1) determinations specific to the various geographic regions of the United States, and, if practical, waiting times for each transplant center by organ and medical status category, and (2) impact of recent changes made by the Organ Procurement and Transplantation Network in patient listing criteria and in measures of medical status.*

Abstract. **There is concern that the current system of organ allocation and transplantation does not ensure that available organs reach the patients most in need of a transplant. Large differences among organ procurement organizations (OPOs) in median waiting times for transplantation have been given as evidence that needier patients in one OPO may be left waiting while less needy patients in another OPO are receiving organs sooner. Median waiting times for liver transplantation in neighboring OPOs have been reported to differ by as much as 100 days.**

The committee examined 68,000 individual records of liver transplant patients and made several observations. Among these are the following. First, median waiting time is a misleading metric as used previously for comparing waiting times among OPOs. As calculated, median waiting time is determined by the waiting time of status 3 patients and has no relationship to the waiting time of status 1 patients. Second, the committee finds that the current system of organ allocation is reasonably equitable within the category of status 1 patients because they are as likely to receive a transplant in a small OPO as in a large one. Third, based on limited data from currently existing sharing arrangements among OPOs, there seems to be (1) a beneficial effect in decreasing mortality among status 2B patients, (2) an increase in status 1 transplantation rates, and (3) a reduction in transplantation for status 3 patients without an increase in mortality. Lastly, the committee concludes that patients awaiting liver transplants will be better served by an allocation system that facilitates broader sharing within a minimum population base of approximately 9 million people than by the current smaller sharing areas.

A transplant candidate's "waiting time" is the period between registration for transplantation and one of three other events: transplantation of a donor organ, death without transplantation, or removal from the waiting list for other reasons. Waiting times for status 1 liver transplant candidates, those most seriously ill, can be measured in days, while the wait for status 2 patients, who are less seriously ill, is measured in months. For status 3 (or 4) patients, who have the least urgent need for transplantation, waiting times may reach years. Historically, more than 50 percent of the patients awaiting liver transplants at any given time have been classified as status 3 (see Table 5-1 and Appendix B, Tables B-1, B-4, B-6, and B-9).

In issuing the Final Rule, the Department of Health and Human Services (1998b) used regional differences in median waiting times for all patients combined as a basis for claiming that inequities exist in the allocation of organs to transplant patients. Panel 1 of Figure 5-1 illustrates the differences in median waiting times among the 11 UNOS regions, grouped by quartiles, for all liver transplant candidates registered between January 20, 1998, and January 19, 1999. Although dividing the waiting time distribution into quartiles oversimplifies these data, this method is similar to that used in previous analyses by DHHS. On this basis, median waiting times are shortest in the South and upper Midwest and longest in New England and the Northwest (including Alaska). However, given that the majority of transplant patients are classified as status 3, these differences principally reflect the differences in waiting time of status 3 patients (see panel 5), who have the least serious need and, therefore, the longest wait for transplantation. Panels 2 and 3 show that statuses 1 and 2A patients contribute little or no regional variability in overall waiting times. Panels 4 and 5 show that variability in overall waiting time is produced almost entirely by statuses 2B and 3 patients.

TABLE 5-1 Characteristics of Liver Transplant Patients by Status, 1995–1999

	Totals	Status 1 (all patients)	Status 2 (all patients)	Status 3 (all patients)
Total patients, 1995–1999	33,286	5,294	14,264	26,907
Percentage receiving a transplant	47.1	52.4	50.2	21.3
Percentage dying prior to transplantation	8.3	9.2	6.1	5.2
Percentage of post-transplant mortality	5.4	11.1	5.0	1.9
Percentage male	58.7	54.1	59.9	58.7
Percentage with A or AB blood type	16.0	15.3	15.4	15.8
Percentage African American	7.7	11.2	8.3	6.9
Mean age	45.0	36.3	44.9	46.1
Mean waiting time	255.6	4.8	56.8	285.1

NB: The "Totals" columns involve the number of unique listings and therefore does not involve the sum of the other three columns which involve patients within status levels (i.e., a given patient may occupy one to three status levels for a particular listing).

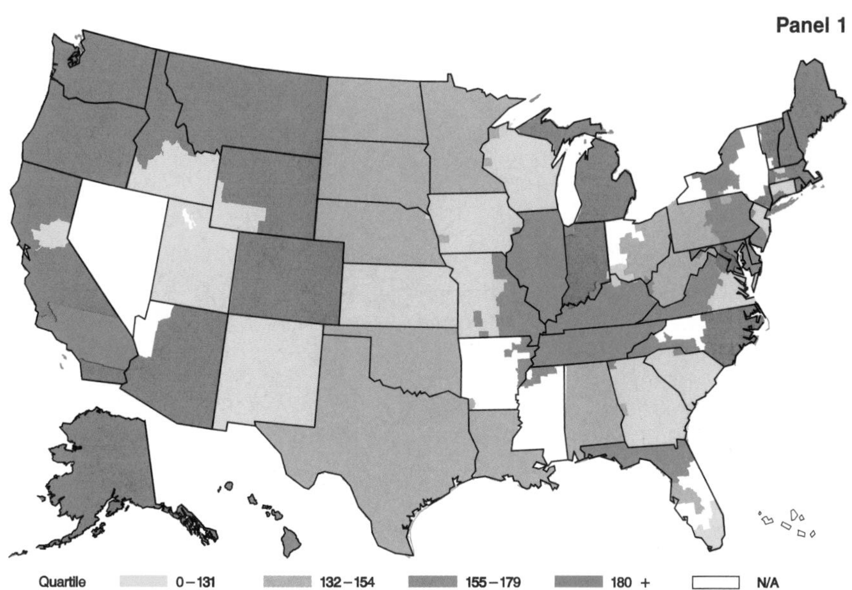

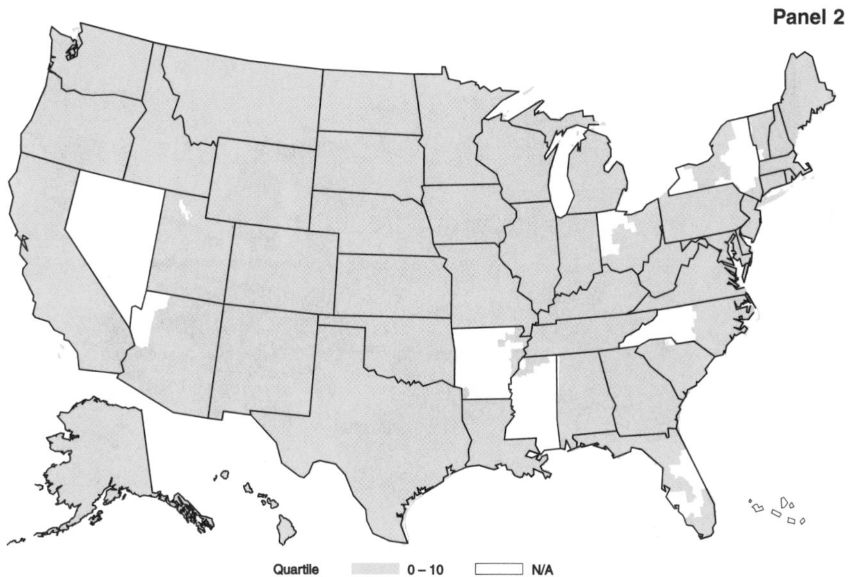

FIGURE 5-1 Median waiting times for liver transplantation, all status groups, registrations added January 20, 1998 to January 19, 1999. **Panel 1:** all patients; **panel 2:** patients ever in Status 1; **panel 3:** patients ever in Status 2A; **panel 4:** patients ever in Status 2B; and **panel 5:** patients ever in Status 3. SOURCE: M. D. Ellison, UNOS, personal communication, May 10, 1999.

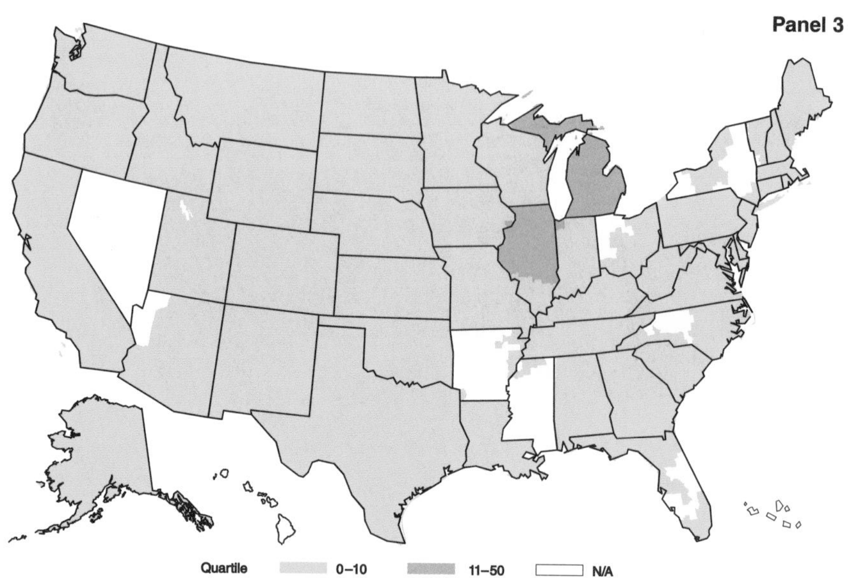

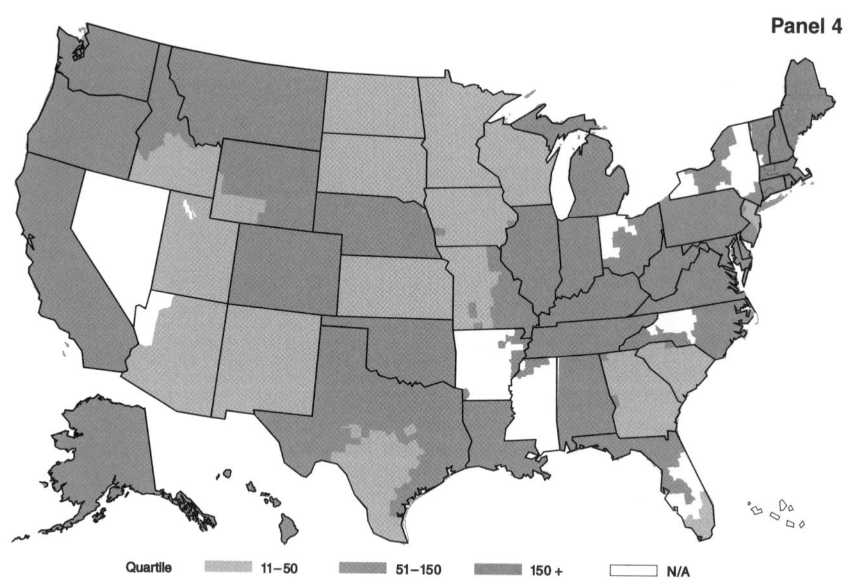

FIGURE 5-1 *Continued*

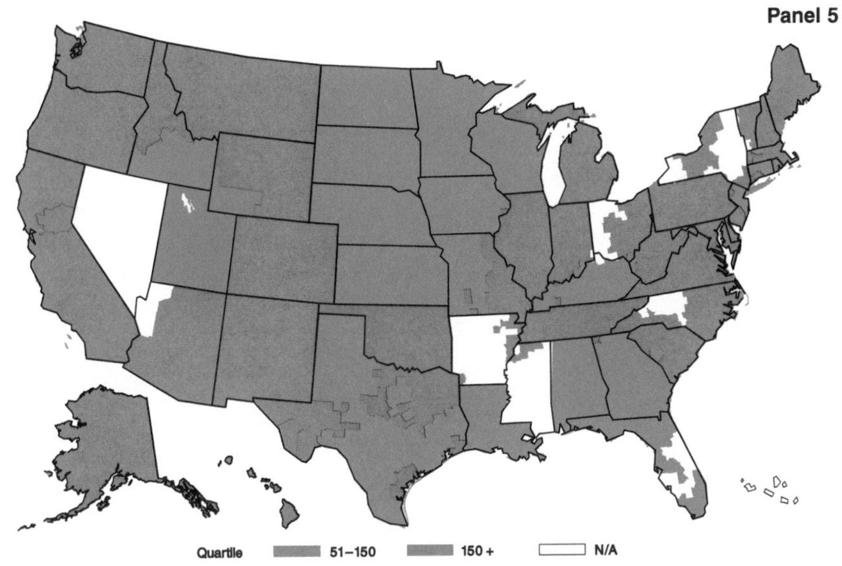

FIGURE 5-1 *Continued*

As discussed later in this chapter, numerous factors influence the waiting times of status 3 patients; none of these are related to severity of illness, or the likelihood of transplantation or death. For example, transplant centers vary in their policies for listing statuses 2B and 3 patients, with some centers choosing to list statuses 2B and 3 patients much earlier in the course of their illness than others.

The remainder of this chapter presents the results of the committee's more detailed statistical analysis of data on transplantation waiting time. The analysis is based on approximately 68,000 records representing each transition made by each patient on the waiting list for liver transplantation from 1995 through the first quarter of 1999. This analysis reveals the strengths and weaknesses of the current organ allocation system and points to directions for change.

METHOD OF ANALYSIS

Analysis of the existing organ allocation program was performed using a mixed-effects multinomial logistic regression model, which is a simple generalization of the mixed effects ordinal logistic regression model originally developed by Hedeker and Gibbons (1994) as described by Hedeker (in press) and is presented in Appendix A. Because of the large differences in waiting times by status, analyses were performed separately for status levels 1, 2B, and 3. (There were insufficient data to evaluate waiting time in status 2A.) The majority of status 1 patients receive a transplant or die within 7 days. For patients in status 2B, the typical waiting time is a few months, whereas status 3 patients may wait a year or more. Patients also change status frequently and can shift from status 1 to status 2 or 3 as well as from a less urgent to a more urgent status.

The unit of analysis is time (number of days or months) spent within a particular status level. For example, in the analysis of status 1, a patient who is initially listed as status 1 for 2 days, shifts to status 2 for 1 month, and returns to status 1 for 1 day and is transplanted would have an outcome of transplant and a status 1 waiting time of 3 days. A patient who is in status 1 for 3 days and dies would have an outcome of death and a status 1 waiting time of 3 days. A patient listed as status 1 for 4 days who is then delisted because he or she is too sick to undergo the transplant (status 9) has an outcome of "other" (i.e., censored) and has a status 1 waiting time of 4 days. The same outcome and number of status 1 days would be recorded if this patient transitioned to status 2 or 3 and did not return to status 1. The time spent by the patient in another status would be used in the analysis for that status level. Similar analyses were performed for time spent in statuses 2B and 3.

At the beginning of 1998, the status categories were changed by the OPTN from 1, 2, 3, and 4 to 1, 2A, 2B, and 3 to create more homogeneous and reliable patient listings. All statistical analyses were performed on these more recent data (i.e., 1998–1999). However, to provide a more complete view of the overall system, tabular displays of various summary statistics (e.g., mean waiting times within status categories, percentages of patients receiving transplants or dying) used all data from 1995 to 1999 and used status categories 1, 2 (2, 2A, and 2B) and 3 (3 and 4). The analysis applies to the 52 OPOs that include liver transplant centers within their service area. Ten OPOs do not do so.

Additional details of the statistical model are presented in Appendix A. Conceptually, the model allows evaluation of the competing risks of transplantation and pretransplantation mortality over time as a function of certain variables such as age, gender, race, blood type, and volume of transplants in OPOs. A further distinguishing feature of the model is that it allows for an analysis of OPO-specific rates for transplantation and pretransplantation mortality by representing OPO as a random effect. A large OPO variance component indicates that the experience of patients within certain OPOs differs systematically from the overall population average experience (e.g., members of a particular OPO may have an increased likelihood of transplantation or death), which suggests inequity in the system of organ transplantation. A small OPO variance component (i.e., not statistically significant or accounting for a small percentage of the total variance; e.g., <5%) indicates that transplantation (or mortality) rates can be considered homogeneous among OPOs and that the system is equitable, or at least consistent, among OPOs.

Expressing the OPO variance component as a proportion of the total variance leads to the intraclass correlation. For this analysis, the intraclass correlation describes the percentage of variability associated with a particular risk (e.g., transplantation or death) attributable to the OPO, once the effects of the model covariates (e.g., age, gender, race, and blood type) have been removed. Thus, the intraclass correlation as employed in this analysis is a useful statistic in determining the extent to which OPOs systematically vary in their rates of transplantation or mortality. Separate variance components and intraclass correlations are associated with each competing risk (i.e., transplantation and death); therefore it is possible for OPOs to systematically vary in one, both, or neither rate.

Waiting time is handled in the committee's analysis by use of the alternative parameterization of the Cox proportional hazards model in terms of a "partial logistic regression" model (Efron, 1988) or "person-time logistic regression" model (Ingram and Kleinman, 1989). This approach to survival analysis involves the use of a series of sequential records from each subject for the period of time he or she was observed in the study.

Efron (1988) and Ingram and Kleinman (1989) have shown that modeling time-to-event data in this manner provides excellent agreement with the traditional proportional hazards survival model and becomes identical to it as the time intervals approach zero (i.e., continuous time). The advantage of this approach for the committee's analysis is the ability to (1) simultaneously model both transplantation and pretransplantation mortality rates, and (2) accommodate OPO-specific components of variability in these rates (i.e., a mixed-effects model).

For each record in the analyses, outcomes are designated as transplantation (coded as 1), death prior to transplantation (coded as 2), or other end points (coded as 0). Several conditions could result in an outcome of "other": shifting to another status level and never returning to the status level in question, being too sick to receive a transplant, being delisted, receiving a transplant at another OPO, or still waiting. For example, a patient listed for 4 days in status 1 who received a transplant on day 4 would have four records, three with an outcome of 0 (other) for days 1–3 and one with an outcome of 1 (transplantation) for day 4. A patient listed for 5 days as a status 1 patient who died on day 5, would have four records with an outcome of 0 for days 1–4 and one record with an outcome of 2 (death) for day 5. A patient listed for 2 days as a status 1 who then was reclassified as a status 2 and was never again classified as status 1, would have two records (as a status 1 patient) with an outcome of 0 (other).

The covariates used in the analysis were age (0–5, 6–17, 18 and over), gender (male = 1, female = 0), race (African American = 1, else = 0), blood type (O or B = 1, else = 0), and OPO transplant volume (small, medium, and large). For blood type, the contrast between type O or B and type A or AB was selected because patients with either of the first two types can receive organs only from a subset of donors, whereas the patients with A or AB blood type can receive organs from almost all potential donors. The 52 OPOs were divided into thirds (large = 17, medium = 17, small = 18) on the basis of number of transplants in 1995–1999. This breakdown corresponds generally to 300 or more transplants over the four year period for large volume OPOs and fewer than 150 transplants for small OPOs. Categorical variables such as age and OPO transplant volume were dummy-coded in the analysis so individual groups could be compared without assuming a functional form for the relationship (e.g., linearity).

RESULTS

In the following sections, the results of the analysis of the liver transplant data for each waiting list status are described. Overall, the committee found reasonable equity among OPOs in terms of waiting time for transplantation and in pretransplantation mortality for (status 1) patients, but greater variation in waiting times for patients in statuses 2B and 3. Among the latter two groups, it also appears that some patients are able to survive for extended periods without transplantation and without an increase in the urgency for transplantation. Thus, for these patients, waiting time is not an optimal criterion for determining the urgency of transplantation, especially for status 3 patients. The committee also saw higher rates of transplantation for status 2B and 3 patients in OPOs serving smaller populations and in those OPOs doing fewer transplants. The results of the statistical analysis are summarized in Table 5-2 for likelihood of transplantation and in Table 5-3 for likelihood of pretransplant mortality.

Status 1

Status 1 includes the most severely ill patients who, in general, are expected to survive approximately 1 week without a liver transplant. Overall characteristics of status 1 patients are described in Table 5-1. Additional detail is provided in Table B-1 in Appendix B, which presents average waiting times, transplantation rates, pre- and posttransplantation mortality rates, and demographic information for status 1 patients for each OPO, sorted by the number of status 1 patients in the OPOs. Average waiting times are relatively similar, generally 3 to 4 days, across the 52 OPOs having liver transplant programs within their service areas. Two possible outliers are OPO 42 (average waiting time 11 days) and OPO 14 (average waiting time 9 days). The average age of patients in OPO 42 is among the lowest for the larger-volume OPOs. When the tabulation is restricted to adults (i.e., patients 18 and over), the number of patients in OPO 42 drops from 203 to 92 and the average waiting time falls to 7 days (see Table B-2 in Appendix B), which is more consistent with, but still slightly higher than, the other OPOs. These changes suggest that the longer overall waiting time for OPO 42 is in large part due to the fact that more than half of the patients in this OPO are children, whose smaller size may give them more limited access to matching organs, resulting in longer waiting times.

Results of the risk analysis of these data (Table 5-2; also see Table B-3 in Appendix B) reveal no significant effects on transplantation rates for status 1 patients with regard to gender, race, blood type, or OPO transplant volume. By contrast, there was a statistically significant decrease in the transplantation rate for children age 5 and under, consistent with the previous observation that young status 1 patients may have less access to organs. The effect of waiting time (i.e., the variable "day") was not significant, indicating that the probability of transplantation for status 1 patients is relatively constant over time. This finding is important because it indicates that even if transplantation does not occur within the first few days of status 1 listing, the likelihood of transplantation in the following days is not diminished.

The OPO random-effect variance was found to be statistically significant, indicating that transplantation rates of status 1 patients differ systematically over OPOs. The intraclass correlation (r = 0.045) indicates, however, that this effect is modest, accounting for less than 5 percent of the total variation in transplantation rates. Once the effects of the model covariates (i.e., gender, race, blood type, and OPO volume) are accounted for.

In terms of mortality rates (Table 5-3; also see Table B-3 in Appendix B), the analysis reveals that (1) variability in pretransplantation mortality rates over OPOs was not significant (intraclass correlation r = 0.001, accounting for 0.1 percent of the variability in mortality rates); (2) the mortality rates are lower for children and adolescents than adults; (3) there are no significant associations between gender, race, blood type, or OPO transplant volume and mortality rates; and (4) the mortality rates are relatively constant over time. Tables B-1 to B-3 in Appendix B support these conclusions. Pretransplantation mortality rates are similar across the OPOs that had a sufficient number of patients with which to estimate them accurately.

These results confirm that the small differences in status 1 transplantation rates observed among OPOs are not associated with differential pretransplantation mortality rates. Moreover, the observed large variations in waiting times for all patients, regardless of status, disguise the narrow variations within the status 1 category. Thus, looking only within the category of the most severely ill patients (status 1), the current system appears to be reasonably equitable. As discussed below, however, a higher proportion of status 1 patients would receive transplants if organs were shared over larger populations.

Tables B-1 and B-2 in Appendix B also reveal that posttransplantation mortality rates are relatively similar across OPOs, with the majority of rates in the range of 5 to 15 percent.

TABLE 5-2 Parameter Estimates (standard errors) for Likelihood of Liver Transplantation as a Function of Time, Age, Gender, Race, and OPO Volume: Individual Models for Statuses 1, 2B, and 3 for All Available Data in 1998–1999

	Status 1	Status 2B	Status 3
Intercept	–1.829*	–2.077*	–3.593*
	(0.276)	(0.129)	(0.210)
Waiting time	0.016[a]	–0.092*[b]	–0.220*[b]
	(0.015)	(0.016)	(0.030)
Age (0–5 vs. adult)	–0.907*	0.470*	1.156*
	(0.188)	(0.103)	(0.154)
Age (6–17 vs. adult)	–0.362	0.135	0.844*
	(0.234)	(0.243)	(0.268)
Gender (1 = male)	–0.098	0.126	0.054
	(0.198)	(0.087)	(0.186)
Race (1 = African American)	–0.275	0.134	0.158
	(0.268)	(0.222)	(0.304)
Blood type (1 = B or O)	–0.076	–0.577*	–0.477*
	(0.196)	(0.062)	(0.098)
OPO volume (M vs. L)	–0.054	0.590*	1.179*
	(0.319)	(0.157)	(0.149)
OPO volume (S vs. L)	0.261	0.560*	0.757*
	(0.336)	(0.187)	(0.228)
Random OPO effect	0.393*	0.689*	1.335*
	(0.144)	(0.064)	(0.162)
Interclass correlation	0.045	0.126	0.351

[a]Time in days. [b]Time in months.

*$p < 0.05$.

TABLE 5-3 Parameter Estimates (standard errors) for Likelihood of Pretransplant Mortality as a Function of Time, Age, Gender, Race, and OPO Volume: Individual Models for Statuses 1, 2B, and 3 for All Available Data in 1998–1999

	Status 1	Status 2B	Status 3
Intercept	–3.685*	–3.313	–3.654*
	(0.482)	(0.227)	(0.172)
Waiting time	0.023[a]	–0.213*[b]	–0.216*[b]
	(0.047)	(0.039)	(0.041)
Age (0–5 vs. adult)	–0.968*	–0.195	–2.119
	(0.378)	(0.381)	(2.099)
Age (6–17 vs. adult)	–1.001	–0.516	–1.193
	(0.551)	(0.641)	(2.000)
Gender (1 = male)	0.077	0.014	–0.063
	(0.371)	(0.191)	(0.268)
Race (1 = African American)	0.162	–0.082	0.027
	(0.448)	(0.359)	(0.544)
Blood type (1 = B or O)	0.003	–0.005	–0.017
	(0.433)	(0.164)	(0.231)
OPO volume (M vs. L)	0.203	0.202	–0.526
	(0.491)	(0.126)	(0.300)
OPO volume (S vs. L)	–0.230	0.355*	–0.658
	(0.930)	(0.151)	(0.358)
Random OPO effect	0.042	0.116*	0.137
	(0.298)	(0.049)	(0.157)
Interclass correlation	0.001	0.004	0.006

[a]Time in days. [b]Time in months.

*$p < 0.05$.

To help illustrate these effects, Figure 5-2a displays the estimated hazard functions for transplantation and death prior to transplantation over the first 12 days patients were listed in status 1. Figure 5-2b displays the estimated cumulative time-to-event distributions.[1] These estimated rates hold the effects of the covariates constant at adult, female, white, A or AB blood type, and large-volume OPO. Inspection of Figure 5-2a reveals that the hazard rates are relatively constant over

[1]Details of the computation of these hazard rates and cumulative survival distributions are provided in Appendix A. The hazard functions were derived from marginal predicted probabilities from the estimated mixed-effects competing risk survival model, and the cumulative time-to-event distributions were derived from the corresponding hazard functions, accounting for the competing risks. The hazard rate describes the likelihood of transplantation or mortality at a given point in time adjusted for the competing risks (i.e., transplantation or mortality) and the model covariates (e.g., gender, race, blood type). The cumulative time-to-event distribution describes the overall adjusted likelihood of transplantation or mortality up to a particular point in time.

the first 12 days in status 1 at approximately 15 to 17 percent for transplantation and 2 to 3 percent for pretransplantation mortality per day. Figure 5-2b shows that after 12 days in status 1, approximately 80 percent of the patients would receive a transplant and approximately 12 percent would die.

Status 2

For status 2 patients (2, 2A, and 2B) during 1995–1999 (see Table 5-1 and Table B-4 in Appendix B), average waiting times range from 40 to 70 days, with greater variability across OPOs than was seen for status 1 patients. In general, smaller-volume OPOs appear to have somewhat higher transplantation rates for their status 2 patients. Both pre- and posttransplantation mortality rates are relatively homogeneous over OPOs and generally lower than the mortality rates for status 1 patients. This is consistent with the greater severity of illness for status 1 patients.

The statistical analysis of the status 2B patient data for 1998–1999 shows that younger status 2B patients have an increased likelihood of transplantation (see Table 5-2 and Table B-5 in Appendix B), but young age is not associated with the pretransplant mortality rate (as noted above, there were too few status 2A patients during this recent time to perform a meaningful statistical analysis) (see Table 5-3 and Table B-5 in Appendix B). Having a blood type that hinders matching to available donor organs (i.e., B or O) decreases the chance of a status 2B transplant, but does not affect pretransplant mortality. Table B-4 in Appendix B demonstrates that a higher percentage of status 2B patients in small- and medium-volume OPOs receive transplants than patients treated at the larger-volume OPOs. This indicates that, although status 1 patients in OPOs with a smaller volume of transplants, receive organs at a rate similar to status 1 patients in other OPOs, there are fewer status 1 patients in these small-volume OPOs. Therefore, more status 2B patients in small volume OPOs ultimately receive transplants. Of concern was evidence of a statistically significant increase in the risk of pretransplantation mortality in those OPOs with smaller transplant volumes. This is reflected in data shown in Table B-4 in Appendix B on the percentage of patients who die before receiving a transplant.

Finally, significant time effects on both transplantation and pretransplantation mortality rates were observed, indicating that the longer patients are listed as status 2B, the lower is their likelihood of either dying or receiving a transplant. This finding suggests that there is heterogeneity in the population of status 2B patients, with a subgroup who need transplantation more quickly or they will die after a relatively short time on the status 2B waiting list. By contrast, those patients who remain on the list for more than 4 months have considerably decreased risk of pretransplantation mortality or transplantation. It may be that the treating physicians are aware of this heterogeneity and are effectively screening the more severely ill status 2B (and status 3) patients for early transplantation, leaving the less severely ill patients on the list, sometimes indefinitely. The increased mortality rates seen among the smaller volume OPOs may indicate that although they are transplanting more status 2B patients, they may not be transplanting the most severely ill status 2B patients.

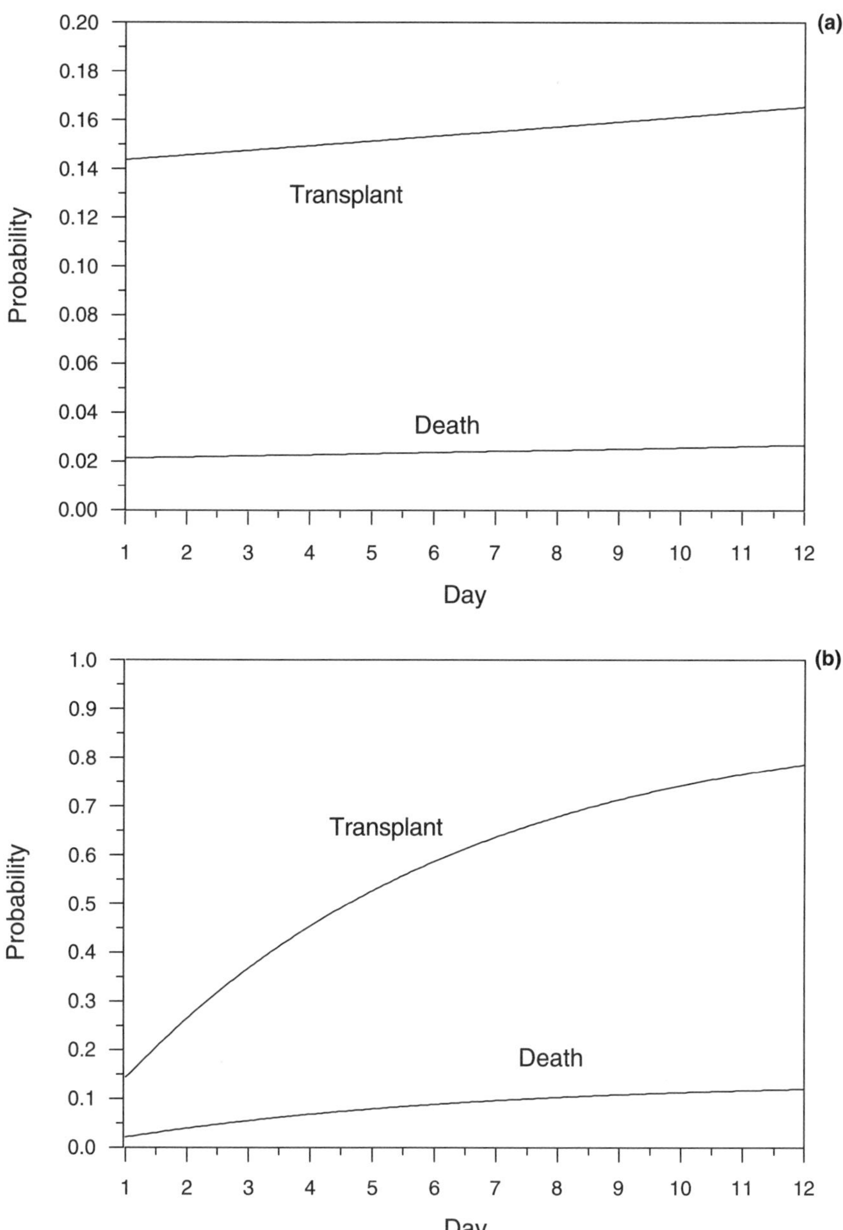

FIGURE 5-2 Estimated daily hazard rates (a) and cumulative time-event distribution (b) for status 1 patients awaiting liver transplantation. The hazard rate describes the likelihood of transplantation or mortality at a given point in time adjusted for the competing risks (i.e., transplantation or mortality) and the model covariates (e.g., gender, race, blood type). The cumulative time-to-event distribution describes the overall adjusted likelihood of transplantation or mortality up to a particular point in time.

The intraclass correlation for OPO-specific effects on transplantation rates was statistically significant and three times that of status 1 patients (i.e., $r = 0.126$ versus $r = 0.045$). This statistic indicates that 13 percent of the variability in transplantation rates for status 2B patients is due to OPO-specific influences even after OPO volume and the other covariates are accounted for. By contrast, the intraclass correlation for mortality rates was $r = 0.004$, which, although significantly different from zero in this large sample, accounts for less than 0.5 percent of the total variability in mortality rates. This finding indicates that differences in transplantation rates across the OPOs (once the covariates, including OPO size, are accounted for) are not leading to differential pretransplantation mortality rates (i.e., once the effects of competing risks and model covariates including OPO volume are accounted for).

To help illustrate these effects, Figure 5-3a displays the estimated hazard functions for transplantation and death rates over the first 12 months in status 2B, and Figure 5-3b displays the cumulative time-to-event distributions. These estimated rates hold the effects of the covariates constant at adult, female, white, A or AB blood type, and large-volume OPO. Figure 5-3a reveals that the probability of transplantation decreases from 12 to 5 percent per month over the 12-month period and death rates decrease from 3 to 0.3 percent per month over the 12-month period. Figure 5-3b reveals that after 12 months as a status 2B patient, approximately 60 percent of patients would have received transplants and approximately 10 percent would have died.

Statuses 3 and 4

For statuses 3 and 4 patients for 1995–1999[2] (see Table 5-1 and Tables B-6 and B-8 in Appendix B), average waiting times on the order of 100 to 400 days are much greater in variability across OPOs relative to statuses 1 and 2B patients. The tendency for smaller-volume OPOs to have somewhat higher transplantation rates, which was observed for status 2B patients, is even stronger for statuses 3 or 4 patients. Again, the OPOs with a smaller volume of transplants appear to be transplanting a greater percentage of status 3 patients relative to the larger-volume OPOs. Both pre- and posttransplantation mortality rates are homogeneous over OPOs and, in general, lower than the mortality rates for either status 1 or 2B patients.

As noted at the beginning of the chapter, concern about differential regional waiting time distributions, which led in large part to this committee's assignment, is driven by status 3 or 4 patients. (It is clear from Table B-9 in Appendix B that the status 3 or 4 patients constitute more than 50 percent of all patients waiting to receive a transplant.) Thus, the previously described large differences in waiting times among OPOs (e.g., DHHS's Final Rule) are primarily a function of status 3 patient listings and not of access to or allocation of organs among OPOs for patients in status 1 or 2.

[2]The status 4 category was eliminated in 1998.

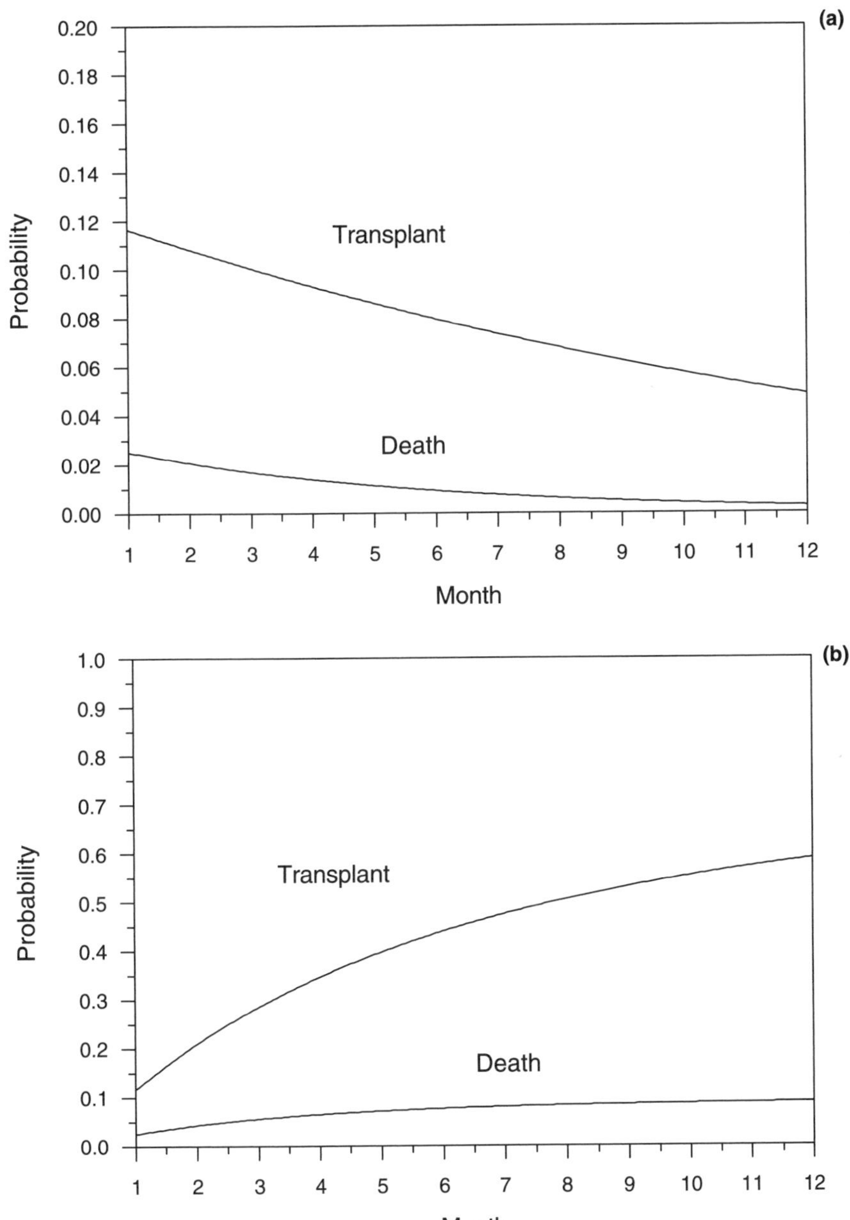

FIGURE 5-3 Estimated monthly hazard rates (a) and cumulative time-event distribution (b) for status 2B patients awaiting liver transplantation. The hazard rate describes the likelihood of transplantation or mortality at a given point in time adjusted for the competing risks (i.e., transplantation or mortality) and the model covariates (e.g., gender, race, blood type). The cumulative time-to-event distribution describes the overall adjusted likelihood of transplantation or mortality up to a particular point in time.

The statistical analysis of the status 3 patient data for 1998–1999 reveals that younger status 3 patients have an increased likelihood over older patients of receiving a transplant (see Table 5-2 and Table B-7 in Appendix B), but age does not affect the pretransplant mortality rate for status 3 patients (see Table 5-3 and Table B-7 in Appendix B). Having a blood type that limits matches with donated organs (i.e., type B or O) decreases the chance of a status 3 transplant, but is not associated with increases in pretransplant mortality.

The analysis also confirms that status 3 patients in small- to medium-volume OPOs have an even greater increased likelihood of receiving transplants relative to patients treated by the larger OPOs. Similar to patients in status 2B, status 3 patients have a decreased likelihood of receiving a transplant the longer they are on the list as status 3 (i.e., as shown in Table 5-2, the effect of waiting time [the variable "month"] was negative). This finding suggests that there is heterogeneity among the listing conditions for less severely ill statuses 2B and 3 patients and that, shortly after listing, a subset of statuses 2B and 3 patients receive transplants more rapidly than the others. Note that the same effect of time on mortality rates is observed with decreased pretransplantation mortality for statuses 2B and 3 patients who remain on the list for longer periods, indicating that the subset of statuses 2B and 3 patients who do not receive transplants are less at risk of death.

The intraclass correlation for OPO-specific effects on transplantation rates was statistically significant and eight times greater than that for status 1 patients (i.e., $r = 0.351$ versus $r = 0.045$) and almost three times greater than that for status 2B patients (i.e., $r = 0.351$ versus $r = 0.126$). This statistic indicates that 35 percent of the variability in status 3 transplantation rates is due to OPO-specific influences even after OPO volume and the other covariates are accounted for. By contrast, the intraclass correlation for pretransplantation mortality rates was not significant, once again indicating that the differences in transplantation rates across OPOs are not leading to differential mortality rates.

To help illustrate these effects, Figure 5-4a displays the estimated hazard functions, and Figure 5-4b displays the estimated cumulative time-to-event distributions for transplantation and mortality rates over the first 12 months of status 3 listings. These estimated rates hold the effects of the covariates constant at adult, female, white, A or AB blood type, and large-volume OPO. Inspection of Figure 5-4a reveals that the hazard rates for both transplantation and death decrease over the first 12 months from 4.3 to 0.05 percent per month for transplantation, and 2.0 to 0.2 percent per month for mortality. Figure 5-4b reveals that after 12 months as a status 3 patient, approximately 20 percent of the patients would have received a transplant and approximately 8 percent would have died.

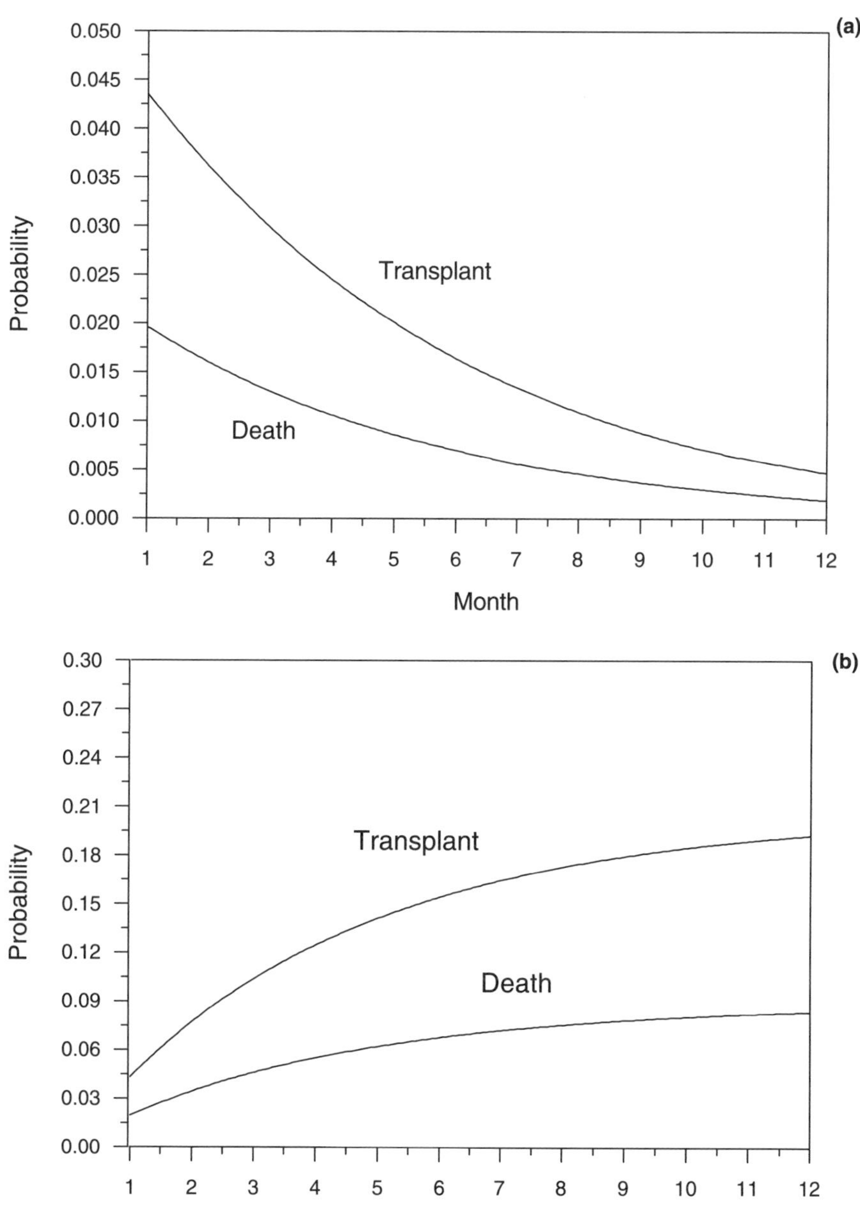

FIGURE 5-4 Estimated monthly hazard rates (a) and cumulative time-event distribution (b) for status 3 patients awaiting liver transplantation. The hazard rate describes the likelihood of transplantation or mortality at a given point in time adjusted for the competing risks (i.e., transplantation or mortality) and the model covariates (e.g., gender, race, blood type). The cumulative time-to-event distribution describes the overall adjusted likelihood of transplantation or mortality up to a particular point in time.

Status Levels of Transplanted Patients

In an attempt to reassemble the information presented to this point on the likelihood of transplantation for each status level across OPOs, Table B-8 in Appendix B shows, for each OPO, the percentage distribution by status (1, 2, 3, 4, 7, or 9) of patients who received transplants during 1995–1999. (Status 7 refers to patients who are too sick to survive a transplant and were therefore temporarily delisted. Status 9 refers to patients who were delisted from the OPO for any other reason [e.g., moved to a different OPO or no longer needed a transplant].)

Table B-8 in Appendix B shows that, in general, a higher percentage of transplants performed in larger-volume OPOs were for status 1 patients and a lower percentage were for status 3 patients, compared to the smaller-volume OPOs. This difference does not appear to be associated with differences across OPOs in the distribution of patients by initial listing status (see Table B-9 in Appendix B), which appear similar regardless of OPO transplant volume.

As discussed previously, under the current system, status 1 patients receive transplants at similar rates among OPOs and have similar mortality and outcomes. However, the equity of the current system, and its effectiveness in getting organs to the neediest patients, might be improved if it were possible to identify a minimum OPO population size or transplant volume that would promote both greater consistency in transplantation rates across OPOs and a higher rate of transplantation for patients with the greatest medical need.

OPO Size

To better understand the relationship between the size of the population served by an allocation system and the probability of transplantation or death, a mixed-effects competing risk survival model was fit to the data using day (status 1) or month (statuses 2B and 3), and the linear and quadratic effects of OPO size measured in millions of people served. The results of the analysis are summarized in Tables 5-4 (transplantation) and 5-5 (mortality). Of the 52 OPOs in the committee's analysis, 11 served populations of 2 million or fewer, 11 served approximately 3 million people, 11 served approximately 4 million people, 4 served approximately 5 million people, 3 served approximately 6 million people, 5 served approximately 7 million people, and 7 served approximately 9 million or more people.

Results of the analysis for status 1 patients (also see Table B-10 in Appendix B) show that OPO size plays no significant role in the transplantation or pretransplantation mortality rates of status 1 patients. As an aid in interpreting these results, Figures 5-5a and 5-5b display a three-dimensional view of the relationships among waiting-list time (measured in days), OPO size, and estimated rates for transplantation and pretransplantation mortality, respectively. Figures 5-5a and 5-5b reveal that both transplantation and mortality rates are essentially constant over waiting time (days 1–12) and OPO size.

TABLE 5-4 Parameter Estimates (standard errors) for Likelihood of Liver Transplantation as a Function of Time, and Linear and Nonlinear Effects of OPO Size (in millions): Individual Models for Statuses 1, 2B, and 3 for All Available Data in 1998–1999

	Status 1	Status 2B	Status 3
Intercept	–2.071*	–2.527*	–4.837*
	(0.561)	(0.432)	(0.604)
Waiting time	–0.003[a]	–0.105*[b]	–0.233*[b]
	(0.012)	(0.010)	(0.023)
Size (linear)	0.018	0.505*	0.841*
	(0.243)	(0.154)	(0.243)
Size (quadratic)	–0.005	–0.063*	–0.079*
	(0.023)	(0.013)	(0.021)
Random OPO effect	0.404*	0.596*	1.196*
	(0.142)	(0.050)	(0.105)

[a]Time in days.
[b]Time in months.

*$p < 0.05$.

TABLE 5-5 Parameter Estimates (standard errors) for Likelihood of Pretransplantation Mortality as a Function of Time, and Linear and Nonlinear Effects of OPO Size (in millions): Individual Models for Statuses 1, 2B, and 3 for All Available Data in 1998–1999

	Status 1	Status 2B	Status 3
Intercept	–4.539*	–3.886*	–4.904*
	(1.349)	(0.361)	(0.694)
Waiting time	0.008[a]	–0.209*[b]	–0.213*[b]
	(0.027)	(0.027)	(0.029)
Size (linear)	0.234	0.328*	0.280
	(0.473)	(0.127)	(0.226)
Size (quadratic)	–0.019	–0.033*	–0.018
	(0.039)	(0.011)	(0.017)
Random OPO effect	0.052	0.076	0.067
	(0.183)	(0.047)	(0.150)

[a]Time in days.
[b]Time in months.

*$p < 0.05$.

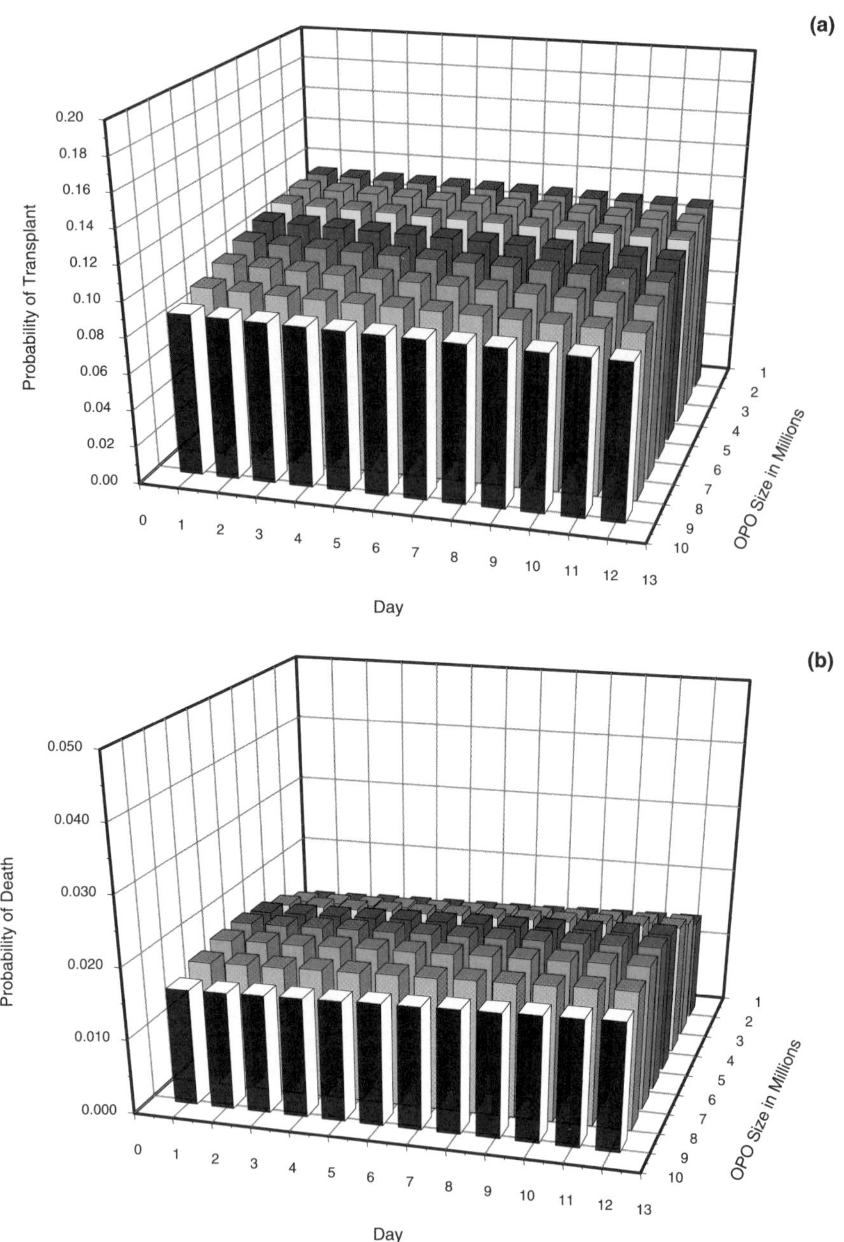

FIGURE 5-5 A three-dimensional view of the relationships among waiting-list time (measured in days), OPO population (in millions), and probability of transplant (a) and death (b) for status 1 patients.

The analysis for status 2B patients (also see Table B-11 in Appendix B) shows that the linear and quadratic size coefficients are significant for both transplantation and pretransplantation mortality and that when OPO size is accounted for, both mortality and transplantation rates decrease over time. At 1 month, transplantation rates range from less than 5 percent for OPOs serving a population 9 million or more to 17 percent for those serving a population of approximately 4 million. OPOs serving populations of 7 million or more have relatively homogeneous estimated transplantation rates, from 5 to 10 percent in month 1 and from 3 to 8 percent in month 4. For patients on the list for 12 months in status 2B, the rate of transplantation is approximately 2 to 5 percent per month regardless of OPO size (see Figure 5-6a). Figure 5-6b displays results for estimated pretransplantation mortality rates. Here OPO size has a smaller effect. At 1 month, the mortality rate is 2 to 3 percent, and at 4 months the rate is approximately 1 percent, regardless of OPO size. At 12 months, the mortality rate is approximately 0.3 percent for all OPOs.

The pattern of results for status 3 is similar to that for status 2B, although the transplantation and mortality rates are somewhat lower (also see Table B-12 in Appendix B). Significant OPO size-related effects are seen for transplantation but not for mortality. Both transplantation and mortality rates show a statistically significant decrease over time. Figure 5-7a reveals that, again, after 4 months of waiting in status 3, the effect of OPO size on transplantation is diminished, but at 1 month, rates vary by size of OPO from a low of 3 percent (>9 million) to a high of 9 percent (5 million). Using an OPO size cutoff of approximately 9 million substantially reduces transplant rates across the entire 12-month period. Figure 5-7b displays a similar graphic for pretransplantation mortality rates and, again, there is a much smaller effect of OPO size. At 1 month the mortality rate is approximately 1 to 1.5 percent, at 4 months the rate is approximately 0.5 to 1 percent, and at 12 months the mortality rate is approximately 0.1 percent, regardless of OPO size.

In sum, as OPO size increases to 9 million people, the probability of transplantation falls for both status 2B and status 3 patients, and the pretransplant mortality also declines for status 2B patients. Thus, the number of status 2B and 3 patients receiving transplant could be reduced to allow more status 1 and 2A patients to receive transplants, without an increase in pretransplant mortality for the status 2B and 3 patients.

A question arises as to why the smaller OPOs have more statuses 2B and 3 patients receiving transplants relative to the larger OPOs. Tables B-13 and B-14 (see Appendix B) shed some light on this issue. Table B-13 reveals that the ratio of transplantations to listings for status 1 patients is generally higher in the larger volume and larger population size OPOs relative to the OPOs serving smaller populations and having a lower transplant volume. Conversely, for statuses 3 to 4 patients, the ratio of transplants to listings is generally larger for the small-volume and small-population OPOs. Based on this result, it could be argued that the reason more status 3 patients are receiving transplants in small OPOs is that these OPOs are more efficient in organ procurement and can therefore provide transplants to patients farther down the waiting list. To test this hypothesis, Table B-14 displays transplantation and listing rates expressed as the number of patients listed or receiving transplants per million people served in the OPO. Table B-14 shows that the smaller OPOs in fact have a smaller number of transplants and listings for their population size than the larger OPOs. The OPO with the greatest number of patients receiving transplants has rates of 107 transplants and 270 listings per million people served, whereas smaller OPOs have transplantation and listing rates on the order of 10–50 transplants and 30–100 listings per million people served, respectively. These results suggest that, although smaller OPOs have lower transplantation rates than larger OPOs, their listing rates are even further reduced relative to larger OPOs. This means that smaller OPOs are able to allocate organs to patients farther down their shorter waiting lists than are larger OPOs. Whether this phenomenon is due to patients listing with OPOs in other states or to decreased access or awareness of transplantation as an option in the smaller OPOs remains unclear. In either case, some degree of regional sharing would be expected to help equalize these rates across the country. By increasing regional sharing, both listings and availability of organs should increase to levels comparable to the larger OPOs. A demonstration of this anticipated result is provided in the following section.

THE EFFECT OF SHARING

Although not rigorously implemented, a number of statewide and regional sharing arrangements have been active in 1998 and 1999. Analysis of the preliminary data points to sharing having the effect of increasing transplantation rates for status 1 patients, decreasing pretransplantation mortality for status 2B patients, and decreasing transplantation rates for status 3 patients without increasing mortality.

To shed light on the anticipated benefits of regional and statewide sharing, the previously described models were expanded to include the effects of a new sharing variable coded 0 (no sharing) or 1 (regional or statewide sharing of any kind). In this way, the unique effect of sharing adjusted for age, gender, race, blood type, transplant volume, and OPO-specific effects can be assessed.

For status 1 patients, the effect of sharing on transplantation rates was positive (Maximum Marginal Likelihood Estimates [MMLE] = 0.51, standard error [SE] = 0.28, $p = .07$) and approached statistical significance, indicating increased likelihood of transplantation of status 1 patients in OPOs that had sharing. The marginal frequency of transplantation increased from 42 percent without sharing to 52 percent with sharing, with average waiting times of 4 and 3 days, respectively. Although the change was not statistically significant, pretransplantation mortality rates decreased from 9 percent without sharing to 7 percent with sharing. The lack of statistical significance for the effect of sharing on mortality may be due to the small number of status 1 patients.

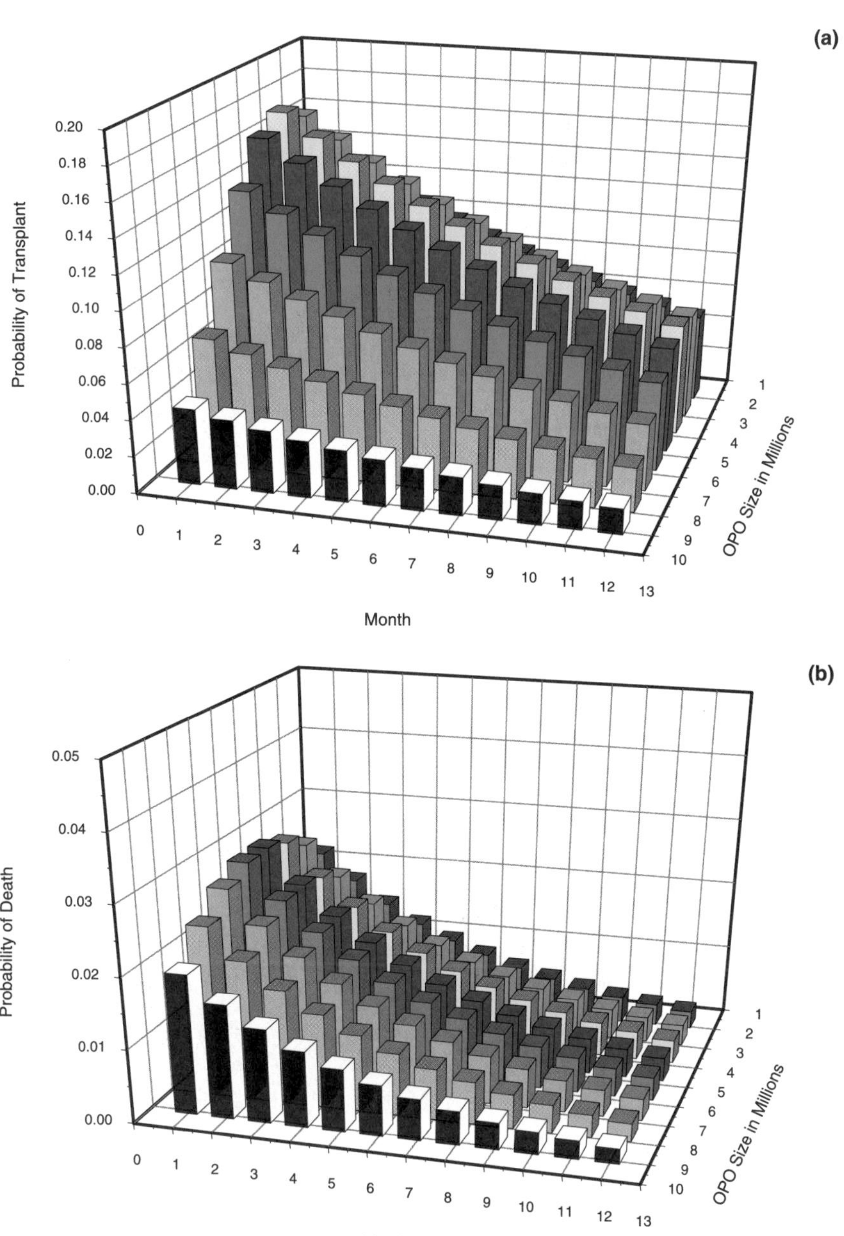

FIGURE 5-6 A three-dimensional view of the relationships among waiting-list time (measured in months), OPO population (in millions), and probability of transplant (a) and death (b) for status 2B patients.

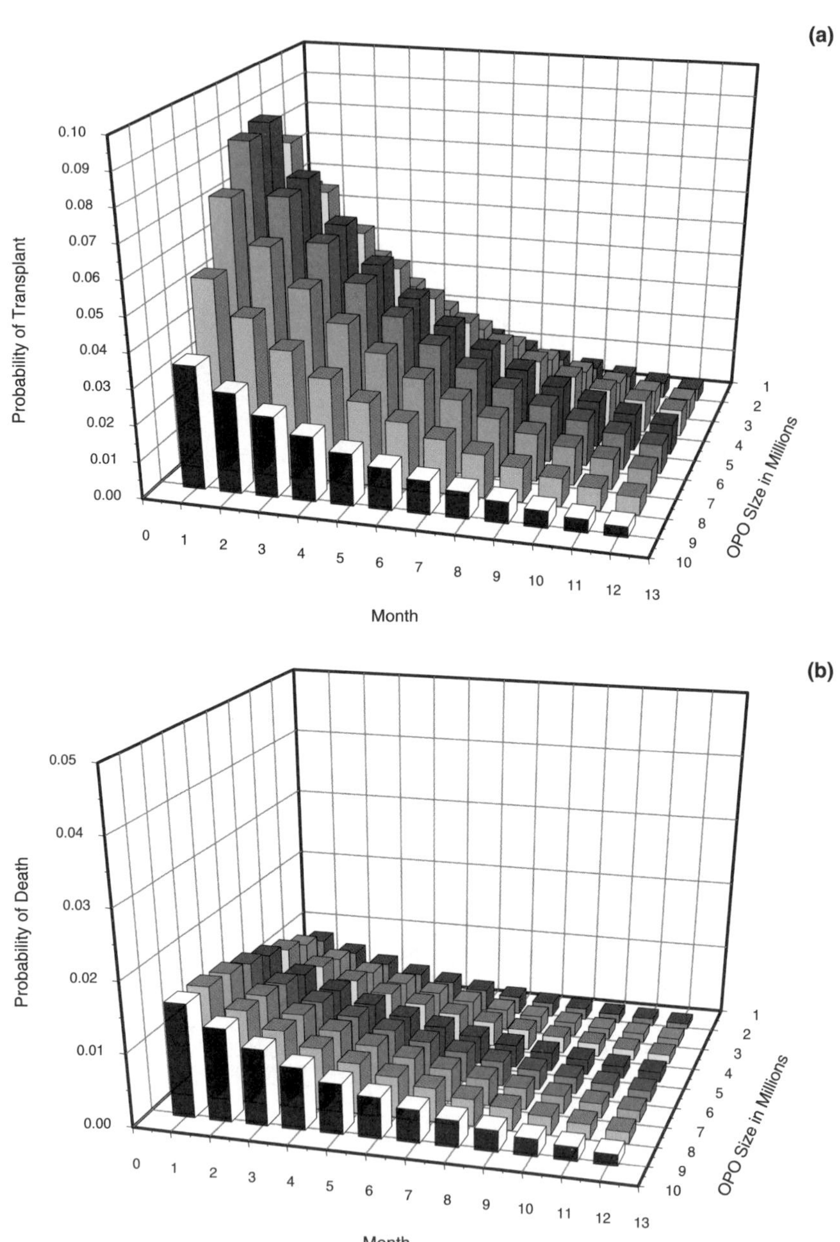

FIGURE 5-7 A three-dimensional view of the relationships among waiting-list time (measured in months), OPO population (in millions), and probability of transplant (a) and death (b) for status 3 patients.

For status 2B patients, the effect of sharing on transplantation rates was not significant, but the effect of sharing on pretransplantation mortality was (MMLE = –0.30, SE = 0.15, $p = 0.05$). The negative coefficient implies that sharing decreases mortality for status 2B patients, presumably due to the ability to transplant more of the neediest status 2B patients (although there was no overall increase in the total number of status 2B patient transplants). The observed overall mortality rate decreased from 6 percent without sharing to 5 percent with sharing. Even though the overall difference in mortality is small, the number of patients is large and the statistical model is adjusting for a large number of factors including OPO transplant volume. This is important because small-volume OPOs had a significantly increased pretransplantation mortality rate for status 2B patients relative to the large-volume OPOs (see Table B-5 in Appendix B) and the OPOs participating in regional sharing had lower transplant volume and served a smaller population size than the OPOs that did not share (average population size of 5 million versus 7 million). Therefore, if sharing had no effect, the OPOs that were participating in sharing arrangements should have had higher mortality rates than those that did not. In fact, the OPOs with sharing had lower mortality rates, which accounts for the significant difference.

For status 3 patients, sharing had a large effect on transplantation rates (MMLE = –1.89, SE = 0.37, $p = 0.001$), but no significant effect on pretransplantation mortality. The large negative coefficient indicates that sharing significantly decreases the probability of transplantation for status 3 patients. In the previous analyses (see Table 5-2; also Table B-7 in Appendix B), the rate of transplantation for status 3 patients was significantly higher for smaller-volume OPOs than for the larger-volume OPOs, leading to the expectation that in the absence of a sharing effect, the OPOs with sharing arrangements would have increased transplantation rates for status 3 patients because they are smaller. In fact, sharing equalizes this effect, because the observed marginal transplantation rates are the same for sharing and nonsharing OPOs (i.e., 5 percent). Average time to transplantation is also the same (138 and 136 days, respectively). As a further illustration, the status 3 transplantation rate among the OPOs serving the smallest population (i.e., 2 million or less) is 31 percent for OPOs that do not share and 6 percent for those that do.

In summary, the preliminary naturalistic data on regional and statewide sharing reveal that (1) sharing increases status 1 transplantation rates, (2) sharing decreases status 2B pretransplantation mortality rates, and (3) sharing decreases the rate of transplantation of status 3 patients, therefore providing more available organs for more seriously ill patients. The effect of sharing, which decreased status 3 transplantation rates for these smaller OPOs, did not, however, produce a concomitant increase in mortality of status 3 patients.

SUMMARY

The results of these analyses reveal that systematic OPO variability in transplantation rates increases from 5 percent for status 1 patients to 13 percent for status 2B patients to 35 percent for status 3 patients when expressed as a percentage of total variability in transplantation rates (i.e., an intraclass correlation). In no case was systematic OPO variability in pretransplantation mortality rates larger than 1 percent of the total variability. These results indicate that the large differences in median waiting times that are the basis for claims of inequity are driven by differences in waiting times for status 3 patients across the OPOs and most likely due to differences in listing practices for status 3 patients across the OPOs. Average mean waiting times for status 1 patients across all OPOs were about 4 days, plus or minus 2 days. Thus, the current system appears to be reasonably equitable within the category of status 1 patients. By contrast, average waiting times for status 3 patients were on the order of 100 to 400 days, with considerable variability across OPOs. However, the overall differences among OPOs are somewhat underestimated by the intraclass correlations, which reflect OPO variability controlling for the effects of OPO size.

Race and gender appear to play no significant role as predictors of transplantation rates and pretransplantation mortality rates. By contrast, young children have a lower likelihood than adults of transplantation in status 1, but a higher likelihood when listed as status 2B or 3. Despite the decreased likelihood of transplantation for status 1 children, they have lower pretransplantation mortality than adult patients. This is most likely related to issues of organ size and of childhood illnesses that are severe but less life-threatening than in adults.

Blood type (B and O versus A and AB) has no effect on transplantation or mortality rates in status 1 patients, but in statuses 2B and 3 patients it is associated with a reduced likelihood of transplantation, but not pretransplant death. This effect is presumed to reflect supply and demand considerations that lead less severely ill patients to wait for a donor with a matching blood type and lead status 1 patients, who are likely to die without transplantation, to accept an organ that is not matched for blood type. Finally, OPO transplant volume and population size have no effect on status 1 transplantation rates or pretransplantation mortality rates, but smaller OPOs (defined both in terms of transplant volume and population served) have higher transplantation rates for statuses 2B and 3 patients relative to larger OPOs.

Thus, smaller OPOs, by generally transplanting more statuses 2B and 3 patients than larger OPOs, may contribute to a situation in which more severely ill patients are required to wait longer for organs at increased risk of death.

The duration of waiting time had no effect on either rate for status 1 patients. By contrast, the longer statuses 2B and 3 patients remain on the list, the less is the likelihood that they will die or receive a transplant. This finding suggests that there may be a subgroup of status 2B and 3 patients that are more severely ill and have increased likelihood of either being transplanted or dying earlier in the course of their illness.

A detailed evaluation of the effects of OPO size (defined by millions of people served) confirmed that transplantation rates for statuses 2B and 3 patients are higher for those OPOs serving fewer people, but pretransplantation mortality rates are constant across OPOs of varying size for status 3 patients. For status 2B patients, there appears to be increased pretransplant mortality in the smaller OPOs. Statuses 2B and 3 transplantation rates were lower in OPOs that serve populations of approximately 9 million, relative to the smaller OPOs. Smaller OPOs have lower transplantation rates per million people served, but even lower listing rates per million people served, relative to larger OPOs. The lower listing rates at small OPOs appear to permit these small OPOs to perform transplants on patients who are farther down the waiting list than do the larger OPOs, rather than reflecting greater efficiency.

Finally, analysis of the preliminary data on regional and statewide sharing showed that sharing (1) increases status 1 transplantation rates, (2) decreases status 2B pretransplantation mortality rates, and (3) decreases the rate of transplantation of status 3 patients, therefore providing more available organs for more seriously ill patients with no concomitant increase in mortality of status 3 patients.

CONCLUSIONS AND RECOMMENDATIONS

The results of the analyses of data on OPO size (defined as either population served or number of transplants per year) provide several insights concerning (1) the determinants and utility of waiting time as a listing criterion and (2) the impact of the size of the organ allocation area on the ability to satisfy the needs of the medically urgent.

Assuming it is more important from a medical urgency standpoint for a status 1 or 2A patient to receive a transplant than it is for a status 2B or 3 patient (a position implicitly endorsed by the internal allocation policies adopted by the OPTN), utilizing the geographical areas served by smaller OPOs as allocation areas for livers results in the allocation of organs to patients for whom transplantation is less medically urgent. Current procedures and policies result, in general, in more statuses 2B and 3 patients receiving transplants in areas served by smaller OPOs than in areas served by larger OPOs. Consequently, more severely ill patients may be required to wait longer for organs, at increased risk of mortality.

A reasonable improvement in the current allocation scheme could be achieved by creating allocation areas of sufficient size to shift some of the transplants from status 3 to statuses 1 and 2. Smaller OPOs could be grouped into regional sharing arrangements such that the minimum population level served would be above the critical level for equitable allocation. The statistical analysis of the data summarized in Table B-8 revealed that OPOs that had fewer than 300 transplants performed in their service area over the four year period were significantly more likely to provide organs for status 2B and status 3 patients than

OPOs that exceed that total volume. In addition, status 2B patients served by OPOs with a volume of less than 160 transplants within their service area had a significantly increased risk of pretransplant mortality while on the waiting list. This suggests that the appropriate scale for organ allocation would be an area in which at least 75 liver transplants are performed per year (i.e., approximately 300 transplants over the 4-year period 1995–1999).

An analysis done with respect to the size of the OPOs (in millions of population) revealed a nonlinear relationship between size and the probability that a status 2B or status 3 patient would receive a transplant. These results are displayed in Figures 5-6a and 5-7a. The estimated marginal probabilities from the committee's statistical model indicate that a minimum population size of about 9 million provides an allocation area with the lowest estimated probability of transplantation of status 2B and status 3 patients, without a statistically significant increase in pretransplant mortality. The OPOs serving a minimum population of 9 million people in all cases also had 75 or more transplants within their service areas (see Table B-14). Based on this analysis, the committee reached the following conclusion:

> *Creation of organ allocation areas based on a minimum population of approximately 9 million persons would substantially increase the allocation of organs to patients with more urgent need of organs.*

Although the policy discussion about variations in waiting time across regions has focused on overall median waiting times, the committee's analyses demonstrate that overall median waiting times are a poor measure of the fairness or effectiveness of organ allocations. This is because the median waiting times, as previously calculated by others, are determined primarily by the waiting times of status 3 patients, who have the least urgent need for transplantation.

> *Overall median waiting time, which has dominated the policy debate, is a poor measure of differences in access to transplantation. Status-specific rates of pretransplantation mortality and transplantation are more meaningful indicators of equitable access.*

Examination of status-specific average waiting times across OPO areas demonstrates that they are typically only about 3–4 days for status 1 patients and 40–70 days for status 2 patients, compared to 100–400 days for status 3 patients. Moreover, there is far less variability in waiting times across OPO areas for status 1 patients than for statuses 2B and 3 patients. Similarly, pretransplant mortality did not vary substantially across OPO areas for all three status levels.

> *The current system appears to generate reasonably little variation in waiting times across OPOs for statuses 1 and 2A patients, indicating that waiting time is an appropriate criterion for organ allocation,*

along with necessary medical criteria, within these categories. Greater amounts of variation occur for statuses 2B and 3 patients across OPOs.

The committee's analysis demonstrates that statuses 2B and 3 patients have a decreased likelihood of either transplantation or mortality the longer they are on the list, suggesting that a subgroup of statuses 2B and 3 patients, despite meeting criteria for listing for transplantation, have little likelihood of receiving a transplant and are also at little risk of dying. It may be that some patients are listed early in some centers to earn "seniority points."

The committee's analysis suggests that one consequence of this practice has been to contribute to the appearance of an inequitable allocation system. Eliminating the use of waiting time in statuses 2B and 3 as a component of the priority score would be one means of reducing the incentive to list patients in status 2B or 3 who are unlikely to require a transplant within a reasonable period of time.

Among the statuses 2B and 3 patients there appears to be a subgroup of patients who are more likely to require a transplant within a shorter period of time than the remainder of patients in that status. The remaining patients in that status will live a relatively long time with chronic liver disease, not become medically urgent, and not receive a transplant. Thus, the length of waiting time in statuses 2B and 3 is not a good indicator of medical urgency or priority.

The committee believes that all parties involved in organ procurement, allocation, and transplantation are carrying out these responsibilities conscientiously and trying to be as effective as possible within the constraints of the current structures and procedures. Moreover, there is broad agreement that the ultimate objective of the organ procurement and allocation system is the extended life and improved health of the patients. On the basis of the analyses in this report, it seems apparent that patients on liver transplant waiting lists will be better served by an allocation system that facilitates broader sharing within larger populations.

RECOMMENDATION 5.1: ***Establish Organ Allocation Areas for Livers***

The committee recommends that the DHHS Final Rule be implemented by the establishment of Organ Allocation Areas (OAAs) for livers—each serving a population base of at least 9 million people (unless such area exceeds the limits of acceptable cold ischemic time). OAAs should generally be established through sharing arrangements among organ procurement organizations to avoid disrupting effective current procurement activities.

If broader sharing is implemented, as recommended, patients who are status 2B or 3 should be told that they are less likely to receive a transplant. This information should be accompanied by a clear statement describing their condition, the risks and benefits of transplantation, and their likely quality of life without it.

They should also be told that if their status changes to 2A or 1 they will have a greater chance of transplantation given broader sharing. Telling patients that transplantation is highly unlikely may help them adjust to life with chronic liver disease.

Physicians must develop an informed consent process to address this range of issues with their patients.

RECOMMENDATION 5.2: ***Discontinue Use of Waiting Time as an Allocation Criterion for Patients in Statuses 2B and 3***

The heterogeneity and wide range of severity of illness in statuses 2B and 3 make waiting time relatively misleading within these categories. For this reason, waiting time should be discontinued as an allocation criterion for status 2B and 3 patients. An appropriate medical triage system should be developed to ensure equitable allocation of organs to patients in these categories. Such a system may, for example, be based on a point system arising out of medical characteristics and disease prognoses rather than waiting times.

6

Organ Failure and Patient Survival

Task 4: *Assess current policies and the potential impact of the Final Rule on patient survival rates and organ failure rates leading to retransplantation, including variances by income status, ethnicity, gender, race, or blood type.*

Abstract. **The effects of solid organ ischemic times on transplant outcomes has not been rigorously evaluated in the past. The committee reviewed existing literature and made judgments based on this information that are in general agreement with current practices. Data analysis also supports the previously reported association between volume and outcome—in this case, larger OPOs are associated with decreased mortality rates following transplantation.**

A number of biological factors can influence both short-term and long-term function of transplanted solid organs. The function of the liver, kidney, heart, lung, and pancreas depends on the continuous flow of blood through them. *Ischemic time* refers to the amount of time that elapses when blood flow to an organ is interrupted (e.g., when the organ is removed for transplantation).

Some organs appear more sensitive to ischemic damage than others. For example, with current technology, common general practice suggests that acceptable clinical results cannot be obtained with heart grafts exposed to much more than 4 hours of ischemia. Livers have longer acceptable ischemic times, and kidneys even longer, using preservation fluids such as University of Wisconsin solution and technologies such as pulsatile perfusion.

The duration of ischemic time is positively correlated with the incidence *of primary nonfunction* (failure to function after a transplant). A lengthy ischemic time may also impair long-term graft function. Increased donor age and other aspects of the donor's health status, such as condition of the organ, can accentuate the impact of ischemic time on primary graft nonfunction.

Primary nonfunction refers to a situation in which the organ, after it has been transplanted, fails to function and must be replaced. For kidney graft failure, dialysis is available as a backup. For failing hearts, ventricular assist devices may be used, at least for short periods of time. With lungs and livers, no substitute is available as a therapeutic bridge. As a result, the recipient of a failed or failing transplanted lung or liver, for example, is at risk of death if he or she does not receive a replacement. However, replacement of the failed organ with a second transplant (i.e., retransplantation) means that an organ has been used that could potentially have saved the life of another individual.

Strategies that minimize the number of organs lost to primary nonfunction are essential. This goal may be accomplished by technological advances that extend maximal achievable and, in turn medically acceptable, ischemic time. Alternatively, the more immediately available approach is to minimize ischemic time. For example, it has been suggested that the rates of primary nonfunction after liver transplantation double from approximately 4 to 8 percent when cold ischemic time is extended beyond 12 hours (Ploeg et al., 1993).

Longer ischemic time is also associated with an increased rate of *delayed graft function*, i.e., a situation in which the graft eventually functions, but only after a prolonged period of time. Delayed graft function, in turn, is associated with longer hospital stays, a higher rate of morbidity and mortality in the recipient, and a higher rate of late graft loss.

An approximate 4.2 percent reduction in primary graft nonfunction, achieved by eliminating severely steatotic (i.e., "fatty") livers, reducing ischemic times, and using selected patients has been reported to reduce the need for retransplantation due to primary nonfunction or initial poor function (D'Allesandro et al., 1998). Extrapolating these data to the 4,000 transplants performed nationally would mean that 170 additional patients could receive a liver transplant. This compares favorably with the increase in recovered cadaveric livers of only 231 between 1997 and 1998. This example does not prove that this strategy is correct or should be universally adopted. Rather, the example illustrates how careful scrutiny of procurement and utilization practices and subsequent clinical outcomes may be used to model and then measure optimal management of a scarce human resource.

ORGAN PRESERVATION AND DONOR INFLUENCES

In the early days of transplantation, the optimal approach to preserve and protect the function of organs deprived of their blood flow had not been well explored. As a result, the donor and recipient had to be located very close to each other to minimize ischemic time. Methods to improve the medically acceptable ischemic time became an intense focus of research that continues. As organ preservation and technical aspects of transplantation improve, the geographic limitations for organ transport have been eased, but not totally eliminated.

The medical literature addressing the impact of cold ischemic time on outcome is expanding but is not yet sufficiently developed to state with certainty the optimal times on an organ-by-organ basis. Even the basic criteria by which viability and function are judged in laboratory-based studies are subject to scientific debate. More to the point, the number of patient and donor variables that confound the interpretation of clinical transplant results is large. Moreover, variability among transplant programs in their philosophy regarding the use of extended criteria donors and organs, as well as the role of retransplantation, significantly affects the results produced in any series.

In addition to ischemic time, several donor factors also influence graft survival. As a result of the shortage of organs for transplantation, the criteria for organ donation have been expanded to include marginal donors (i.e., extended criteria donors) for those candidates awaiting a transplant who could face death if a donor does not become available within a limited time. Donor age, health at the time of donation, and the presence of fatty change on donor liver biopsy are all representative of donor and donor organ characteristics that may influence graft survival.

The transplant team needs to have the flexibility to apply medical judgment in selecting extended criteria donors for candidate recipients with life-threatening organ failure. These decisions may relate solely to the donor source or to the recipient's medical status, and the results of such transplantation decisions must be weighed in clinical context. As an example, approximately 50 percent of candidates for a cardiac transplant die before a donor becomes available. In this circumstance, a 10–15 percent risk of primary graft nonfunction, hypothetically, might be acceptable if the patient was medically decompensating and likely to die if no donor were available. However, the increased use of non-heartbeating donors and other extended criteria donors must be prospectively evaluated within the context of current and novel technology. The impact on total organ allocation among potential recipients must also be assessed. These analyses must be formulated in a manner that recognizes that clinical and programmatic philosophies will influence perceived differences in outcome.

REVIEW OF LITERATURE

As the science of organ preservation continues to advance, the duration of tolerable ischemic time from organ procurement to organ transplantation may increase. An important distinction must be made, for purposes of this analysis, between what might be labeled "maximal achievable cold ischemic time" (i.e., the longest duration of cold storage to which an ideal organ can be exposed and still have some measurable chance of functioning when reanastomosed to a blood supply) and "medically acceptable ischemic time" (i.e., the duration of cold ischemia that has been associated in clinical experience with an appropriate and acceptable percentage of acute and long-term organ survival). These times may differ significantly. Improvements in the former rely primarily on advances in technology, which are then explored in clinical studies to determine the rates of acute and long-term graft function. In addition, although the maximal achievable ischemic time may be an absolute, the medically acceptable ischemic time will differ depending on the relative scarcity of the organ, the opportunities for retransplantation, the condition of the patient, and increasing knowledge of synergistic variables that influence ultimate organ survival.

Based on a review of the existing literature on organ preservation and patient survival, outlined in Tables 6-2 through 6-6, the committee generated a summary of its findings, which are presented in Table 6-1. The figures presented in Table 6-1 are not meant to be standards of practice, but rather approximations that will vary as a function of other factors (described above). Although these findings should not be interpreted as absolute standards, they tend to agree in general with the current practice among transplant professionals.

ASSESSING THE IMPACT

Any strategy to expand organ allocation areas, for example, as described in this report, would have to take into account the very significant efforts devoted to matching a suitable donor with a suitable recipient, including the mechanisms currently used by the OPO system to expedite organ recovery and distribution. Given current biological constraints, any format must have as a central goal an organ allocation policy that serves to minimize ischemic time within reasonable limits in locating a potential recipient. That this function can be performed for some organs on a large geographic basis with some efficiency is attested to by current practice nationwide as well as the results within regional sharing programs.

Health outcomes data of several different types will be needed to assess and monitor the impact of biological factors on the organ distribution and allocation system. The data collected should inform the evaluation of minimum performance criteria for the organ procurement process and the transplantation process itself because they may have an impact on organ viability. Rigorous evaluation of the procurement process would appear to be a sound principle.

TABLE 6-1 Summary of Literature on Cold Ischemic Time for Solid Organs

Organ	Medically Acceptable Cold Ischemic Time* (simple cold storage using appropriate preservation fluids) (hrs)
Liver	12
Pancreas	17
Kidney	2
Heart	4
Lung	6–8

*The committee defines medically acceptable cold ischemic time as the duration of cold ischemia that has been associated in clinical experience with an appropriate and acceptable percentage of acute and long-term graft function and survival. The times presented in this table are based on the committee's review of peer reviewed literature. Longer times are sometimes reported in clinical practice with acceptable outcomes. Outcomes vary as a function of many other factors, including age of donor and quality of organ.

Data provided by the United Network of Organ Sharing (UNOS) suggest that between 450 and 550 (or 10–13 percent) of livers recovered per year (1994–1998) are not transplanted. It is difficult to ascertain the exact reasons for this, although possibilities include a marginal donor, difficulty in finding a second center in a timely manner after the first choice rejects the organ, or the finding of extensive steatosis or hepatitis in the donor organ. Each of these losses may be unavoidable. Alternatively, many of these lost opportunities might be avoided by improved communication and tracking—for example, data on the time from notification of a possible donor to the time that formal contact between the OPO and family is established; time to obtain permission for donation; time to scheduling of organ harvest; duration of the organ harvest procedure; number of organs procured but not used; and cold ischemic time of procured organs stratified by appropriate geographic criteria (e.g., miles traveled).

Transplant center-based measures would likely include the number of delivered but discarded organs; number of transplanted organs with primary nonfunction or delayed graft function; and the number of patients requiring retransplantation. Both acute and chronic organ survival could be followed and analyzed by appropriate demographics to suggest where more efficient organ allocation might be implemented to maximize organ utilization. A method to ensure the accuracy of data reporting as well as the timely availability of data is essential.

Despite the variable nature of patients and donors, other parameters that are well within the control of the system may be associated with divergent results. Appropriate and timely data analysis will strengthen the ability of the medical and allied communities to make strategic decisions in this regard. Promulgation and enforcement of minimum performance guidelines should help optimize graft survival of the overall population. Given the critical nature of this system, all involved parties should be monitored for quality control and quality assurance and for compliance with recommended methods and processes. Lastly, appropriate measures are needed to assess the impact of the Final Rule on the biological and practical measures that affect organ failure and patient survival. It must also be recognized that as methods for preservation or other technologies change, the system must be flexible enough to incorporate new data. The National Marrow Donor Program is offered as an example of a system that has operated well with respect to many of these factors (see Box 6-1).

Computer Simulation Models

Historically, the primary approach to exploring the impact of various changes on the allocation system has been through the use of computer simulation models. These models allow the user to input various characteristics of the organ allocation system (e.g., initial waiting list composition, recipient stream, status changes, donor stream, allocation policy, liver offer/acceptance process, post-transplant relisting/mortality) and then simulate the impact that various changes in organ allocation policies have on relevant outcomes (e.g., numbers of primary and repeat transplants; distribution of transplants by medical urgency status; posttransplant survival rates; percentage of transplants performed locally, regionally, and nationally; cost-related measures; and waiting times).

As an illustration, change from the current allocation policy to a system using expanded allocation areas is generally expected to increase the number of status 1 patients receiving liver transplants and decrease the number of status 3 patients receiving transplants. Depending on the assumptions of the model, this change can lead to either increased or decreased posttransplant survival. The outcomes and conclusions of the simulation models are highly dependent on the assumptions upon which they are based.

This has largely been the case for the two major simulation models used in this area; the Pritsker model used by UNOS and the CONSAD model used by the University of Pittsburgh. In general, the Pritsker model shows that national organ sharing will result in more repeat transplants and poorer posttransplant survival than will the current system (Edwards and Harper, 1995). Although there is some evidence of reduced pretransplant mortality, it is at the expense of increased posttransplant mortality.

The CONSAD model also shows a decrease in pretransplant deaths but an increase in posttransplant deaths (CONSAD, 1995). The two models differ slightly because the CONSAD model assumes that, under a national sharing system, status 3 patients are at increased risk of death following transplant. The CONSAD model also shows a larger number of status 1 patients would die under a national system than does the Pritsker model.

Those developing the Pritsker model had an advantage over the CONSAD model because of their complete access to all center-level data from UNOS. Furthermore, they were able to validate their simulation model results using the rates actually observed in the population of transplant patients over time.

POSTTRANSPLANT PATIENT SURVIVAL

In an effort to better understand the determinants of organ failure and posttransplant survival, the committee examined posttransplant mortality data for liver transplant recipients who were transplanted in 1998 and 1999, using the data provided to this committee by UNOS. Attention was restricted to this more current period because of the change by UNOS in 1998 to the definitions of medical urgency status categories. This time restriction severely limits both the length of follow-up and the number of transplanted patients for which follow-up information was available. Therefore, this analysis should be replicated as more follow-up data under the new status system become available.

BOX 6-1 National Marrow Donor Program

The National Marrow Donor Program (NMDP) is a nonprofit organization that has a cooperative agreement with the Department of the Navy and a competitively renewed contract with the Health Resources and Services Administration. The mission of NMDP is to identify hematopoietic stem cell donors and then procure and deliver stem cell transplants to patients who do not have a suitably matched family member donor. This organization has a clearly stated set of minimum performance criteria for both donor harvest (procurement) and transplant centers. NMDP has also developed criteria that govern allocation (e.g., donors must match at five or more of six prescribed histocompatibility loci), and there is centralized training and retraining of personnel involved in the donor search process (which is the closest analogue of the solid organ allocation process). There is a requirement that any change in the ability of the center to meet any of the above as well as many other criteria must be reported immediately. Acceptance as a center of any sort (transplant, donor harvest) is dependent on having appropriate computer and communication software and hardware on-site and operational. Strict time criteria exist for merging data with the NMDP central data file. For example, donor recruitment centers must merge these data at least monthly and must use either NMDP-developed software or other software that meets NMDP standards. All centers must meet or exceed the NMDP continuous process improvement indicators. Centers are given frequent feedback on task-appropriate indicators. Data are analyzed centrally, not locally, and feedback enables the center to measure its own performance as well as compare its performance to that of other centers. In addition, an NMDP statistician analyzes the aggregate data to ascertain whether there is systematic improvement or deviation from standards and then recommends actions.

There are significant medical differences between solid organ and bone marrow transplantation, as well as many differences in the processes of donor recruitment and organ procurement. However, there are also significant commonalities in making a scarce human resource available to critically ill individuals in a reproducible, effective, and safe fashion. Many of the issues that concern access for the socioeconomically underserved as well as the particular biologic issues that influence organ availability for minority populations are common to both groups. Thus, with due acknowledgment of the divergence between these disciplines, NMDP serves as an illustration of a federally funded organ procurement and allocation organization with a highly regulated set of performance standards for itself and its participating centers. This program demonstrates that a sophisticated data monitoring process that includes a significant quality assurance–quality improvement component can serve a diverse national constituency of small to large procurement and transplant centers. Central data analysis and analyses performed after application by interested parties are made available to the community in a timely fashion. This and other models, thoughtfully adjusted for discipline-specific issues, may provide practical tools to improve and enforce more regularized practice in the area of solid organ procurement, allocation, and transplant.

The sample was comprised of 1,095 transplanted patients in status categories 1, 2B, and 3. The follow-up period ranged from 0.03 month to 17.83 months, with an average follow-up of 3.30 months. The committee examined blood type (O and B versus A and AB), age (0–5, 6–17, and 18 and older), gender, race (black versus other), status (1, 2B, and 3), OPO volume (small, medium, and large),* and follow-up time as potential predictors of patient survival. In addition, OPO-specific effects were included as a random effect in the model. A mixed-effects "person–time" logistic regression model was used to analyze these data and follows directly from the previously described mixed-effect multinomial logistic regression model, where interest is restricted to only two outcomes (i.e., dead or alive).

Results of the analysis revealed that risk of posttransplant mortality for status 1 patients significantly decreased over time (MMLE = –0.58, SE = 0.089, $p < .001$). Similarly, patients transplanted in status 2B (MMLE = –0.74, SE = 0.298, $p < .01$) and status 3 (MMLE = –1.37, SE = 0.529, $p < .01$) both had decreased risk of mortality relative to patients transplanted in status 1.

The analysis also showed that patients located in smaller-volume OPOs had increased risk of posttransplant mortality relative to those in larger-volume OPOs (MMLE = 0.79, SE = 0.323, $p < .01$). These results are not readily explainable. Because smaller OPOs have a larger proportion of status 2B and status 3 patients receiving transplants than larger OPOs, smaller OPOs should be expected to have lower mortality rates. The results found may be explained with the fact that, as a general rule, smaller OPOs are serving lower volume transplant centers. There is considerable health services research indicating that, for a variety of other surgical procedures, there is a positive correlation between volume and patient outcomes (Hannan, 1995; Hosenpud, 1994). Although the committee did not find comparable research for liver transplantation, it did find that the 1997 Report of Center Specific Graft and Patient Survival Rates, produced by UNOS (UNOS, 1997), contains a table showing that several of the transplant centers doing 25 or fewer liver transplants had 1-year graft survival rates significantly lower than expected, given the health status of their patients (see Fig. II-2, p. 15, UNOS, 1997). Further research is needed before any definitive conclusion can be drawn. Therefore, the committee is reluctant to draw any inference as to whether or how graft and patient survival might be affected by the broader sharing of organs.

CONCLUSIONS

Ischemic times for solid organs have not been rigorously evaluated in the past and they are an important factor in the calculus of allocation. The committee re-

*OPOs were split into three groups (17, 17, and 18 for large, medium, and small OPOs, respectively) on the basis of number of transplants performed during 1995–1998. In general this breakdown corresponded to the following definitions: small (S) OPOs performed < 150 transplants during the period 1995–1999; medium (M) OPOs performed 150–300 transplants in the same period; and large (L) OPOs performed > 300 transplants.

viewed existing literature and made judgments based on this information that are in general agreement with current practices. Data analysis also supports the previously reported association between volume and outcome—in this case, larger OPOs are associated with decreased mortality rates following transplantation.

Tables 6-2 through 6-6 follow beginning on page100.

TABLE 6-2 Heart: Summary of Literature on Cold Ischemic Times

Source	Solution	No. of Transplants	Preservation Time	Comments
Korner et al., 1997	HTK solution (Bretschneider), University of Wisconsin Solution (UW)	100	> 4-hr CIT vs. < 4-hr CIT	• Retrospective Evaluation • A preservation time of up to 5.5 hrs using HTK-solution satisfies early and long-term survival rates compared to heart transplants with ischemic times of < 4 hours. • Demonstrated no survival differences in either the short term or long term.
Briganti et al., 1995	Euro-Collins	151	< 4 hrs, 4–5 hrs, > 5 hrs	• Short and Long-Term Outcome Study • An increase in the available donor pool has been facilitated by the use of allografts with prolonged ischemic time (>4 hrs). • No difference in allograft functional capacity, development of transplant-associated coronary disease, or actuarial survival in the short and the long term. • Conclusion: Improved population treatment with prolonged ischemic time cardiac allografts can be safely undertaken without long-term risk to heart transplant recipients. • Intermediate- and long-term survival has not been compromised by the use of cardiac allografts with ischemic times up to 441 minutes. • Prolonged ischemic time cardiac allografts (> 5 hrs) can be successfully used in clinical heart transplantation with acceptable outcome.

Young et al., 1994	1,719	• Consecutive Primary Transplantation • Probability of death within one month increases with longer ischemic time (i.e., > 4 hrs). • Transplants performed at 27 institutions between Jan. 1, 1990, and June 30, 1992, were analyzed. • Mean follow-up of survivors was 13.9 months, and actuarial survival was 85% at 1 year. • Most common causes of death were infection (22%), acute rejection (18%), and early graft failure (18%). Forty-five percent of the deaths occurred within 30 days of transplantation. • The risk of failure increases with donor age and the interaction of advanced age with other risk factors. • Mean follow-up of survivors was 13.9 mos., and actuarial survival was 85% at 1 year.

CIT = Cold ischemic time.

TABLE 6-3 Kidney: Summary of Literature on Cold Ischemic Times

Source	Solution	No. of Transplants	Preservation Time	Comments
D'Alessandro et al., 1991	UW	68	Mean 18.3 ± 4.3 hrs, range 6–28 hrs	• Retrospective Analysis • Actuarial renal allograft survival as 97.8% and 86.6% at 1 month and 2 years, respectively.
Belzer et al., 1992	UW	163	Kidney: 19.2 ± 4.3 hrs, range 4–27 hrs	• Retrospective Analysis • Time period: May 1997-November 1991. • Simultaneous pancreas–kidney transplants. • No differences in allograft function or graft-related complications in organs preserved for <12 or >12 hrs. • Liver, kidney, and pancreas can be safely preserved for times that currently meet most clinical needs (i.e., 24–40 hrs). • After transplant kidney–pancreas, the actuarial patient survival was 97.5% and 96.8% at 1 month, and 83.0% and 83.4% at 4 years, respectively.
Lange and Kuhlmann, 1998				• Literature Review • No correlation between CIT and histopathological changes or serum creatinine levels. • Conclusion: Immunological factors such as human leukocyte antigen mismatches, preformed cytotoxic antibodies, and the number of previous grafts have had a greater impact on graft survival than CIT. • Conclusion: Organ sharing would be almost completely abandoned and HLA mismatch rate would increase tremendously with the introduction of ultrashort CIT (<6 hrs) into clinical practice.

Offermann, 1998			• Literature Review • Long-term graft outcome clearly depends on the length of CIT, with significantly inferior results after CIT > 36 hrs. • A reasonable CIT (<18–24 hrs) allows surgery to be performed during the day.
Opelz, 1998	UW	• Group 1: 7 to 12 hrs • Group 2: 13 to 24 hrs • Group 3: 0 to 6 hrs	• Collaborative transplant study • Time period: 1986–1996. • Group 1 had the best long-term survival (75% at 5 years); Group 2 was slightly worse; Group 3 was worst (65% at 5 years). • Conclusion: No clear relationship between the length of warm ischemia and graft outcome. • Decrease in the success rate as cold ischemia increased from 7 to 12 hrs to 37 to 48 hrs. • Some centers believe that short ischemia times eliminate the need for HLA matching. • Only kidneys preserved with the cold storage method were analyzed: machine perfused kidneys were excluded.
Shaheen et al., 1994	CyA (cyclosporine)	Mean CIT: 46 hrs, range: 18–72 hrs	• Time period: 1983–1987. • Patients received kidneys from Eurotransplant. **Actuarial graft survival:** • 1 year: 88.6% • 3 years: 70.2% • 5 years: 58.4% • 7 years: 55.1%

Continued

TABLE 6-3 *Continued*

Source	Solution	No. of Transplants	Preservation Time	Comments
Shaheen et al., 1994 (*continued*)				**Actuarial patient survival:** • 1 year: 94.3% • 3 years: 91.4% • 5 years: 88.5% • 7 years: 88.5% • Good prognosis for patients with prolonged CIT (even when immunosuppressed with CyA). • 35 patients whose grafts survived for > 6 months. • Long-term results unknown.
Pita et al., 1997	UW	858	• Group 1: 0–24 hrs • Group 2: >24 hrs	• Used consecutive patients in a Spanish hospital Cadaveric Kidney Transplants **Graft survival, Group 1:** • 1 year: 86.4% • 2 years: 83% • 3 years: 80% • 5 years: 72.8% **Graft survival, Group 2:** • 1 year: 77.9% • 2 years: 73.5% • 3 years: 65.1% • 5 years: 58.7% • CIT > 24 hrs vs. 0–24 hrs has an RR = 1.75 (95% CI: 1.052–2.91); prolonged CIT (>24 hrs) exerts an independent adverse effect on graft survival.

NOTE: CI = confidence interval; CIT = cold ischemic time; RR = relative risk; and UW = University of Wisconsin solution.

This page intentionally left blank.

TABLE 6-4 Liver: Summary of Literature on Cold Ischemic Times

Source	Solution	No. of Transplants	Preservation Time	Comments
Kalayoglu et al., 1988	UW	17 transplants, 13 with storage > 8 hrs	• Group 1: 8 livers ≤10 hrs (mean 8 hrs) • Group 2: 9 livers >10 hrs (mean 12.7 hrs; range 11–20 hrs) Total Preservation time: 6–20 hrs (mean: 10.5 hrs)	• All had good liver function, even when preservation time > 10 hrs (mean 12.7 hrs, range 11–20 hrs). • No differences between groups in: – total bilirubin concentration in the first postoperative week, – serum aspartate aminotransferase, – prothrombin, and – partial thromboplastin time. • Other liver enzymes showed normal levels within 5 days. • All patients discharged with normal liver function and enzyme values. • Acceptable liver function when preservation ≤ 8 hrs
Todo et al., 1989	UW, 4–24 cadaveric liver homografts: 185 (mean 10.1 ± 5.0) Euro-Collins solution 3–9, 5 hrs: 180 (mean 5.9 ± 1.4 hrs)	UW: 185 cadaveric liver homografts Euro-Collins: 180 grafts	• With UW: 4–24 hrs • With Euro-Collins: 3–9.5 hrs	• Comparison between liver preserved with UW and Euro-Collins solution. • UW-preserved grafts survived at higher rate. • Permitted equal patient survival. • Lower rate of primary nonfunction. • Reduced need for retransplantation. • Lower rate of hepatic artery thrombosis—no correlation between time of preservation with UW preserved grafts up to 24 hrs and liver function abnormalities in the first postoperative week. • Maximum increase in serum aspartate aminotransferase and serum alanine aminotransferase in first week was not greater than with Euro-Collins-preserved livers. • No differences in prothrombin for UW livers.

				• Livers preserved with Euro-Collins solution for >5 hrs had significantly increased perturbation of hepatic function tests (significant increases in serum aspartate aminotransferase and serum alanine aminotransferase levels).
D'Alessandro et al., 1991	UW	181	Mean 12.6 ± 4.5 hrs, range 2–24 hrs	• Retrospective Analysis • Time period: May 1987 to June 1990 • No differences in primary nonfunction or hepatic artery thrombosis were seen for those preserved <6 hrs, 6–12 hrs, or >12 hrs. • Serum aminotransferase levels and prothrombin times were lower on the first postoperative days in livers preserved for <6 hrs when compared to 6–12 hrs or >12 hrs. • Comparison of rates of PNF for reduced and nonreduced liver transplantation also failed to demonstrate a statistical difference. Likewise, the length of preservation for up to 4 hours did not impact on the development of PNF. • The actuarial 1-month patient survival for liver transplant was 91.5%. Actuarial 1-month allocation survival for liver transplants was 83.0%.
Belzer et al., 1992	UW	288	Mean 12.7 ± 4.4 hrs,	• Retrospective analysis from May 1987 to Nov. 1991 • No differences in allograft function or graft-related complications in organs preserved for <12 hrs or >12 hrs; no differences in rates of PNF, hepatic artery thrombosis, or bile duct stenosis for < 12 hrs or > 12 hrs preservation. • Grafts preserved for <6 hrs: less hepatocellular injury (lower serum enzymes including aminotransferases and lactate dehydrogenase).

Continued

TABLE 6-4 *Continued*

Source	Solution	No. of Transplants	Preservation Time	Comments
Belzer et al., 1992 (*continued*)				• Length of stay in intensive care unit after liver transplantation did not correlate with length of preservation but appeared to correlate with the patient's condition before transplant. • One-month patient and graft survival was 91.4% and 80.2% respectively.
Porte et al., 1998	UW	315		• Retrospective European multi-center analysis • Overall patient survival: 3 months, 83%; after 6 years, 63%. • Median CIT was significantly longer in grafts with primary nonfunction (PNF) compared to initial poor function (IPF) or immediate function. • Long-term graft survival was significantly influenced at a lower CIT threshold, with a 6-year graft survival of 67% for CIT of 16 hrs compared to 46%% for CIT > 16 hrs. • Patients with PNF but not IPF have significantly lower CITs. • There is a definitive effect of length of CIT on graft survival. • Follow-up analysis after 3 months indicates that preservation times up to 18 hrs with UW are without adverse effects on long-term graft survival after transplantation. • Long-term data with a 6-year follow up indicate that CIT should be kept to <16 hrs to avoid detrimental effects on graft survival.

			• Complete follow-up of at least 6 years was available for 296 grafts in 277 patients. • Patients with IPF had a 34% lower GS at 3 months than those with immediate function. • 315 transplants were performed in 288 patients in participating European centers.
Furukawa et al., 1991	593	Groups (CIT): • 1: <10 hrs, N = 223; • 2: 10–14 hrs, N = 188; • 3: 15–19 hrs, N = 101; • 4: 20–24 hrs, N = 52; and • 5: ≥25 hrs, N = 29. Mean CIT: 12.8 hrs, range 2.4–34.7 hrs	• 13–32 Months of post-transplant observation • Cadaveric livers were used for primary liver transplant between Oct. 1987 and May 1989 at the University of Pittsburgh • No difference among the five groups in 1-year patient survival; highest serum glutamic oxaloacetic transaminase (SGOT) occurred in the first week after operation and the highest SGOT and total bilirubin during the first month after operation. • However, the retransplantation rate and primary nonfunction rate rose significantly as CIT increased (using a logistic regression model). • Equivalency of patient survival was increasingly dependent on aggressive retransplantation. • Results reported caution against undue procrastination in the use of these livers. • Most of the organs preserved for ≥20 hrs were satisfactory, attesting to the efficiency of the method used. The necessity for life-saving retransplantation because of primary graft nonfunction or other reasons became progressively more frequent. • Effective use of retransplantation prevented a commensurate increase in mortality.

Continued

TABLE 6-4 *Continued*

Source	Solution	No. of Transplants	Preservation Time	Comments
Furukawa et al., 1991 (*continued*)				Policy formulated from findings of the study: • Need to revascularize liver grafts within 20 hrs because the early graft failure rate was increasingly nonlinear beyond this time. • Patient survival was 77.2% at the end of 1 year; there was no difference in patient survival between the different CIT groups. • Differences existed in early graft survival. • When the CIT was less than 10 hrs, the retransplantation rate was 5.4%, whereas it was double, triple, or quadruple this rate with successively longer preservation times. • Primary nonfunction was the principal cause of graft loss during the first 2 weeks no matter what the CIT, and rejection was the least important factor.
Rossi et al., 1993	UW	62	Mean: 12.6 hours Range: 6–20 hours	• In 51.5% of cases with CIT > 12 hrs, incidence of delayed liver function (DLF) has not exceeded 29.5%, as retransplantation due to PNF or technical failure has never been required. • Results may be partially attributed to homogeneous, careful donor selection and liver harvesting procedures. • Even if UW allows one to safely extend liver preservation up to 24 hrs, such a prolonged CIT is associated with an increased incidence of delayed liver function; thus, they concluded that these organs should not be transplanted into marginal recipients, but only into those who could tolerate a more complicated postoperative course.

Marino et al., 1997	UW	2,376	• Transplantations performed from November 1987 to December 1993. • Purpose of the study was to identify the risk factors associated with an unfavorable outcome following orthotopic liver transplantation (OLTx). • Total ischemic time was found to be associated with outcome of liver transplant (graft failure): Odds ratio = 1.3 for each 6-hr increase in CIT after the first 8 hrs; 95% CIT 1.1–1.5. • Three donor variables (donor age, female donor sex, and total CIT) and 7 recipient variables (recipient age, indication for OLTx, history of prior OLTx, need for preoperative mechanical ventilation, preoperative bilirubin and creatinine, type of primary immunosuppressant) were found to be independently associated with graft failure. • Number of successful transplants: 1,635 • Number of transplants that failed: 741
Haller et al., 1995	UW (for majority of grafts: 433 of transplants, or 95.8%)	452	• Transplantation occurred between September 1988 and December 1993 in 414 patients. • Grafts developing primary dysfunction (PDF) had significantly longer CIT: 12 hrs for PDF vs. 10 hrs for initial function (IF). • Donor age was significantly higher: PDF, 38 years; IF, 29 years. • One-year graft survival was 88.0% in the IPF group and 85.1% in the IF group. • The extent of CIT was the most important risk factor leading to PDF in this population. • Concluded: CIT should be kept below 12 hrs whenever possible to avoid the development of PDF.

Continued

TABLE 6-4 *Continued*

Source	Solution	No. of Transplants	Preservation Time	Comments
Adam et al., 1995	UW, Euro-Collins	789		• Retrospective analysis of implants at one center • Study conducted: November 1984–March 1992 • Compared survival of livers from donors of different age groups: – Group 1: <30 years (281 livers) – Group 2: 30–49 years (206 livers) – Group 3: ≥50 years (51 livers) • Graft survival was comparable among groups both within 1 month and 1 year after liver transplant. • However, as far as grafts preserved for an ischemic time exceeding 12 hrs, maximal alanine transaminase levels were higher and PT and bile output decreased with increasing time. • No difference in 1-month graft survival was noted, but a difference in graft survival existed at 1 year when CIT > 12 hrs. • Liver grafts from donors > 50 years old and submitted to CIT exceeding 12 hrs demonstrated increased transaminase levels, lower PT, and lower bile output as compared to young livers. • 1-year survival of grafts also decreased with increasing age. • Cumulative effects of advanced age and extended ischemia may be deleterious.
Deschenes et al., 1998	Retrospective analysis of transplants at 3 centers		710	• Authors evaluated the incidence of early allograft dysfunction (EAD), its effect on long-term allograft survival, and factors contributing to this. • EAD occurred in 23% of recipients who had a worse clinical outcome. • Those with EAD had worse 3-year graft survival (68% vs. 83%).

					• EAD was independently associated with CIT ≥ 15 hrs.
Ploeg et al., 1993	UW (n = 277) Euro-Collins (n = 46)	323		• Group 1: 1–6 hrs • Group 2: 6–12 hrs • Group 3: 12–17 hrs • Group 4: > 17 hrs	• Retrospective analysis • Analysis conducted: November 1984 to March 1992 • This series reviewed 323 orthotopic liver transplants to identify possible risk factors for 2 forms of primary dysfunction (PDF) of the liver: primary nonfunction (PNF) and initial poor function (IPF). • Group 1: 83% IF (initial function), 14% IPF, 3% PNF • Group 2: 83% IF, 13% IPF, 4% PNF • Group 3: 74% IF, 18% IPF, 8% PNF • Group 4: 62% IF, 27% IPF, 11% PNF • Occurrence of both IPF and PNF resulted in a higher graft failure rate, retransplantation rate, and patient mortality within the first 3 months after liver transplantation. • Multivariate analysis of potential risk factors showed that reduced-size liver, fatty changes on donor liver biopsy, older donor age, retransplantation, renal insufficiency, and prolonged ischemia times were independently associated with a higher incidence of IPF and PNF. • Post liver transplantation: PDF was 22% (73/323), PNF occurred in 6% (20/323), and 16% (53/323) IPF found. **Risk factors for the development of PDF included:** • older donor age (>49 years), • longer donor hospitalization (>3 days), • extended preservation times (>18 hrs), • fatty change on donor biopsy, • renal insufficiency, • reduced liver size, and • younger recipient age.

Continued

TABLE 6-4 *Continued*

Source	Solution	No. of Transplants	Preservation Time	Comments
Ploeg et al., 1993 (*continued*)				**No significant correlation was observed between:** • etiology of end-stage liver disease, • nutritional status of patient, • UNOS status, • child's (Child-Pugh) classification, and • PDF. • Note: the lack of statistically significant correlation between some of these factors and IPF or PNF does not necessarily prove lack of relationship between these variables and PDF. **Conclusions:** • Results of study highlight the importance of IF of the liver after transplantation. • Impact of PNF and IPF are significant as 2 separate forms of PDF. • IPF of livers should be recognized as a separate clinical entity with its own significant effects.
Kadmon et al., 1993	UW	59	Range: 4–22 hours; used a cut-off time of 10 hrs	• The objective in this report was to examine the possibility that long CIT has an adverse effect on the biliary system in allografts not damaged by ABO incompatibility or thrombosis. • 59 Patients were identified using 10 hrs of CIT as the cutoff; unknown etiologies for biliary complications occurred in 7% of patients with <10 hrs of CIT and 27% of patients with >10 hrs of CIT. • Conclusion: cold preservation appears to represent the major causative explanation for bile complications occurring after CIT of longer than 10 hours.

Sanchez-Urdazpal et al., 1992	UW (91) Euro-Collins (97)	188	• UW: 5–19 hrs • Euro-Collins: 4–9 hrs	• Retrospective study of transplants at one center • Purpose: To evaluate risk factors for ischemic-type biliary complications (ITBC) (excluding ABO incompatibilities, chronic rejection, and hepatic artery thrombosis). • Results: 17% of these patients had ITBC. With UW, grafts with ischemic times of <11.5 hrs had 2% ITBC; in contrast, grafts with ischemic times of >11.5 hrs had 35% ITBC. With Euro-Collins, ischemic time < 6.5 hrs had 2% ITBC; ischemic time >6.5 hrs yielded 24% ITBC. • Prolonged CIT may cause either direct ischemic injury or predisposes to reperfusion injury.
Mor et al., 1993	UW	419	< 12 hrs > 12 hrs	• Retrospective study of transplants at one center • Authors evaluated the incidence of hepatic artery thrombosis (HAT) with prolonged preservation with UW; background for this study included prior work showing that prolonged preservation with Euro-Collins is associated with HAT. • 12 patients (3.3%) developed HAT. • Results: Graft survival after HAT is 33.3%, with patient survival at 75% in this population. • 7 Out of 165 patients with CIT > 12 hrs developed HAT. • 3 Out of 234 patients with CIT < 12 hrs developed HAT. • Warm ischemic time was the same in patients who developed HAT and those who did not. • Conclusion: This is the first study to report an association between UW and HAT similar to that seen with Euro-Collins solution; a possible explanation for this finding is that a disturbance of the vascular microcirculation due to endothelial damage during CIT may activate coagulation factors predisposing to thrombosis.

Continued

TABLE 6-4 *Continued*

Source	Solution	No. of Transplants	Preservation Time	Comments
Strasberg et al., 1994	Not applicable	Not applicable		• Literature Review • Injury is a microvascular injury; it appears to be delayed rather than changed by UW. • CIT of 30 hrs seems to be *absolute risk factor* for development of PNF using UW. • Two large studies identified CIT = *12 hrs as a relative risk factor* for IPF. • It is not yet clear how long the period of cold preservation must be to lead to increased relative risk; shortest cold preservation time to be a relative risk factor has not been established.
Angelescu et al., 1999		44	• No injury mean = 10.1 hrs • Moderate injury mean = 14.9 hrs • Severe injury mean = 12.9 hrs	• Histologic examination of graft biopsies obtained 1 hr after graft revascularization. • Associated with CIT (≤12 hrs); increased damage to the liver allograft as demonstrated by propagation of intrasinusoidal granulocytes. • Evaluated histologically the outcome of orthotopic liver transplants after prolonged ischemic times

NOTE: CIT = cold ischemia time; IF= immediate function; IPF = initial poor function; ITBC = ischemic-type billiary complication; PNF = primary nonfunction; PT = prothrombin time; and UW = University of Wisconsin solution.

This page intentionally left blank.

TABLE 6-5 Lung: Summary of Literature on Cold Ischemic Times

Source	Solution	No. of Transplants	Preservation Time	Comments
Kirk et al., 1993				• Literature review • Authors reviewed 10 years of pulmonary transplantations and reviewed the relative merits of current preservation techniques of core-cooling and single flush perfusion. • Solution most commonly used for flushing is Euro-Collins; clinical experience with single flush perfusion is greatest with this solution. • Steroids are used widely as an adjunct to preservation. • Ischemia of the lung is better tolerated in conditions of hypothermia than normothermia; it is common practice to flush lungs with a solution at 4°C and to store and transport them at 4°C on ice. • Preservation of the lung is better when it is inflated. • The optimal gas mixture with which to ventilate and store lungs is not known. • Double lung transplantation is perhaps the ideal model for assessing lung preservation, but operative mortality is high. • Concluded that safe limits of such techniques extend only to 6 hours of ischemia.
Wahlers et al., 1991	First four patients: core cooling of the donor; for the rest: modified Euro-Collins and prostacyclin	44	Mean: 241; 176–390 minutes Range: 3–6.5 hours	• Prospective single-, double-, or heart–lung transplants • December 1987 to February 1991: 44 patients underwent either single-, double-, or heart–lung transplantation. • Authors concluded that lung preservation with modified Euro-Collins solution and prostacyclin for flush perfusion of the pulmonary artery will result in excellent lung function early postperatively with ischemic times up to 6.5 hrs.

Grover et al., 1997		• Review of studies for the past 10 years • Review covering the history of and recent advances in lung transplantation. • Article reviewed the results of single, double sequential, and heart–lung transplantation over the past 10 years as reported by the International Society for Heart and Lung Transplantation Database; also reviewed the statistics of the lung and heart–lung transplantation program at the Univ. of Colorado Health Sciences Center. • Lung preservation techniques are now capable of preserving lung for up to 8 hours of CIT, utilizing cold modified Euro-Collins pulmonoplegia and intravenous PGE to the donor. • Concluded: during the past decade, significant improvements have resulted in single and double-sequential lung transplants. • Areas for continuing and future investigation: living related lobar transplantation, new antirejection agents, chimerism, and xenograft transplantation.
Hopkinson et al., 1998	UW, Euro-Collins, and Papworthy	• Survey • Worldwide survey of the 125 centers performing lung transplantation was conducted by questionnaire; 112 (90%) replies were received. • Maximum ischemic period accepted by centers varies from 4 to 12 hrs, with median periods of 8, 7, 6, and 6 hrs for the UW, Euro-Collins, Papworth, and donor core-cooling centers, respectively. • Beginnings of a trend toward the use of UW and a slightly warmer storage temperature. • Conclusion: there has been a trend toward the use of UW solution and a slightly warmer storage temperature. However, for most centers, graft storage techniques have changed little over the past decade.

NOTE: CIT= cold ischemic time.

TABLE 6-6 Pancreas: Summary of Literature on Cold Ischemic Time

Source	Solution	No. of Transplants	Preservation Time	Comments
D'Alessandro et al., 1991	UW	92 (combined pancreas–kidney)	Mean 16.7 ± 4.4 hrs, range 4–27 hrs	• Retrospective analysis • Analysis conducted: May 1987 to June 1990. • Early pancreatic allograft function was excellent for up to 24 hrs of cold storage preservation. • No differences in pancreatic function were noted for organs that were preserved for <6 hrs, 6–12 hrs, or >12 hrs.
Belzer et al., 1992	UW	163 (simultaneous pancreas–kidney transplants)	17.2 ± 4.4 hrs, range 4–27 hrs	• Retrospective Analysis • Analysis conducted: May 1987 to Nov. 1991. • No differences in pancreas allograft function or rate of graft-related complications in organs preserved for <12 hrs or >12 hrs. • After combined kidney–pancreas transplantation, there was one initial nonfunction (0.6%) and 2 episodes of vascular thrombosis (1.2%). • Pancreatic allograft survival at 1 month and 4 years was 97.5% and 83.0%, respectively.
Stratta, 1997		134 (combined kidney–pancreas transplants)	< 20 hrs (mean CIT 15.3 hours) and ≥ 20 hrs (mean CIT 21.9 hours)	• Retrospective Analysis • Combined kidney–pancreas transplants • In this study, donor age above 45 years and CIT above 20 hours were both associated with a significantly increased incidence of posttransplant dialysis and early technical problems/pancreatitis. However, neither of these factors had an adverse effect on patient survival or early graft survival. • Results suggest that the outcomes of simultaneous kidney–pancreas transplantation from older donors can be optimized when experienced surgeons perform the organ retrieval with short CIT.

Belzer et al., 1994	UW	253 (combined pancreas–kidney transplants)	Average preservation time: 17 hrs	• Safe preservation time with UW for up to 30 hrs without any obvious deleterious effects on immediate pancreas function. • Concluded: preservation with the UW solution is safe, effective, and virtually meets all clinical needs.

NOTE: CIT = cold ischemic time, and UW = University of Wisconsin solution.

7

Costs

Task 5: *Assess current policies and the potential impact of the Final Rule on costs of organ transplantation services.*

Abstract. **Based on data provided to the committee by the GAO, as well as the published literature, the committee finds that total expenditures associated with organ procurement and transplantation are likely to increase as a result of broader sharing. OPOs and transplant teams may both experience higher transportation costs. In addition, a larger number of sicker patients will receive transplants and there will likely be more retransplants—both of which would increase costs. The committee was unable to estimate the magnitude of the increase, but believes it would be marginal compared to the total expenditures for transplantation. The committee also believes the health benefits of implementing broader sharing will be substantial and outweigh any net increase in expenditures.**

Some of those who have commented on the implications of the Final Rule believe it will increase the total expenditures associated with transplantation because of the combined effects of sharing donated organs over a greater geographic area and using donated organs in patients who are more severely ill. Sharing donated organs over a greater area will increase expenditures, they argue, because it will cost more to transport organs greater distances. In addition, the increased travel time will decrease the viability of the organs, decrease the graft survival rate, and increase the number of retransplants. Transplantation in more seriously ill patients will increase costs and expenditures, it is claimed, because it is more expensive to transplant sicker patients. Moreover, transplanting sicker patients will result in a higher rate of graft failure and an increase in retransplantations. The committee, with the assistance of the General Accounting Office (GAO), gathered and analyzed data for each of these points.

DEFINING THE COMPONENTS OF COST

Previous analyses of the financial aspects of transplantation by Evans (1993, 1995b; Evans and Kitzmann, 1997) have underscored the importance of distinguishing among accounting costs, billed charges, estimated reimbursement, and contracted prices. Definitions for each of these concepts are provided in Table 7-1.

TABLE 7-1 Economic Concepts in Health Care

Concept	Definition
Cost	The economic value of both the labor and resource inputs required to provide a service or perform a procedure, excluding markup (i.e., production cost).
Charge	The amount a patient or third-party payer is actually billed by a health care organization (i.e., list price).
Reimbursement	The amount a patient or third-party payer actually pays based on billed charges, determined retrospectively or prospectively. There is often a shortfall between billed charges and payment.
Price	The amount a third-party payer, usually a managed care plan, has determined in advance (i.e., prospectively) it will pay for a service or procedure (i.e., capitated) payment.

SOURCE: Reprinted by permission of Evans, 1995b. All rights reserved.

More often than not, economic analyses of transplantation have been based on billed charges. Actual reimbursements are typically less than billed charges, particularly in a managed care environment, where contracted prices have become the norm. Nonetheless, data on accounting costs and contracted prices are rarely available and, therefore, charges have been the basis for most economic studies. The analysis in this chapter is based on billed charges.

The overall charges associated with solid organ transplantation are substantial. Table 7-2 shows the total billed charges for 1996 for each category of organ transplants, as well as the average billed charge per transplant procedure and the average total charges billed by each transplant program.

The major components of these billed charges include hospitalization of the patient before, during, and after the transplant; evaluation of the patient's condition and suitability for a transplant; acquisition of the donated organ and evaluation of its suitability; transportation of the organ from the site of donation to the site of transplantation; use of the operating room; fees of the various physicians; and posttransplant therapy, including immunosuppressive medications (Evans, 1985, 1986).

The charges associated with each component can vary, sometimes substantially, depending on the condition of the patient, the condition of the donor, the location and standard practices of the donor site and transplant program, and other factors. Summary estimates of the average charges billed for major categories of expense are shown in Table 7-3. As noted previously, the actual cost incurred by health care providers, as well as the amount reimbursed by third-party payers, is typically lower than the billed charges, sometimes by a significant amount.

TABLE 7-2 Estimated Billed Charges ($1,000s) for Transplants, 1996

Major Organ	No. of Programs	No. of Transplants	Total Program-Billed Charges	Average Billed Charges per Transplant	Average Program-Billed Charges
Kidney	253	11,099	$1,043,306	$94	$4,124
Liver	120	4,058	1,176,820	290	9,807
Pancreas	120	1,022	112,420	110	937
Heart	166	2,342	533,976	228	3,217
Lung	94	805	194,005	241	2,064
Total programs	753	19,366	3,060,527	—	—
Total hospitals	281	19,366	3,060,527	—	10,892

SOURCE: Table reprinted from DHHS, 1998b, page 16322.

TABLE 7-3 Average Billed Charges (1996 Dollars) per Transplantation, First Year After Transplantation, 1996

	Heart	Lung	Heart–Lung	Kidney	Pancreas	Kidney–Pancreas	Liver
Evaluation	$11,000	$11,000	$11,000	$11,000	$11,000	$11,000	$11,000
Candidacy (per month)	10,600	10,600	10,600	0	0	0	10,600
Procurement	25,200	24,800	24,800	22,400	16,200	26,000	24,700
Hospital	155,800	160,400	160,400	50,600	76,200	67,300	188,900
Physician	21,800	26,300	31,800	8,900	12,600	12,600	42,600
Follow-up	18,500	22,500	22,500	11,900	4,700	11,900	26,400
Immunosuppressants	10,300	10,300	10,300	11,300	5,100	12,500	10,300
Total	253,200	265,900	271,800	116,100	125,800	141,300	314,500

NOTE: " Charges" refers to the amount billed by the provider and may not be the actual expense incurred by the provider in performing the services.

The committee assumed, based on the discussion in Chapter 5, that the Final Rule would result in the transplantation of more status 1 and, possibly, more status 2A patients and fewer status 2B and status 3 patients. It also assumed there would be more retransplantations, and increased organ acquisition costs due to greater distances, on average, between the site of donation and the site of transplantation. Although there may be some offsetting decreases in expenditures, the committee concluded that these assumptions will result in a net increase in the overall expenditures associated with transplantation.

TABLE 7-4 Information on Medicare-Covered Liver Transplant Recipients, Calendar Year 1995 through 1998

	Status 1	Status 2	Status 3
Number of Patients	199	555	737
Length of Stay, Days			
Mean	39	32	19
Range	1–185	1–727	1–266
Days from Hospital Admission to Transplant			
Mean	16	12	1
Range	0–142	0–440	0–72
Days from Transplant to Discharge			
Mean	23	20	17
Range	0–178	0–287	0–246
Total Charges (U.S. dollars)			
Mean	300,692	185,135	140,518
Range	57,370–2,569,086	35,267–2,683,110	30,027–1,454,216

NOTE: The UNOS severity of illness status codes changed during the period of this analysis; therefore, the committee created uniform status codes. Status 1 patients are the most severely ill and have < 7 days to live without a transplant. Status 2 patients are cared for in the hospital either in acute or intensive care. Status 3 patients are under continuous medical care and are generally at home with some hospital stays.

SOURCE: R. Hogberg, GAO, personal communication, June 29, 1999.

INCREASED EXPENDITURES DUE TO TRANSPLANTATION OF SICKER PATIENTS

The GAO provided IOM with data on Medicare expenditures for liver and heart transplantation (R. Hogberg, GAO, personal communication, June 29, 1999). For liver transplants, the GAO data showed that status 1 patients who received a transplant had longer hospital stays, both before and after transplantation, and higher total charges than did status 2 patients (see Table 7-4). Similarly, status 2 patients had longer hospital stays and higher total charges than status 3 patients. The GAO data showed similar results for status 1 and status 2 heart transplant patients. If, as the committee assumes, implementation of the Final Rule results in more status 1 (and status 2A), but fewer status 3 patients receiving transplants, there would likely be an increase in total Medicare expenditures, even if there was no change in the total number of transplants performed.

Because the GAO data were based on Medicare data, one question for the committee was whether this conclusion was valid for all other transplant patients. To answer this, the GAO examined whether Medicare patients undergoing liver and heart transplantation were reasonably representative of all patients undergoing these procedures. The results indicate that Medicare patients were comparable with respect to gender, race, and ethnicity, but were significantly older, than non-Medicare patients. This finding is consistent with studies reported by Evans (1993; 1994; 1995a; and Evans and Kitzmann, 1997), Whiting et al. (1998; 1999), and by Showstack et al. (1999). These studies concluded that status 2 patients were significantly more expensive to transplant than status 3 patients, with length of hospitalization being a major factor. Therefore, although the committee did not assume that the amount of the expenditures for non-Medicare patients would be exactly the same as those for Medicare patients, it did accept the pattern of cost differentials among different status patients described in the GAO analysis as comparable to what would be seen in the general population.

Thus, the committee concluded that implementation of the Final Rule would result in a net increase in total expenditures due to the transplantation of more severely ill patients. However, the committee was not able to estimate how large that increase would be, for several reasons. First, it is not clear exactly how the Final Rule will be implemented and, therefore, it is not clear how many patients would be affected in each status.

Second, it is not clear how large the net charge differential would be, on average, for transplanting a status 1 or status 2A patient rather than a status 2B or 3 patient. In the data provided to the committee by the GAO, for example, a substantial part of the higher charges for status 1 and 2 patients was due to a longer length of stay prior to transplantation. (Status 1 and 2A patients on the waiting list are typically in an intensive care unit, many status 2B patients are in acute care settings but many are not, and status 3 patients are normally being cared for in a non-hospital setting.) If more status 1 and 2A patients were transplanted, presumably there would be a decrease in the number of hospital days used by these patients awaiting a transplant. The resulting savings would partially offset the increased expenditures associated with transplanting these patients. Similarly, the pretransplant hospital stay apparently contributed, in part, to the increased expenditures for status 2 patients in the Whiting et al. study (1999) (but not in the Showstack et al. [1999] study). This adjustment to savings would, in turn, be further offset by an increase in the treatment-related expenditures for status 3 patients awaiting transplantation.

Liver retransplantation is a more expensive procedure than first-time transplantation, according to the studies by Evans (1993; 1994; 1995a; and Evans and Kitzmann, 1997), Whiting (1999), and Markmann et al. (1997). The committee concluded that implementation of the Final Rule (or establishing organ allocation areas that serve a population of at least 9 million people, as recommended in Chapter 5 of this report) by increasing the number of severely ill patients receiving transplants, would increase total expenditures to some degree because of an increase in the number of retransplants. It was unable, however, to estimate either the average differential in cost or the increase in number of retransplants.

INCREASED EXPENSES FOR ORGAN ACQUISITION

For the purpose of providing the committee with information about organ acquisition practices and expenses, the GAO collected data from a sample of six OPOs and some of their associated transplant centers. The results suggest that the acquisition practices and, therefore, acquisition expenses vary considerably among transplant centers and OPOs (Evans et al., 1993). OPOs are reimbursed by transplant centers for their role in acquiring, preserving, and transporting a donated organ. Reimbursement is typically a prospectively set fee, reflecting each OPO's standard acquisition costs. The committee assumes for the reasons set forth below, that the actual cost to the OPO for the procurement of organs will increase under broader sharing and, in turn, these added costs will be passed on to transplant centers in the form of higher fees. These higher fees represent an increase in cost to the transplant centers.

The process of matching an available organ with a prospective transplant recipient begins before the organ is removed from the donor. Once the organ has been accepted by a transplant center, a decision must be made regarding who will remove the organ from the donor. Sometimes a surgical team from the transplant hospital travels to the site of the organ donor to excise the organ; at other times, the transplant center relies on a local surgical team to do so. In its survey of OPOs for this committee, the GAO found that a surgical team from the transplant center almost always travels to retrieve hearts and lungs, but seldom does so for kidneys. The practice with respect to livers seems to vary considerably, depending on whether experienced transplant surgeons are available at the donor site.

The transportation expenses associated with sending a surgical team from the transplant center to retrieve an organ can be substantial, depending on the size of the surgical team and the distance and mode of travel. Because of the need to proceed expeditiously with organ retrieval and transplantation, the preferred mode of travel is often air, frequently by chartered aircraft.

Similarly, the expense of transporting an organ will vary considerably depending on the distance and mode of travel. The GAO found that the costs of transporting organs varied from a few hundred dollars for ground travel to several thousand dollars for air travel. The committee assumed that the expense of organ acquisition would be increased under broader sharing because of the sharing of organs over a greater geographical area. However, the committee was unable to estimate the magnitude of this change, given uncertainties about how the Final Rule will be implemented, how much larger the new geographical areas will be and how they will affect travel times, and how the organ acquisition practices of transplant centers might change over time. The potential increase might appear significant in absolute dollars. However, as shown in Table 7-3, expenditures for procurement are a relatively minor component of overall expenditures for transplantation. Therefore, such an increase would likely have a marginal impact on total cost.

The committee confined its analysis to the expenses and expenditures directly associated with organ acquisition and transplantation. It did not attempt to evaluate other aspects that might appropriately be taken into consideration, such as the value of additional lives saved for status 1 and status 2A patients who receive a transplant or the cost of additional years of impaired health incurred by status 3 patients who do not receive a transplant.

CONCLUSION

Expenditures for organ procurement and transplantation are likely to increase as a result of broader sharing. The committee is not, however, able to estimate with confidence how large the increase might be because it is not clear how the Final Rule will be implemented and how many patients in each status will be affected. In addition to transportation expenses, implementation will alter multiple factors affecting transplant expenditures. These factors can vary widely from one case to another. Any increase in expenditures must, however, be weighed against the additional health benefits gained through broader sharing, which the committee believes will be substantial and could outweigh any net increase in expenditures.

8

Oversight and Review

Abstract. **The committee concluded that achieving the goals of the National Organ Transplant Act requires an active federal role in review and oversight, and that this should be in collaboration with representatives from all those involved in transplantation, including patients, donor families, physicians and nurses, OPOs, and transplant centers. To assist in this activity there needs to be independent scientific review and better performance measures for various aspects of the system. In addition, data about the system must be reliably and regularly gathered, independently assessed, and made widely available.**

In conducting its review, the committee concluded that oversight and review of the nation's organ procurement and transplantation system needs to be enhanced to improve the system's accountability to the public and to ensure that it operates effectively in the public interest. The committee's concerns cut across the individual issues specified in its charge and relate in general to all organ transplantation, not just liver transplantation. The committee addresses these matters—the role of the federal government and the need for improved data—separately in this final chapter.

ROLE OF THE FEDERAL GOVERNMENT

The federal government, as well as the transplantation community, has a legitimate and appropriate role to play in ensuring that the organ procurement and transplantation system serves the public interest, especially the needs and concerns of patients, donors, and families affected by it. The committee learned of numerous instances in which weak governance tends to undermine the effectiveness of the system. Specifically, responsibilities are dispersed throughout the system, creating impediments to oversight and review. Weak oversight has compromised accountability at all levels, permitted poor procedures for data collection and analysis to persist, and allowed the system to operate without adequate assessment of performance.

The committee acknowledges that many aspects of organ procurement and transplantation require effective arrangements and decision making at a local level. However, a more centralized mechanism for oversight and review would improve the quality assurance that donors and recipients deserve. This is not to say that the federal government should be making medical judgments regarding individual patients, or that DHHS ever intended to do so, but rather that its responsibility is to ensure that the policies that guide the operation of the system are equitable and well-grounded in medical science.

Vigilant and conscientious oversight and review of programs and policies are critically important to ensuring accountability on the part of the OPTN and other participants in the organ procurement and transplantation system. The Final Rule appropriately places this responsibility with the federal government. The committee believes that this is an important aspect of the Final Rule and a charge that should be pursued by the federal government in close cooperation with the full range of participants in the transplant community.

Some of the activities that could be undertaken in a more proactive manner include, but are not limited to, assessing the equity of access to transplantation, including fairness across socioeconomic, racial, and ethnic groups, and monitoring short- and long-term patient outcomes.

Performance Measures

The various participants in the transplantation system (including the federal government) and the general public would be better served if there were a comprehensive set of reliable, informative, and patient-centered performance measures for the various key components of the overall system of organ procurement and transplantation. As noted in Chapter 2, the Health Care Financing Administration (HCFA) has established performance measures for OPOs. However, the General Accounting Office (GAO) and others have noted several improvements that could be made in these measures to focus them more sharply on the most important determinants of effective performance and improve their fairness among the OPOs (GAO, 1997). The committee believes that the standards for successful performance could be raised to a higher level.

HCFA has also established performance standards that transplantation centers must meet to be eligible for Medicare reimbursement. The committee believes it would be appropriate for the independent scientific review board (see Recommendation 8.2), to review these measures and standards on a periodic basis to make sure they are consistent with current medical science and are as useful as possible to patients and policy makers.

The committee also believes that the OPTN should be rigorously evaluated against performance measures. The committee recognizes that some of these measures would necessarily be process-oriented but urges that, to the degree possible, they focus on patient outcomes and on the equity of the overall system in serving the needs of America's diverse population.

A few summary statistics that could be used to assess outcomes might include: (1) transplantation rate by medical status; (2) pre-transplant mortality rate by medical status; (3) post-transplant mortality rate by medical status; (4) median waiting time in the status 1 category; and (5) graft survival as a function of such variables as cold ischemic time and donor characteristics. The improved data collection and analysis (Recommendation 8.3) and the independent scientific oversight called for in this chapter (Recommendation 8.2) would facilitate the development and reporting of such performance measures.

RECOMMENDATION 8.1: ***Exercise Federal Oversight***
The Department of Health and Human Services should exercise the legitimate oversight responsibilities assigned to it by the National Organ Transplant Act, and articulated in the Final Rule, in order to manage the system of organ procurement and transplantation in the public interest. This oversight should include greater use of patient-centered, outcome-oriented performance measures for OPOs, transplant centers, and the OPTN.

Independent Scientific Review

The science of organ transplantation has been continuously evolving and improving, sometimes at a rapid pace. A process for periodic, independent, and comprehensive review by a body reporting to the Secretary and not affiliated with the OPTN contractor is needed to help provide objective information and advice for the future directions of the system. Timely, nonpartisan review will assist the Secretary in managing the system in a manner that best serves the public interest and advances the health of the public. An independent, external, scientific review board would help ensure that policies and procedures are evidence-based and guided by the best available medical and scientific precepts. It would also enhance public confidence in the integrity and effectiveness of the system. The independent scientific review board should include a broad spectrum of medical and scientific experts, including epidemiologists and health services researchers, as well as representatives from the community of transplant patients and donor families.

RECOMMENDATION 8.2: ***Establish Independent Scientific Review***
The Department of Health and Human Services should establish an external, independent, multidisciplinary scientific review board responsible for assisting the Secretary in ensuring that the system of organ procurement and transplantation is grounded on the best available medical science and is as effective and as equitable as possible.

DATA COLLECTION, ANALYSIS, AND DISSEMINATION

The committee's analysis and deliberations were hampered by a lack of publicly available, comprehensive, and timely data. For this reason, in part, the committee had great difficulty establishing a sufficient baseline of information from which to make its determinations. Too frequently, important data were either unavailable or were several years old. Although UNOS has been collecting a substantial amount of data, and the UNOS staff responded promptly and fully to committee requests, the committee was puzzled that its requests appeared to be unique or first-time inquiries. The committee believes that the data and analyses it requested were essential to assessing the status and adequacy of the existing system. The fact that these types of analyses are not conducted routinely and made publicly available in a timely manner should be a matter of concern.

Modern computing and information technologies provide mechanisms for facilitating the collection, analysis, and reporting of information essential to the evaluation of the system of organ procurement and transplantation—for example, donor information; OPO and transplant center performance data; biological factors; and, socioeconomic and demographic data on patients, outcomes of donation, organ wastage, primary graft nonfunction, transplant outcomes, and patient outcomes. The power of these technologies to process large amounts of information from numerous sites should be employed to improve the system of data collection and analysis.

In addition, the data that are available need to be shared more widely with the scientific and clinical communities. The lack of access to data has limited the analytical and scientific work being conducted and published. Moreover, this situation has fostered a poorly informed debate over the important issues. Making the raw data available to a broader audience is essential to improving the quality and reliability of analyses that might be used to set policy.

Broader public access to reliable data in a timely manner will facilitate better assessment of such issues as:

- conformity of patient classifications to standardized medical listing criteria,
- effectiveness of organ procurement activities,
- equity of organ allocation and sharing arrangements, and
- graft and patient transplantation outcomes.

Data needs are likely to change over time—requiring continual review and revision. Thus, routine review of the system of data collection and dissemination would help to assure the quality, timeliness, and accuracy of data over time. Review by an external organization, experienced in data management and statistics, but independent of the OPTN contractor and not drawn from the transplant community, could help to ensure the validity, accuracy, and usefulness of the data.

RECOMMENDATION 8.3: *Improve Data Collection and Dissemination*

Within the bounds of donor and recipient confidentiality and sound medical judgment, the OPTN contractor should improve its collection of standardized and useful data regarding the system of organ procurement and transplantation and make it widely avail-

able to independent investigators and scientific reviewers in a timely manner. DHHS should provide an independent, objective assessment of the quality and effectiveness of the data that are collected and how they are analyzed and disseminated by the OPTN.

References

Adam, R., C. Sanchez, I. Astarcioglu, and H. Bismuth. 1995. Deleterious effect of extended cold ischemia time on the posttransplant outcome of aged livers. *Transplantation Proceedings* 27(1):1181–1183.

Alexander, G.C., and A.R. Sehgal. 1998. Barriers to cadaveric renal transplatation among blacks, women, and the poor. *Journal of the American Medical Association* 280(13): 1148–1152.

American Hospital Association, American Medical Association, and United Network for Organ Sharing. 1988. *Required Request Legislation: A Guide for Hospitals on Organ and Tissue Donation.* Richmond, Va. United Network for Organ Sharing.

Angelescu, M., W. Hofmann, C. Zapletal, M. Bredt, T. Kraus, C. Herfarth, and E. Klar. 1999. Histomorphological analysis of preservation injury as determinant of graft quality in clinical liver transplantation. *Transplantation Proceedings* 31(1–2):1074–1076.

Association of Organ Procurement Organizations. 1997. Alternatives Being Developed to More Accurately Assess Performance. Report to the ranking minority member, Committee on Labor and Human Resources, U.S. Senate, Washington, D.C.

Ayanian, J.Z., P.D. Cleary, J.S. Weissman, and A.M. Epstein. 1999. Do patients' preferences explain racial differences in access to renal transplantation? (Abstract.) *Journal of General Internal Medicine* 14:8.

Belzer, F.O., A.M. D'Alessandro, R.M. Hoffman, S.J. Knechtle, A. Reed, J.D. Pirsch, M. Kalayoglu, and H.W. Sollinger. 1992. The use of UW solution in clinical transplantation. A 4-year experience. *Annals of Surgery* 215(6):579–583; discussion, 584–585.

Belzer, F.O., R.J. Ploeg, S.J. Knechtle, A.M. D'Alessandro, J.D. Pirsch, M.M. Kalayoglu, and H.W. Sollinger. 1994. Clinical pancreas preservation and transplantation. *Transplantation Proceedings* 26(2):550–551.

Benjamin, M.R. 1999. Testimony presented to the Institute of Medicine Committee on Organ Procurement and Transplantation Policy, March 11, Washington, D.C.

Bock, R.D. 1970. Estimating multinomial response relations. In: *Contributions to Statistics and Probability*. R.C. Bose, ed. Chapel Hill: University of North Carolina Press.

Bock, R.D. 1972. Estimating item parameters and latent ability when responses are scored in two or more nominal categories. *Psychometrika* 37:29–51.

Bock, R.D., and M. Aitkin. 1981. Marginal maximum likelihood estimation of item parameters: An application of the EM algorithm. *Psychometrika* 46:443–459.

Bock, R.D., R.D. Gibbons, and E. Muraki. 1988. Full-information item-factor analysis. *Applied Psychological Measurement* 12:261–280.

Briganti, E.M., P.J. Bergin, F.L. Rosenfeldt, D.S. Esmore, and M. Rabinov. 1995. Successful long-term outcome with prolonged ischemic time cardiac allografts. *The Journal of Heart and Lung Transplantation* 14(5):840–845.

Bryk, A.S., and S.W. Raudenbush. 1992. *Hierarchical Liner Models: Applications and Data Analysis Methods*. Thousand Oaks, Calif.: Sage Publications, Inc.

Callender, C.O. 1999. Testimony presented to the Institute of Medicine Committee on Organ Procurement and Transplantation Policy, April 16, Washington, D.C.

Cate, F.H., and S.S. Laudicina. 1991. *Transplantation White Paper: Current Statistical Information About Transplantation in America.* Washington, D.C.: The Annenberg Washington Program Communications Policy Studies, Northwestern University, and the United Network for Organ Sharing.

CCH Medicare and Medicaid Guide. Undated. Paragraph 15,501 ff.

Christiansen, C.L., S.L. Gortmaker, J.M. Williams, C.L. Beasley, L.E. Brigham, C. Capossela, M.E. Matthiesen, and S. Gunderson. 1998. A method for estimating solid organ donor potential by organ procurement region. *American Journal of Public Health* 88:1645–1650.

CONSAD Research Corporation. *An Analysis of Alternative National Policies for Allocating Donor Livers for Transplantation*. Pittsburgh, Pa.: CONSAD Research Corporation.

D'Alessandro, A.M., M. Kalayoglu, H.W. Sollinger, J.D. Pirsch, J.H. Southard, and F.O. Belzer. 1991. Current status of organ preservation with University of Wisconsin solution. *Archives of Pathology and Laboratory Medicine* 115(3):306–310.

D'Alessandro, A.M., S.J. Knechtle, J.S. Odorico, J.D. Pirsch, W.J. Van der Werf, B. Collins, Y. Becker, H.W. Sollinger, and M. Kalayoglu. 1998. Retransplantation of the liver: A single center experience. Paper presented at the American Society of Transplant Surgeons, 24th Annual Scientific Meeting, May 13–15, Chicago.

Dejong, W., J. Drachman, and S.L. Gortmanker. 1995. Options for increasing organ donation: The potential role of financial incentives, standardized hospital procedures, and public education to promote family discussion. *Milbank Quarterly* 73:463–479.

Deschenes, M., S.H. Belle, R.A. Krom, R.K. Zetterman, and J.R. Lake. 1998. Early allograft dysfunction after liver transplantation: A definition and predictors of outcome. *Transplantation* 66(3):302–310.

DHHS (U.S. Department of Health and Human Services). 1999a. Organ donations increase in 1998 following national initiative and new regulations. *HHS News,* April 16. Located at http://www.hhs.gov/news/press/1999pres/990416b.html. Accessed on April 19, 1999.

DHHS. 1999b. *Organ Procurement Organization (OPO) Directory—January,1999 (revised 12/98)*. Washington, D.C.: Center for Health Plans and Providers, Health Care Financing Administration.

DHHS. 1998a. *HHS News,* March 26. HHS rule calls for organ allocation based on medical criteria, not geography: Calls on private transplant network to develop policies.

Located at http://www.hhs.gov/news/press/1998pres/980326a.html. Accessed on May 3, 1999.

DHHS. 1998b. Organ Procurement and Transplantation Network; Final Rule (42 CFR Part 121). *Federal Register* 63(63):16296–16338.

DHHS, Office of the Inspector General. 1998c. *Racial and Geographic Disparity in the Distribution of Organs for Transplantation*. Washington, D.C.: DHHS.

Eckhoff, D.E., B.M. McGuire, C.J. Young, M.T. Sellers, L.R. Frenette, S.L. Hudson, J.L. Contreras, and S. Bynon. 1998. Race: A critical factor in organ donation, patient referral and selection, and orthotopic liver transplantation? *Liver Transplantation and Surgery* 4(6):499–505.

Edwards, E.B., and A.M. Harper. 1995. The UNOS model for liver allocation. Prepared for the United Network for Organ Sharing, Richmond, Va.

Efron, B. 1988. Logistic regression, survival analysis, and the Kaplan-Meier curve. *Journal of the American Statistical Association* 83:414–425.

Eggers, P.W. 1995. Racial differences in access to kidney transplantation. *Health Care Financing Review* 17:(2)89.

Ehrle, R.N., T.J. Shafer, and K.R. Nelson. 1999. Referral, request, and consent for organ donation: Best practice—A blueprint for success. *Critical Care Nurse* 19(2):21–33.

Evans, R.W. 1995a. Liver transplantation in a managed care environment. *Liver Transplantation and Surgery* 1:61–75.

Evans, R.W. 1995b. Organ transplantation in an era of economic constraint: Liver transplantation as a case study. *Seminars in Anesthesiology* 14:127–135.

Evans, R.W. 1994. Organ transplantation and the inevitable debate as to what constitutes a basic health care benefit. In: *Clinical Transplants 1993,* P.I. Terasaki, and J.M. Cecka (eds). Los Angeles: UCLA Tissue Typing Laboratory. Pp. 359–391.

Evans, R.W. 1993. Organ procurement expenditures and the role of financial incentives. *Journal of the American Medical Association* 269:3113–3118.

Evans, R.W. 1986. Cost-effectiveness analysis of transplantation. *Surgical Clinics of North America* 66:603–616.

Evans, R.W. 1985. The socioeconomics of organ transplantation. *Transplantation Proceedings* 17(6):129–136.

Evans, R.W., and D.J. Kitzmann. 1997. Contracting for services: Liver transplantation in the era of mismanaged care. *Clinics in Liver Disease* 1(2):287–303.

Evans, R.W., D.L. Manninen, and F.B. Dong. 1993. An economic analysis of liver transplantation: Costs, insurance coverage, and reimbursement. *Gastroenterology Clinics of North America* 22:451–473.

First, M.R. 1997. Controversies in organ donation: Minority donation and living unrelated donors. *Transplantation Proceedings* 29:67–69.

Franz, H.G., W. DeJong, S.M. Wolfe, H. Nathan, D. Payne, W. Reitsma, and C. Beasley. 1997. Explaining brain death: A critical feature of the donation process. *Journal of Transplant Coordination* 7:14–21.

Furukawa, H., S. Todo, O. Imventarza, A. Casavilla, Y.M. Wu, C. Scott-Foglieni, B. Broznick, J. Bryant, R. Day, and T.E. Starzl. 1991. Effect of cold ischemia time on the early outcome of human hepatic allografts preserved with UW solution. *Transplantation* 51(5):1000–1004.

Gallup Organization, Inc. 1998. *Adults' Opinions Concerning Organ Allocation Policies and Their Effects on Organ Donation.* Prepared for the National Transplant Action Committee. Princeton, N.J.: Gallup Organization, Inc.

GAO (U.S. General Accounting Office). 1999. Office of the General Counsel. GAO/OGC-99-47R OPTN: Legal Liability and Data Confidentiality. Washington, D.C.: GAO.

GAO. 1997. *Organ Procurement Organizations: Alternatives Being Developed to More Accurately Assess Performance* (GAO/HEHS-98-26). Report to the ranking minority member, Committee on Labor and Human Resources, U.S. Senate. Washington, D.C.: GAO.

Gaylin, D.S., P.J. Held, F.K. Port, L.G. Hunsicker, R.A. Wolfe, B.D. Kahan, C.A. Jones, and L.Y. Agodoa. 1993. The impact of comorbid and sociodemographic factors on access to renal transplantation. *Journal of the American Medical Association* 269(5):603–608.

Gentry, D., J. Brown-Holbert, and C. Andrews. 1997. Racial impact: Increasing minority consent rate by altering the racial mix of an organ procurement organization. *Transplantation Proceedings* 29:3758–3759.

Gift of Life Donor Program. 1999. Delaware Valley Transplant Program Changes Name to Gift of Life Donor Program (News release). Located at http://www.donors1.org/pages/newname.html. Accessed on July 13, 1999.

Goldstein, H. 1995. *Multilevel Statistical Models.* New York: Halsted Press.

Gortmaker, S.L., C.L. Beasley, L.E. Brigham, H.G. Franz, R.N. Garrison, B.A. Lucas, R.H. Patterson, A.M. Sobol, A.N.A. Grenvik, and M.J. Evanisko. 1996. Organ donor potential and performance: Size and nature of the organ donor shortfall. *Critical Care Medicine* 24(3):432–439.

Gortmaker, S.L., C.L. Beasley, E. Sheehy, B.A. Lucas, L.E. Brigham, A. Grenvik, R. Patterson, N. Garrison, P. McNamara, and M.J. Evanisko. 1998. Improving the request process to increase family consent for organ donation. *Journal of Transplant Coordination* 8:210–217.

Grover, F.L., D.A. Fullerton, M.R. Zamora, C. Mills, B. Ackerman, D. Badesch, J.M. Brown, D.N. Campbell, P. Chetham, A. Dhaliwal, M. Diercks, T. Kinnard, K. Niejadlik, and M. Ochs. 1997. The past, present, and future of lung transplantation. *American Journal of Surgery* 173(6):523–533.

Haller, G.W., J.M. Langrehr, G. Blumhardt, K.P. Platz, A. Muller, W.O. Bechstein, S. Bisson, S. Jonas, H. Lobeck, M. Knoop, and P. Neuhaus. 1995. Factors relevant to the development of primary dysfunction in liver allografts. *Transplantation Proceedings* 27(1):1192.

Hanto, D.W. 1999. Testimony presented to the Institute of Medicine Committee on Organ Procurement and Transplantation Policy, April 16, Washington, D.C.

Hannan, E.L., A.L. Siu, D. Kumar, H. Kilburn, Jr., and M.R. Chassin. 1995. The decline in coronary artery bypass graft surgery mortality in New York State. *Journal of the American Medical Association* 273(3):209–213.

Hauboldt, R.H. 1996. *Cost Implications of Human Organ and Tissue Transplantations, An Update: 1996.* Milliman and Robertson, Inc. http://www2.milliman.com/milliman/publications/reports/HRR16/.

HCFA (Health Care Financing Administration). 1989. Medicare and Medicaid programs. Organ Procurement and Transplantation Network rules and membership actions. *Federal Register* 54(241):51802–51803.

Hedeker, D.R. In press. MIXNO: A computer program for mixed-effects nominal logistic regression. *Journal of Statistical Software.*

Hedeker, D.R., and R.D. Gibbons. 1994. A random-effects ordinal regression model for multilevel analysis. *Biometrics* 50:933–944.

Held, P.J., M.V. Pauly, R.R. Bovbjerg, J. Newmann, and O. Salvatierra, Jr. 1988. Access to kidney transplantation. Has the United States eliminated income and racial differences? *Archives of Internal Medicine* 148(12):2594–2600.

Held, P.J., M.V. Pauly, and L. Diamond. 1987. Survival analysis of patients undergoing dialysis. *Journal of the American Medical Association* 257(5):645–650.

Holman, G. 1999. Executive update and summary: Medication coverage and access to transplantation services. Unpublished manuscript.

Hopkinson, D.N., M.S. Bhabra, and T.L. Hooper. 1998. Pulmonary graft preservation: A worldwide survey of current clinical practice. *The Journal of Heart and Lung Transplantation* 17(5):525–531.

Hosenpud, J.D., T.J. Breen, E.B. Edwards, O.P. Daily, and L.G. Hunsicker. 1994. The effect of transplant center volume on cardiac transplant outcome. *Journal of the American Medical Association* 271(23):1844–1849.

Ingram, D.D., and J.C. Kleinman. 1989. Empirical comparisons of proportional hazards and logistic regression models. *Statistics in Medicine* 8(5):525–538.

Kadmon, M., J. Bleyl, B. Kuppers, G. Otto, and C. Herfarth. 1993. Biliary complications after prolonged University of Wisconsin preservation of liver allografts. *Transplantation Proceedings* 25(1):1651–1652.

Kalayoglu, M., H.W. Sollinger, R.J. Stratta, A.M. D'Alessandro, R.M. Hoffmann, J.D. Pirsch, and F.O. Belzer. 1988. Extended preservation of the liver for clinical transplantation. *Lancet* 1:617–619.

Kallich, J.D., T. Wyant, and M. Krushat. 1990. The effect of DR antigens, race, sex, and peak PRA on estimated median waiting time for a first cadaver kidney transplant. *Clinical Transplantation* 311–318.

Kappel, D.F., M.E. Whitlock, T.D. Parks-Thomas, B.A. Hong, and B.K. Freedman. 1993. Increasing African American organ donation: The St. Louis experience. *Transplantation Proceedings* 25:2489–2490.

Kasiske, B.L., J.F. Neylan, R.R. Riggio, G.M. Danovitch, L. Kahana, S.R. Alexander, and M.G. White. 1991. The effect of race on access and outcome in transplantation. *New England Journal of Medicine* 324:320–327.

Keeffe, E.B. 1998. Summary of guidelines on organ allocation and patient listing for liver transplantation. *Liver Transplantation and Surgery* 4(5):S108–S114.

Kirk, A.J., I.W. Colquhoun, and J.H. Dark. 1993. Lung preservation: A review of current practice and future directions. *Annals of Thoracic Surgery* 56(4):990–1000.

Kjellstrand, C.M. 1988. Age, sex, and race inequality in renal transplantation. *Archives of Internal Medicine* 148(6):1305–1309.

Korner, M.M., G. Tenderich, D. Baller, H. Mannebach, K. Minami, L. Arusoglu, N. Mirow, A. Bairaktaris, T. Breymann, and R. Korfer. 1997. Accepting prolonged ischemia times for the donor heart. *Transplantation Proceedings* 29(8):3662–3663.

La Hay P.M. 1999. Pa. may become first state to aid kin of organ donors. *The Philadelphia Inquirer*. Wednesday, April 14, 1999, A1, A15.

Lange, H., and U. Kuhlmann. 1998. Organ procurement policy: Should we reduce cold ischemia times? *Transplantation Proceedings* 30(8):4297–4302.

Magnus, J.R. 1988. *Linear Structures*. London: Charles Griffin.

Marino, I.R., F. Morelli, C. Doria, T. Gayowski, J. McMichael, J.J. Fung, T.E. Starzl, and H.R. Doyle. 1997. Preoperative assessment of risk in liver transplantation: A multivariate analysis in 2,376 cases of the UW era. *Transplantation Proceedings* 29(1–2):454–455.

Markmann, J.F., J.S. Markowitz, H. Yersiz, M. Morrisey, D.G. Farmer, D.A. Farmer, J. Goss, R. Ghobrial, S.V. McDiarmid, R. Stribling, P. Martin, L.I. Goldstein, P. Seu,

C. Shackleton, and R.W. Busuttil. 1997. Long-term survival after retransplantation of the liver. *Annals of Surgery* 226:408–420.

McNamara, P., and C.L. Beasley. 1997. Determinants of familial consent to organ donation in the hospital setting. In: *Clinical Transplants 1997,* J.M. Cecka and P.I. Terasaki (eds.). Los Angeles: UCLA Tissue Typing Laboratory. Pp. 219–229.

McNamara, P., H.G. Franz, R.A. Fowler, M.J. Evanisko, and C.L. Beasley. 1997. Medical record review as a measure of the effectiveness of organ procurement practices in the hospital. *Journal on Quality Improvement* 23:321–333.

Meier, E. 1999. Testimony presented to the Institute of Medicine Committee on Organ Procurement and Transplantation Policy, March 11, Washington, D.C.

Mesler, D.E., E.P. McCarthy, S. Byrne-Logan, A.S. Ash, and M.A. Moskowitz. 1999. Does the survival advantage of nonwhite dialysis patients persist after case mix adjustment? *American Journal of Medicine* 106(3):300–306.

Mor, E., M.E. Schwartz, P.A. Sheiner, P. Menesses, P. Hytiroglou, S. Emre, K. Kishikawa, S. Chiodini, and C.M. Miller. 1993. Prolonged preservation in University of Wisconsin solution associated with hepatic artery thrombosis after orthotopic liver transplantation. *Transplantation* 56(6):1399–1402.

Nathan H.M. 1999. Pennsylvania Looks for Answers to the Organ Donor Shortage. Press release, *Gift of Life Donor Program*, Philadelphia, June 10, 1999.

Nathan, H.M. 1998. Implementation of comprehensive state legislation increases organ and tissue donations [abstract]. Presented at the Annual Meeting of the American Society of Transplant Physicians, May 10, Chicago.

Nerlove, M., and S.J. Press. 1973. *Univariate and Multivariate Log-Linear and Logistic Models* (Technical Report R-1306-EDA/NIH). Santa Monica, Calif.: RAND Corporation.

Offermann, G. 1998. What is a reasonably short ischemia time in kidney transplantation? *Transplantation Proceedings* 30(8):4291–4293.

Opelz, G. 1998. Cadaver kidney graft outcome in relation to ischemia time and HLA match. *Transplantation Proceedings* 30(8):4294–4296.

Ozminkowski, R.J., A.J. White, A. Hassol, and M. Murphy. 1997. Minimizing racial disparity regarding receipt of a cadaver kidney transplant. *American Journal of Kidney Diseases* 30:749–759.

Pennsylvania Act 1994-102. 1994. Chapter 86: Anatomical Gifts. Pennsylvania 178th General Assembly—1993–1994 Regular Session, Act 102, Senate Bill No. 1662, pp. 663–673.

Pita, S., F. Valdes, A. Alonso, C.F. Rivera, M. Cao, M.P. Fontan, A.R. Carmona, J. Mongalian, A. Adeva, D. Lorenzo, and J. Oliver. 1997. The role of cold ischemia on graft survival in recipients of renal transplants. *Transplantation Proceedings* 29(8):3596–3597.

Ploeg, R.J., A.M. D'Alessandro, S.J. Knechtle, M.D. Stegall, J.D. Pirsch, R.M. Hoffmann, T. Sasaki, H.W. Sollinger, F.O. Belzer, and M. Kalayoglu. 1993. Risk factors for primary dysfunction after liver transplantation—A multivariate analysis. *Transplantation* 55(4):807–813.

Porte, R.J., R.J. Ploeg, B. Hanson, J.H. van Bockel, J. Thorogood, G.G. Persijn, J. Hermans, O.T. Terpstra, and the European Multicentre Study Group. 1998. Long-term graft survival after liver transplantation in the UW era: Late effects of cold ischemia and primary dysfunction. *Transplant International* 11(Suppl. 1):S164–S167.

Randall, V.R. 1996. Slavery, segregation, and racism: Trusting the health care system ain't always easy! An African American perspective on bioethics. *St. Louis University Public Law Review* 15:191–235.

Rossi, M., D. Alfani, P. Berloco, P. Bruzzone, and R. Cortesini. 1993. Prolonged liver cold ischemia time with University of Wisconsin solution and incidence of delayed graft function after hepatic transplantation: A single center experience. *Transplantation Proceedings* 25(6):3193–3194.

Sanchez-Urdazpal, L., G.J. Gores, E.M. Ward, T.P. Maus, H.E. Wahlstrom, S.B. Moore, R.H. Weisner, and R.A. Krom. 1992. Ischemic-time biliary complications after orthotopic liver transplantation. *Hepatology* 16(1):49–53.

Sanfilippo, F.P., W.K. Vaughn, T.G. Peters, C.F. Shield III, P.L. Adams, M.I. Lorber, and G.M. Williams. 1992. Factors affecting the waiting time of cadaveric kidney transplant candidates in the United States. *Journal of the American Medical Association* 267(2):247–252

Shafer, T.J., J. Orlowski, R.N. Ehrle, R. Gruenenfelder, K. Davis, and D.A. Reyes. 1998. Two years experience with routine notification [abstract]. Presented at the Annual Meeting of the North American Transplant Coordinators Organization, August 10, New York.

Shaheen, F., R.M. Abdur, D. Mousa, M. al-Sulaiman, R.W. Chang, and A.A. al-Khader. 1994. Long-term outcome in transplanted kidneys with long cold ischemia times. *Transplantation Proceedings* 26(5):2580.

Showstack, J., P.P. Katz, J.R. Lake, R.S. Brown, Jr., R.A. Dudley, S. Belle, R.H. Wiesner, R.K. Zetterman, and J. Everhart. 1999. Resource utilization in liver transplantation: Effects of patient characteristics and clinical practice. *Journal of the American Medical Association* 281:1381–1386.

Siminoff, L.A., R.M. Arnold, A.L. Caplan, B.A. Virnig, and D.L. Seltzer. 1995. Public policy governing organ and tissue procurement in the United States. *Annals of Internal Medicine* 123(1):10–17.

Southeastern Institute of Research, Inc. 1994. *General Consumers: American Attitudes Toward the Allocation of Organ Transplantation.* Richmond, Va.: United Network for Organ Sharing.

Strasberg, S.M., T.K. Howard, E.P. Molmenti, and M. Hertl. 1994. Selecting the donor liver: Risk factors for poor function after orthotopic liver transplantation. *Hepatology* 20(4):829–838.

Stratta, R.J. 1997. Donor age, organ import, and cold ischemia: Effect on early outcomes after simultaneous kidney–pancreas transplantation. *Transplantation Proceedings* 29(8):3291–3292.

Stroud, A.H., and D. Sechrest. 1966. *Gaussian Quadrature Form*ulas. Englewood Cliffs, N.J.: Prentice Hall.

Todo, S., J. Nery, K. Yanaga, L. Podesta, R.D. Gordon, and T.E. Starzl. 1989. Extended preservation of human liver grafts with UW solution. *Journal of the American Medical Association* 261(5):711–714.

Tuttle-Newhall, J.E., R. Rutledge, M. Johnson, and J. Fair. 1997. A statewide population-based, time series analysis of access to liver transplantation. *Transplantation* 63: 255–262.

UNOS (United Network for Organ Sharing) 1999. Information and data available on UNOS website at: http://www.unos.org. Accessed July 1, 1999.

UNOS. 1998. *1998 Annual Report—The U.S. Scientific Registry of Transplant Recipients and the Organ Procurement and Transplantation Network: Transplant Data 1988–1997.* Richmond, Va.. UNOS.

UNOS. 1997. *1997 Report of Center Specific Graft and Patient Survival Rates—Liver Volume.* Richmond, Va.: UNOS.

UNOS/OPTN. 1999. United Network for Organ Sharing—Cadaveric Donors Recovered in the U.S.: 1994–1998. (Photocopy.) Richmond, Va.: UNOS.

Wahlers, T., H.J. Schafers, J. Cremer, M. Jurman, S.W. Hirt, H.G. Fieguth, and A. Haverich. 1991. Organ preservation for heart–lung and lung transplantation. *Thoracic and Cardiovascular Surgery* 39(6):344–348.

Wald, A. 1943. Tests of statistical hypotheses concerning several parameters when the number of observations is large. *Transactions of the American Mathematical Society* 54:426–482.

Whiting, J.F., M. Golconda, R. Smith, S. O'Brien, M.R. First, and J.W. Alexander. 1998. Abstract: Economic costs of expanded criteria donors in renal transplantation. *Transplantation* 65:204–207.

Whiting, J.F., J. Martin, E. Zavala, and D. Hanto. 1999. Abstract: The influence of clinical variables on hospital costs after orthotopic liver transplantation. *Surgery* 125: 217–222.

Young, J.B., D.C. Naftel, R.C. Bourge, J.K. Kirklin, B.S. Clemson, C.B. Porter, R.J. Rodeheffer, and J.L. Kenzora. 1994. Matching the heart donor and transplant recipient. Clues for successful expansion of the donor pool: A multivariable, multiinstitutional report. *The Journal of Heart and Lung Transplantation* 13(3):353–364; discussion, 364–365.

Zeger, S.L., K.Y. Liang, and P.S. Albert. 1988. Models for longitudinal data: A generalized estimating equation approach. *Biometrics* 44:1049–1060.

A

Data Sources and Methods

In an effort to be comprehensive in addressing the task of reviewing the current policies of the Organ Procurement and Transplantation Network (OPTN) and the potential impact of the Final Rule, the committee explored various data sources in a concerted effort to cast a broad net for the collection and assessment of information. These sources included public input and testimony from federal agencies, professional societies, organizations, and individuals; a review of recent scientific literature; and statistical analyses of over 68,000 records of patient listings for liver transplantation.

In addition to these fairly traditional sources of data, expert liaisons were assembled for the committee to consult with throughout the project (see Box A-1). The expert liaisons are people with recognized experience and expertise on the issues before the committee. They provided technical advice and guidance in framing the issues, identifying important sources of information, and ensuring a comprehensive analysis. A summary description of the committee's evidence-gathering method follows.

TESTIMONY AND PUBLIC INPUT

Over the course of the study, the committee requested and received written responses and presentations from organizations and individuals representing many perspectives of organ procurement and transplantation. The committee felt it was important to receive as much input as possible from public groups involved with or seeking involvement in the organ allocation process, as well as from health professional and other organizations. To accomplish this, the committee convened public meetings on March 11 and April 16, 1999, to gather information and hear from groups and individuals. The committee made every effort to include as many groups as possible, given the short time available.

Committee members heard presentations and asked questions to explore the particular issues and unique perspectives that each organization represented. In particular, the committee was interested in hearing of the potential impact of the Final Rule on these respective parties. The organizations and individuals that addressed the committee are listed in Box A-2.

BOX A-1 Expert Liaisons

Patients and Donor Families

Vicki Crosier, National Kidney Foundation Donor Family Council
Charlie Fiske, National Transplant Action Committee
Pushkal Garg, Johns Hopkins University
Robert J. Kelly, Recipient Family Member
George Walton, Donor Family Member
Bruce Weir, Transplant Recipient International Organization

Transplantation

Ronald W. Busuttil, University of California at Los Angeles
Clive Callender, Howard University Hospital
Anthony D'Alessandro, University of Wisconsin Hospital and Clinics
Arnold Diethelm, University of Alabama, Birmingham
Ronald M. Ferguson, Ohio State University
John Fung, University of Pittsburgh
William E. Harmon, Children's Hospital, Boston
John F. Neylan, Emory University

Procurement

Carol Beasley, Partnership for Organ Donation
James Childress, University of Virginia
Rudolph C. Morgan, Organ and Tissue Acquisition Center, San Diego, Calif.
Howard Nathan, Gift of Life Transplant Program
Robert M. Sade, Medical University of South Carolina
Rodney Taylor, National Minority Organ Tissue and Transplant Education Program
Charles Thomas, Samaritan Transplant Services, Phoenix, Ariz.
Kathy Witmer, University of Washington

BOX A-2 Organizations and Individuals Appearing Before the Committee

March 11, 1999

Milton Benjamin, American Society of Transplant Surgeons
Vicki Crosier, National Kidney Foundation Donor Family Council
Marcia Crosse, U.S. General Accounting Office
Beverly Dennis, U.S. Department of Health and Human Services
Mike Hall, American Liver Foundation
William Harmon, American Society of Transplantation
Craig Irwin, National Transplant Action Committee
Richard Luskin, Association of Organ Procurement Organizations
Robert Merion, Patient Access to Transplantation Coalition
William W. Pfaff, United Network for Organ Sharing
Bruce Weir, Transplant Recipient International Organization
Andrea Zachary, American Society of Histocompatibility and Immunogenetics

April 16, 1999

Ronald W. Busuttil, University of California at Los Angeles
Clive Callender, Howard University Hospital
Ronald M. Ferguson, Ohio State University
Jameson Forster, University of Kansas
Doug Hanto, University of Cincinnati
Robert Higgins, Henry Ford Hospital
Mark Joensen, CONSAD Research Corporation
Goran Bo Gustaf Klintmalm, Baylor University Medical Center
Patrick McCarthy, Kaufman Center for Heart Failure, Cleveland
Robert Metzger, Translife, Orlando, Fla.
William Minogue, Suburban Hospital, Bethesda, Md.
Paulita Narag, Hendrick Medical Center, Abilene, Texas
Howard Nathan, Delaware Valley Transplant Program
Mary Ann Palumbi, North American Transplant Coordinators Organization
William W. Pfaff, United Network for Organ Sharing
Timothy L. Pruett, University of Virginia
Byers Shaw, University of Nebraska Medical Center
Kevin Stump, Mississippi Organ Recover Agency
Carlton Young, University of Alabama, Birmingham

In addition to the participants listed in Box A-2, many other individuals attended and participated in the public meetings, and/or provided written information to the committee. These individuals are listed below:

OTHER PARTICIPANTS AND CONTRIBUTORS

Patricia Adams
Bowman Gray School of Medicine

Mike Adcock
Patient Access to Transplantation Coalition

Jason Altmire
UPMC Health Systems

Denise Alveranga
Lifelink Transplant Institute

Bill Applegate
American Society of Transplantation

David Benor
Department of Health and Human Services

Audrey Bohnengel
Ohio Solid Organ Transplantation Consortium

Jodi Chappell
American Society of Transplantation

Dolph Chianchiano
National Kidney Foundation

Karen Chiccehitto
United Network for Organ Sharing

Coralyn Colladay
Department of Health and Human Services

Pat Daily
United Network for Organ Sharing

Todd Dickerson
University of Cincinnati

Isabel Dunst
Hogan and Hartson
Washington, D.C.

Gail Durant
American Society of Transplant Surgeons

Erick Edwards
United Network for Organ Sharing

Jon Eiche
The Living Bank International

Mary Ellison
United Network for Organ Sharing

Lorraine Fishback
Department of Health and Human Services

John Ford
U.S. House of Representatives Committee on Commerce

Walton Francis
Department of Health and Human Services

Robert Goldstein
Juvenile Diabetes Foundation

Walter Graham
United Network for Organ Sharing

Carol Green
U.S. Senate Committee on Health Education, Labor, and Pensions

Pamela Guarrera
Transplantation Institute

Ann Harper
United Network for Organ Sharing

Baxter Harrington
American Society of Minority Health and Transplant Professionals

Russell Hereford
Office of Evaluation and Inspections

Roy Hogberg
General Accounting Office

Lesly Hollman
Bureau of National Affairs

A. J. Hostetler
Richmond *Times-Dispatch*

Melody Hughson
Hoffman-LaRoche

Kent Jenkins
United Network for Organ Sharing

Linda Jones
Lifeline of Ohio

Karen Kennedy
Transplant Resource Center of Maryland

Jerry Klepner
United Network for Organ Sharing

Lisa Kory
Transplant Recipient International Organization

Evan Krisely
Patient Access to Transplantation Coalition

Eugene Laska
Nathan Kline Institute

Judy LaSov
Maryland Patient Advocacy Group

William Lawrence
United Network for Organ Sharing

Sue Leffell
American Society of Histocompatibility and Immunogenetics

Becky Levin
Renal Physicians Association

Pearl Lewis
Maryland Patient Advocacy Group

Chris Lu
U.S. House of Representatives Government Reform Committee

Michael Manley
Alaska Regional Organ Recovery Agency

Mark Marin
University of Cincinnati

Mary Mazanec
Senator William Frist's Office

Patrick McCarthy
Kaufman Center for Heart Failure

Eileen Meier
North American Transplant Coordinators Organization

Laura Melkler
Associated Press

Behn Miller
General Accounting Office

Joshua Miller
American Society of Transplant Surgeons

Marlene Mitman
American Society of Transplant Surgeons

Joseph Morton
Maryland Patient Advocacy Group

Elizabeth Neus
Gannett News Service

Jill Nusbaum
National Kidney Foundation

Joseph O'Donnell
Transplant Resource Center of Maryland

Lazar Palnick
University of Pittsburgh

Matthew Piron
Transplant Recipient International Organization

Dave Ress
Richmond *Times-Dispatch*

Lisa Rossi
University of Pittsburgh

Paul Schwab
Association of Organ Procurement Organizations

Timothy Shaver
INOVA Fairfax Hospital

Haimi Shiferaw
The Blue Sheet

Bernice Steinhardt
General Accounting Office

S. John Swanson, III
Organ Transplant Service and Consultant to Army Surgeon General for Transplantation

Alice Thurston
American Association of Kidney Patients

Sibyl Tilson
Congressional Research Service

Jennifer Van Horn
U.S. Senate Committee on Health, Education, Labor, and Pensions
Subcommittee on Public Health

Cliff VanMeter
United Network of Organ Sharing

Angela Vincent
National Medical Association

Jim Warren
Journal of Transplant News

Lynn Wegman
Department of Health and Human Services

Marc Wheat
U.S. House of Representatives Committee on Commerce

J. White
Department of Health and Human Services

Marlene Whiteman
Strategic Alliance Management

Donna Henry Wright
United Network for Organ Sharing

Elaine Young
Juvenile Diabetes Foundation

Troy Zimmerman
National Kidney Foundation

To gain the perspective of people who could not attend the public meetings, a notice was mailed to more than 1,000 professional societies, organizations, and interest groups. The mailing included a one-page description of the study, the committee roster, and a cover letter explaining the committee's purpose for requesting the information. The letter asked those interested to send or fax comments pertinent to the committee's five tasks. The information submitted supplemented the materials obtained by the committee through the literature review, public meetings, and data analyses.

All written materials presented to the committee were reviewed and considered with respect to the five tasks. This material can be examined by the public. The public access files are maintained by the National Research Council Library at 2001 Wisconsin Avenue, N.W., Harris Building, Room HA 152, Washington, DC 20007; tel: (202) 334-3543.

LITERATURE REVIEW

The committee conducted numerous literature searches as part of its effort to be comprehensive. Search terms used included organ donation policy, ethics, organ donation, organ procurement, organ preservation, ischemic time, costs of transplantation, and secondary analyses of existing databases. In addition, many transplant professionals and the expert liaisons provided literature to the committee for review and consideration.

STATISTICAL ANALYSIS

At the committee's request, the United Network for Organ Sharing (UNOS) provided a large amount of data regarding organ-specific allocation policies; waiting list mortality rates; waiting lists from multiple organ procurment organizations (OPOs); citizenship of patients recently added to the waiting lists; survival rates and transplant rates by OPO population size; OPO death rates on the liver waiting list by initial status and status at death; algorithms; and audits regarding classification of recipients.

Analysis of Waiting Time

The statistical development of the model used in this analysis is described by Hedeker and Gibbons (1994). Note that as previously described, the unit of analysis is the patient-day and not the patient. Following Efron (1988) we assume that days within patients are conditionally independent on the prior days as long as the competing risk outcomes of interest (i.e., death or mortality) can only occur on the final day for each subject. Using the terminology of multilevel analysis (Goldstein, 1995) let i denote the level-2 units (OPOs) and let j denote the level-1 units (patient-days within OPOs). Assume that there are $i = 1, \ldots, N$ level-2 units (i.e., OPOs) and $j = 1, \ldots, n_i$ level-1 patient-days nested within each OPO. The n_i patient-day measurements include the set of all available measurement days for all patients in OPO i (i.e., n_i is the total number of daily measurements in OPO i). Let y_{ij} be the value of the nominal variable associated with level-2 unit i and level-1 unit j. In our case, these represent transplant, death, and other and we code the $K + 1$ response categories as 0, 1, 2.

Adding random effects to the multinomial logistic regression model of Bock (1970), Nerlove and Press (1973), and others, we get that the probability, for a given OPO i, and patient-day j, $y_{ij} = k$ (a response occurs in category k), conditional on β and α, is:

$$P_{ijk} = P(y_{ij} = k \mid \boldsymbol{\beta}, \boldsymbol{\alpha}) = \frac{\exp(z_{ijk})}{1 + \sum_{h=1}^{K} \exp(z_{ijh})} \quad \text{for } k = 1, 2, \ldots K \tag{1}$$

$$P_{ij0} = P(y_{ij} = 0 \mid \boldsymbol{\beta}, \boldsymbol{\alpha}) = \frac{1}{1 + \sum_{h=1}^{K} \exp(z_{ijh})} \tag{2}$$

where $z_{ijk} = \boldsymbol{x}'_{ij} \beta_{ik} + \boldsymbol{w}'_{ij} \alpha_k$. Here, $\boldsymbol{w}_{ij}$ is the $p \times 1$ covariate vector and $\boldsymbol{x}_{ij}$ is the design vector for the r random effects, both vectors being for the jth patient-day nested within OPO i. Correspondingly, α_k is a $p \times 1$ vector of unknown fixed regression parameters, and β_{ik} is a $r \times 1$ vector of unknown random effects for OPO i. The distribution of the random effects is assumed to be multivariate normal with mean vector μ_k and covariance matrix Σ_k. Notice that the regression coefficient vectors β and α carry the k subscript. Thus, for each of the p covariates and r random effects, there will be K parameters to be estimated. Additionally, the random effect variance-covariance matrix Σ_k is allowed to vary with k.

It is convenient to standardize the random effects by letting $\beta_{ik} = T_k\theta_i + \mu_k$, where $T_k T'_k = \Sigma_k$ is the Cholesky decomposition of Σ_k. The model is now given as

$$z_{ijk} = \boldsymbol{x}'_{ij}(\boldsymbol{T}_k\boldsymbol{\theta}_i + \boldsymbol{\mu}_k) + \boldsymbol{w}'_{ij}\boldsymbol{\alpha}_k \,. \tag{3}$$

In this form, it is clear that this generalizes Bock's (1972) model for educational test data by including covariates $\boldsymbol{w}_{ij}$, and by allowing a general random-effects design vector $\boldsymbol{x}_{ij}$ including the possibility of multiple random effects θ_i.

Parameter Estimation

Let $\boldsymbol{y}_i$ denote the vector of nominal responses from OPO i for all n_i patient-day measurements nested within. Then the probability of any $\boldsymbol{y}_i$, conditional on the random effects θ and given α_k, μ_k, and T_k, is equal to the product of the probabilities of the patient-day responses:

$$\ell(\boldsymbol{y}_i \mid \boldsymbol{\theta}; \boldsymbol{\alpha}_k, \boldsymbol{\mu}_k, \boldsymbol{T}_k) = \prod_{j=1}^{n_i} \prod_{k=0}^{K} [P(y_{ij} = k \mid \boldsymbol{\theta}; \boldsymbol{\alpha}_k, \boldsymbol{\mu}_k, \boldsymbol{T}_k)]^{d_{ijk}} \tag{4}$$

where $d_{ijk} = 1$ if $y_{ij} = k$, and 0 otherwise. Thus, associated with the response from a particular patient-day, $d_{ijk} = 1$ for only one of the $K + 1$ categories and zero for all others. The marginal density of the response vector $\boldsymbol{y}_i$ in the population is expressed as the following integral of the likelihood, $\ell(\cdot)$, weighted by the prior density $g(\cdot)$:

$$h(\boldsymbol{y}_i) = \int_{\boldsymbol{\theta}} \ell(\boldsymbol{y}_i \mid \boldsymbol{\theta}; \boldsymbol{\alpha}_k, \boldsymbol{\mu}_k, \boldsymbol{T}_k)\; g(\boldsymbol{\theta})\; d\boldsymbol{\theta} \tag{5}$$

where $g(\theta)$ represents the population distribution of the random effects.

For parameter estimation, the marginal log-likelihood from the N OPOs can be written as: $\log L = \Sigma_i^N \log h(\boldsymbol{y}_i)$. Then, using η_k to represent an arbitrary parameter vector,

$$\frac{\partial \log L}{\partial \boldsymbol{\eta}_k} = \sum_{i=1}^{N} h^{-1}(\boldsymbol{y}_i) \int_{\boldsymbol{\theta}} \left[\sum_{j=1}^{n_i} (d_{ijk} - P_{ijk}) \frac{\partial z_{ijk}}{\partial \boldsymbol{\eta}_k} \right] \ell(\boldsymbol{y}_i \mid \boldsymbol{\theta}; \boldsymbol{\alpha}_k, \boldsymbol{\mu}_k, \boldsymbol{T}_k)\; g(\boldsymbol{\theta})\; d\boldsymbol{\theta} \tag{6}$$

where

$$\frac{\partial z_{ijk}}{\partial \boldsymbol{\alpha}_k} = \boldsymbol{w}_{ij}\;, \quad \frac{\partial z_{ijk}}{\partial \boldsymbol{\mu}_k} = \boldsymbol{x}_{ij}\;, \quad \frac{\partial z_{ijk}}{\partial \mathrm{v}(\boldsymbol{T}_k)} = \mathrm{J}_r(\boldsymbol{\theta} \otimes \boldsymbol{x}_{ij})\;, \tag{7}$$

J_r is a transformation matrix eliminating elements above the main diagonal (see Magnus, 1988), and $v(T_k)$ is the vector containing the unique elements of the Cholesky factor T_k. If T_k is a $r \times 1$ vector of independent random effect variance terms, then $\partial z_{ijk} / \partial T_k = \boldsymbol{x}_{ij}\theta$ in the equation above.

Fisher's method of scoring can be used to provide the solution to these likelihood equations. For this, provisional estimates for the vector of parameters Θ, on iteration ι are improved by

$$\Theta_{\iota+1} = \Theta_{\iota} - \mathcal{E}\left[\frac{\partial^2 \log L}{\partial \Theta_{\iota}\, \partial \Theta_{\iota}'}\right]^{-1} \frac{\partial \log L}{\partial \Theta_{\iota}} \tag{8}$$

where the empirical information matrix is given by:

$$\mathcal{E}\left[\frac{\partial^2 \log L}{\partial \Theta_{\iota}\, \partial \Theta_{\iota}'}\right] = -\sum_{i=1}^{N} h^{-2}(\mathbf{Y}_i)\, \frac{\partial h(\mathbf{Y}_i)}{\partial \Theta_{\iota}} \left(\frac{\partial h(\mathbf{Y}_i)}{\partial \Theta_{\iota}}\right)'. \tag{9}$$

In general, the total number of parameters equals the $K \times p$ fixed regression coefficients (α_k; $k = 1, \ldots, K$), plus the $K \times r$ means of the random effects (μ_k; $k = 1, \ldots, K$), and the $K \times r \times (r - 1)/2$ random effect variance-covariance terms ($\mathrm{v}[T_k]$; $k = 1, \ldots, K$). Notice that the parameter vector $\mathrm{v}(T_k)$, which indicates the degree of OPO population variance, is what distinguishes the mixed-effects model from the ordinary fixed-effects multinomial logistic regression model.

At convergence, the MML estimates and their accompanying standard errors can be used to construct asymptotic z-statistics by dividing the parameter estimate by its standard error (Wald, 1943). The computed z-statistic can then be compared with the standard normal table to test whether the parameter is significantly different from zero. While this use of the standard errors to perform hypothesis tests (and construct confidence intervals) for the fixed effects μ_k and α_k is generally reasonable, for the variance and covariance components $\mathrm{v}(T_k)$ this practice is problematic (see Bryk and Raudenbush, 1992, p. 55).

Numerical Quadrature

In order to solve the above likelihood equations, numerical integration on the transformed θ space can be performed. If the assumed random-effect distribution is normal, Gauss-Hermite quadrature can be used to approximate the above integrals to any practical degree of accuracy. In Gauss-Hermite quadrature, the integration is approximated by a summation on a specified number of quadrature points Q for each dimension of the integration; thus, for the transformed θ space, the summation goes over Q^r points. For the standard normal univariate density, optimal points and weights (denoted B_q and $A(B_q)$, respectively) are given in Stroud and Sechrest (1966). For the multivariate density, the r-dimensional vector of quadrature points is denoted by $\boldsymbol{B}_q' = (B_{q1}, B_{q2}, \ldots, B_{qr})$, with its associated (scalar) weight given by the product of the corresponding univariate weights,

$$A(\boldsymbol{B}_q) = \prod_{h=1}^{r} A(B_{qh}) \,. \tag{10}$$

If another distribution is assumed, other points may be chosen and density weights substituted for $A(B_q)$ or $A(B_{qh})$ above (note, the weights must be normalized to sum to unity). For example, if a rectangular or uniform distribution is assumed, then Q points may be set at equal intervals over an appropriate range (for each dimension) and the quadrature weights are then set equal to $1/Q$. Other distributions are possible; Bock and Aitkin (1981) discussed the possibility of empirically estimating the random-effect distribution.

For models with few random effects the quadrature solution is relatively fast and computationally tractable. In particular, if there is only one random effect in the model (as in the present case), there is only one additional summation over Q points relative to the fixed effects solution. As the number of random effects r is increased, the terms in the summation (Q^r) increase exponentially in the quadrature solution. Fortunately, as is noted by Bock, et al., (1988) in the context of a dichotomous factor analysis model, the number of points in each dimension can be reduced as the dimensionality is increased without impairing the accuracy of the approximations; they indicated that for a five-dimensional solution as few as three points per dimension were sufficient to obtain adequate accuracy. In general, specifying between 10 to 20 quadrature points for a unidimensional solution and 7 to 10 points for a two-dimensional solution is usually reasonable.

Hazard Rates and Cumulative Survival

For a model with one random-effect and three categories, we can estimate the probability of each outcome conditional on a particular covariate vector as

$$P_{ij2} = \frac{\exp(\sigma_2\theta_i + \mu_2 + \boldsymbol{w}'_{ij}\boldsymbol{\alpha}_2)}{1 + \exp(\sigma_1\theta_i + \mu_1 + \boldsymbol{w}'_{ij}\boldsymbol{\alpha}_1) + \exp(\sigma_2\theta_i + \mu_2 + \boldsymbol{w}'_{ij}\boldsymbol{\alpha}_2)} \tag{11}$$

$$P_{ij1} = \frac{\exp(\sigma_1\theta_i + \mu_1 + \boldsymbol{w}'_{ij}\boldsymbol{\alpha}_1)}{1 + \exp(\sigma_1\theta_i + \mu_1 + \boldsymbol{w}'_{ij}\boldsymbol{\alpha}_1) + \exp(\sigma_2\theta_i + \mu_2 + \boldsymbol{w}'_{ij}\boldsymbol{\alpha}_2)} \tag{12}$$

$$P_{ij0} = \frac{1}{1 + \exp(\sigma_1\theta_i + \mu_1 + \boldsymbol{w}'_{ij}\boldsymbol{\alpha}_1) + \exp(\sigma_2\theta_i + \mu_2 + \boldsymbol{w}'_{ij}\boldsymbol{\alpha}_2)} \tag{13}$$

These are referred to as "subject-specific" probabilities because they indicate response probabilities for particular values of the random subject effect θ_i (Neuhaus et al., 1991, Zeger et al., 1988). Replacing the parameters with their estimates and denoting the resulting subject-specific probabilities as $\hat{P}_{ss}$, marginal probabilities $\hat{P}_m$ are then obtained by integrating over the random-effect distribution, namely $\hat{P}_m = \int_\theta \hat{P}_{ss}\, g(\theta) d(\theta)$. Numerical quadrature can be used for this integration as well. These marginal probabilities represent the hazard rate for a particular competing risk of interest (i.e., transplant, mortality or other) expressed as a daily rate for status 1 or monthly rate for status 2B and 3 patients. The cumulative survival rate is then computed by summing the daily risk for status 1, or monthly risk in the case of status 2B and 3, over time adjusting for the number of subjects remaining on the list at that time point (i.e., adjusted for the competing risk).

All computations were performed using the MIXNO program developed under a grant from the National Institute of Mental Health and available at no charge at **http://www.uic.edu/labs/biostat/.**

ANALYSIS OF COSTS

The General Accounting Office (GAO) provided the committee with data that were instrumental in analyzing the potential effects of the Final Rule on transplantation costs. These included data on costs of solid organ transplantation, transportation costs, and costs of assembling a transplantation team. Roger Evans assisted Institute of Medicine staff and the committee in the analysis of these cost issues.

B

Guide to Summary Tables

The tables presented in this appendix relate to the discussion in Chapter 5. All tables provide summary data on liver transplantation only.* Because the medical status categories changed in 1998, all statistical analyses were performed on 1998–1999 data. To provide a more complete view of the overall system, tabular displays of summary data from 1995 to 1998 are included, using categories l, 2 (2, 2A, and 2B), and 3 (3 and 4). Column headings for the tables in this appendix are defined below.

Definitions of Terms That Appear as Table Headings

Avg. Wait: The average number of days waited by patients until transplant, death, or removal from the list. Average waiting times for status 1 patients are listed in days. Waiting times for all other status patients are listed in months.

Max. Wait: The maximum number of days waited by any patient in a particular status level until transplant, death, or removal from the list.

% TX: The number of patients transplanted in a particular status level, divided by the number of patients ever in that status level, multiplied by 100.

% Died: The number of patients who died in a particular status level, divided by the number of patients ever in that status level, multiplied by 100.

---

*Data for these analyses were provided by UNOS and are available in the Public Access File. Public access files are maintained by the National Research Council Library at 2001 Wisconsin Avenue N.W., Harris Building, Room HA 152, Washington, DC., 20007; tel: (202) 334-3543.

% Other: The number of patients who neither died nor were transplanted in a particular status level, divided by the number of patients ever in that status level, multiplied by 100.

% Died Post-TX: The number of patients who died following transplantation, divided by the number of patients ever transplanted in that status level, multiplied by 100 for a particular status level at the time of transplantation.

% Male: The percentage of male patients in a particular status level.

% B or AB: The percentage of patients with blood type B or AB out of all patients ever in that status level.

% Black: The percentage of African American patients ever in that status level.

Age: The average for patients in that status level.

***MMLE*:** Maximum marginal likelihood estimate—an estimate of an unknown parameter in a statistical model that produces the greatest probability of the model given the date.

SE: Standard error—a measure of uncertainty in an estimated parameter of a statistical model.

P: The probability associated with a test of the null hypothesis that the true parameter value is zero.

N: The number of patients ever listed in that status category during the period analyzed.

OPO: Organ procurement organization. The numbers in this column are coded. To conduct the analysis, the identities of 52 OPOs were encrypted (10 OPOs do not perform liver transplants). Therefore, the number assigned to each OPO does not match the number assigned to OPOs on the UNOS regional map found in Chapter 1 (Figure 1-1).

Total No. of TX: The total number of transplants performed in an OPO regardless of status level.

Total No. of Listings: The total number of patient listings in an OPO regardless of status.

Overall Percentage: The total number of transplants divided by the total number of patient listings for a particular OPO regardless of listing or transplant status.

This page intentionally left blank.

TABLE B-1 Transplants, Mortality, Waiting Time, and Demographics by OPO Patients During Status 1, Sorted by OPO Volume, 1995–1999

OPO[a]	*N*	Avg. Wait	Max. Wait	% TX	% Died	% Other[b]	% Died Post-TX	% Male	% B or AB	% Black	Age
14	567	9	59	49	12	38	13	53	16	13	37
59	504	6	55	54	8	38	15	61	14	6	40
7	415	4	28	52	8	40	11	57	17	12	37
47	392	3	18	65	5	30	8	51	16	5	37
5	321	4	22	51	9	40	6	52	18	5	34
49	296	3	15	69	6	25	8	48	13	15	40
22	242	3	16	53	5	42	12	55	16	10	36
39	226	4	47	55	3	42	6	65	19	3	45
42	203	11	83	45	17	38	12	54	13	10	25
46	188	5	31	41	11	48	14	58	17	26	39
29	127	4	17	53	9	38	7	50	18	6	32
41	107	4	23	43	10	47	13	50	17	17	33
52	96	4	40	48	18	34	8	52	14	10	34
24	79	4	15	61	6	33	8	48	15	20	33
20	76	4	13	46	8	46	14	50	12	11	41
17	70	4	41	44	14	41	16	43	19	27	29
61	69	3	12	64	3	33	12	58	16	16	29
45	66	4	15	59	6	35	18	55	17	15	23
40	64	4	19	59	16	25	9	47	17	5	35
48	62	4	13	52	2	47	5	60	15	5	35
37	58	4	15	41	10	48	5	47	10	47	36
35	56	4	36	52	11	38	5	43	9	11	34
10	55	3	18	51	7	42	7	55	13	2	43
15	55	3	22	73	5	22	18	53	13	20	33
57	54	3	9	57	9	33	20	57	15	19	41
44	53	4	38	49	6	45	6	66	9	2	44
58	52	5	33	38	15	46	12	48	17	25	47

11	51	4	15	49	8	43	8	45	25	24	18
4	47	3	9	47	9	45	17	60	9	9	43
50	46	4	17	54	7	39	17	61	13	11	35
67	46	5	22	43	13	43	15	46	17	4	33
38	43	5	22	40	28	33	14	49	7	16	35
27	41	5	49	51	2	46	2	32	15	24	27
36	41	5	20	54	10	37	10	49	2	0	34
64	39	5	21	44	18	38	15	62	13	0	36
23	37	4	14	27	27	46	5	43	19	32	32
34	33	3	14	48	9	42	21	55	18	33	27
18	31	3	6	55	16	29	23	52	3	23	38
60	31	3	10	35	6	58	0	42	10	29	39
28	29	4	16	69	14	17	24	66	10	0	33
32	28	4	10	46	7	46	25	54	36	11	47
33	28	2	9	46	4	50	14	50	11	0	38
63	27	3	13	52	4	44	22	67	22	0	45
26	26	7	22	38	12	50	4	46	0	4	27
53	25	4	17	48	12	40	16	60	20	12	35
65	23	2	8	61	4	35	9	78	9	0	46
31	21	3	9	19	24	57	5	48	10	0	29
6	15	3	16	87	0	13	20	53	7	7	43
12	15	3	10	20	20	60	0	87	7	0	50
13	9	2	5	33	33	33	11	67	33	0	36
3	6	3	5	50	17	33	0	33	17	67	36
30	3	4	10	33	0	67	0	67	33	0	33

[a] The numbers in this column are coded. The number assigned to each OPO does not match the number assigned to OPOs on the UNOS regional map found in Chapter 1 (Figure 1-1).

[b] For example, shifting to another status level, being too sick to receive a transplant, being delisted, receiving a transplant at another OPO, or still waiting.

TABLE B-2 Transplants, Mortality, Waiting Time, and Demographics by OPO Patients During Status 1, Sorted by OPO Volume—Adults Only (18 and over), 1995–1999

OPO[a]	*N*	Avg. Wait	Max. Wait	% TX	% Died	% Other[b]	% Died Post-TX	% Male	% B or AB	% Black	Age
14	388	9	59	47	14	39	13	53	17	14	47
59	365	5	27	56	7	36	16	62	15	3	50
7	291	4	27	48	10	42	11	58	18	13	46
47	261	3	18	65	5	30	10	49	16	5	47
5	223	4	19	54	10	36	8	53	20	4	47
49	220	3	15	66	7	27	8	41	13	16	47
39	193	4	19	54	4	42	6	63	20	4	47
22	172	3	16	54	6	40	14	55	17	7	47
46	128	5	29	34	13	53	10	54	18	27	48
42	92	7	43	54	8	38	14	55	15	5	49
29	79	3	16	46	10	44	6	42	15	8	42
41	69	3	12	45	10	45	10	41	17	20	44
52	67	3	10	43	19	37	7	49	16	12	45
20	61	3	13	41	8	51	11	46	13	11	46
24	60	4	15	58	8	33	8	42	18	20	39
10	50	3	18	48	8	44	8	56	14	2	44
44	49	4	38	49	6	45	6	65	10	2	44
40	46	4	12	59	20	22	11	41	15	7	46
37	45	4	15	38	9	53	4	40	9	40	43
4	43	3	9	49	9	42	16	60	9	9	44
48	43	4	13	47	0	53	2	60	14	5	46
58	43	5	33	28	19	53	12	40	19	30	47
15	42	3	12	67	5	29	19	48	17	21	40
57	42	3	9	52	7	40	19	50	14	19	47
35	40	4	15	55	8	38	5	43	8	10	44
17	39	3	12	41	18	41	15	33	10	28	41
61	36	3	10	64	3	33	17	47	14	17	42

38	33	6	22	39	27	33	15	45	6	6	45
67	31	4	8	45	10	45	19	48	19	3	43
36	30	5	20	50	13	37	7	50	0	0	42
50	30	4	15	50	10	40	10	63	20	10	45
64	30	4	11	47	17	37	17	60	17	0	45
45	29	4	15	38	7	55	21	45	7	10	43
63	26	3	13	50	4	46	23	69	19	0	45
18	25	3	6	64	20	16	28	52	4	24	42
32	25	3	10	48	8	44	24	48	28	8	52
27	24	4	12	58	4	38	4	33	13	25	40
23	23	4	9	22	35	43	9	39	22	26	43
33	22	2	9	45	5	50	14	45	14	0	44
60	22	3	10	36	9	55	0	41	5	27	47
28	21	3	9	71	14	14	29	67	14	0	43
11	19	3	9	32	11	58	0	26	21	42	38
26	17	7	17	35	18	47	6	35	0	0	38
34	17	3	8	47	18	35	18	35	24	24	43
53	17	4	17	41	12	47	12	53	18	0	47
31	14	3	7	29	14	57	7	43	14	0	40
6	12	4	16	83	0	17	17	42	8	8	43
65	12	2	8	25	8	67	8	67	8	0	49
12	11	3	10	9	27	64	0	82	9	0	50
13	6	2	5	17	50	33	0	83	50	0	51
3	5	3	5	40	20	40	0	40	20	60	40
30	2	5	10	50	0	50	0	50	50	0	50

[a] The numbers in this column are coded. The number assigned to each OPO does not match the number assigned to OPOs on the UNOS regional map found in Chapter 1 (Figure 1-1).

[b] For example, shifting to another status level, being too sick to receive a transplant, being delisted, receiving a transplant at another OPO, or still waiting.

TABLE B-3 Mixed-Effects Competing Risk Survival Model for Patient Time in Status 1: Maximum Marginal Likelihood Estimates (MMLE), 1998–1999

	MMLE	*SE*	*p*
Transplant vs. Other			
Intercept	–1.829	0.276	0.001
Day	0.016	0.015	0.299
Age 0–5 vs. adult	–0.907	0.188	0.001
Age 6–17 vs. adult	–0.362	0.234	0.123
Gender (1 = male)	–0.098	0.198	0.621
Race (1 = black)	–0.275	0.268	0.306
Blood type (1 = B or O)	–0.076	0.196	0.697
OPO volume (M vs. L)	–0.054	0.319	0.866
OPO volume (S vs. L)	0.261	0.336	0.437
Random OPO effect *SD*	0.393	0.144	0.003
Mortality vs. Other			
Intercept	–3.685	0.482	0.001
Day	0.023	0.047	0.625
Age 0–5 vs. adult	–0.968	0.378	0.010
Age 6–17 vs. adult	–1.001	0.551	0.069
Gender (1 = male)	0.077	0.371	0.835
Race (1 = black)	0.162	0.448	0.717
Blood Type (1 = B or O)	0.003	0.433	0.995
OPO volume (M vs. L)	0.203	0.491	0.679
OPO volume (S vs. L)	–0.230	0.930	0.805
Random OPO effect *SD*	0.042	0.298	0.444

NOTE: L = >300 transplants; M = 150–300 transplants; S = <150 transplants; and SD = standard deviation.

This page intentionally left blank.

TABLE B-4 Transplants, Mortality, Waiting Time, and Demographics by OPO Patients During Status 2, Sorted by OPO Volume, 1995–1999

OPO[a]	*N*	Avg. Wait	Max. Wait	% TX	% Died	% Other[b]	% Died Post-TX	% Male	% B or AB	% Black	Age
49	1,113	62	429	54	3	43	2	61	17	11	50
7	957	79	1,363	42	8	49	4	59	15	12	43
14	913	56	446	37	9	54	5	59	19	11	43
5	863	62	1,426	49	4	47	3	62	15	4	44
59	748	41	720	44	9	47	6	62	16	4	43
47	726	43	1,363	51	5	44	4	55	17	4	46
29	725	110	729	40	10	50	3	64	15	3	46
22	545	30	328	58	6	36	6	57	14	9	43
39	478	62	431	44	5	51	2	63	18	3	49
52	404	41	209	65	4	31	4	56	10	6	46
41	387	70	417	43	4	53	5	64	15	13	45
46	374	67	455	33	9	57	3	59	19	20	47
20	341	48	406	56	4	39	8	61	10	11	44
42	335	46	414	38	3	59	9	50	13	8	34
61	311	55	841	74	4	23	7	61	13	6	46
40	306	43	328	69	5	26	7	55	20	1	44
27	303	78	420	58	4	38	5	57	16	17	44
24	285	40	295	65	7	29	6	58	15	12	44
15	279	40	307	62	6	32	8	62	19	10	50
48	216	79	391	53	2	45	5	66	18	1	45
58	215	65	386	40	6	55	5	62	14	18	50
67	209	73	412	50	11	38	10	61	10	1	44
37	201	53	1,362	53	3	44	6	61	14	19	46
11	195	59	304	43	9	48	3	52	18	12	39
44	184	50	312	51	10	39	2	61	16	2	50
50	173	35	1,430	66	9	25	10	53	11	10	47
17	164	29	175	59	4	38	7	59	12	19	41

45	161	53	421	60	7	34	9	58	14	7	38
10	155	72	426	45	5	51	3	59	17	8	46
38	151	48	356	55	5	40	8	54	13	7	44
23	136	42	238	55	4	40	9	60	13	18	45
6	132	73	324	62	11	27	7	73	13	6	48
63	132	45	315	61	8	31	5	72	14	2	48
4	129	35	214	54	6	40	9	64	14	6	46
57	125	60	394	58	6	37	6	69	15	14	48
60	121	36	210	64	8	27	6	67	21	11	48
32	111	37	180	50	5	45	7	63	15	5	48
35	102	69	400	53	4	43	6	56	10	11	41
18	100	46	340	54	6	40	9	63	12	8	50
65	97	64	324	45	6	48	0	61	18	3	48
64	90	10	63	53	13	33	4	59	17	0	42
3	82	64	296	66	6	28	0	65	15	12	49
36	80	35	300	38	11	51	3	55	8	3	40
34	77	40	206	60	10	30	12	55	18	16	40
28	65	13	58	63	2	35	14	62	15	5	40
33	63	15	105	46	0	54	5	57	16	0	46
26	62	26	157	32	10	58	8	50	6	5	36
53	43	16	102	47	0	53	9	60	14	12	38
12	39	50	212	54	5	41	3	77	10	0	50
31	29	31	135	31	17	52	7	62	21	0	41
13	21	35	206	38	14	48	10	62	29	0	47
30	11	82	254	36	0	64	0	55	18	0	44

[a] The numbers in this column are coded. The number assigned to each OPO does not match the number assigned to OPOs on the UNOS regional map found in Chapter 1 (Figure 1-1).

[b] For example, shifting to another status level, being too sick to receive a transplant, being delisted, receiving a transplant at another OPO, or still waiting.

TABLE B-5 Mixed-Effects Competing Risk Survival Model for Patient Time in Status 2B: Maximum Marginal Likelihood Estimates (MMLE), 1998–1999

	MMLE	*SE*	*p*
Transplant vs. Other			
Intercept	–2.077	0.129	0.001
Month	–0.092	0.016	0.001
Age 0–5 vs. adult	0.470	0.103	0.001
Age 6–17 vs. adult	0.135	0.243	0.577
Gender (1 = male)	0.126	0.087	0.150
Race (1 = black)	0.134	0.222	0.546
Blood type (1 = B or O)	–0.577	0.062	0.001
OPO volume (M vs. L)	0.590	0.157	0.001
OPO volume (S vs. L)	0.560	0.187	0.003
Random OPO effect *SD*	0.689	0.064	0.001
Mortality vs. Other			
Intercept	–3.313	0.227	0.001
Month	–0.213	0.039	0.001
Age 0–5 vs. adult	–0.195	0.381	0.608
Age 6–17 vs. adult	–0.516	0.641	0.421
Gender (1 = male)	0.014	0.191	0.944
Race (1 = black)	–0.082	0.359	0.820
Blood type (1 = B or O)	–0.005	0.164	0.974
OPO volume (M vs. L)	0.202	0.126	0.110
OPO volume (S vs. L)	0.355	0.151	0.019
Random OPO effect *SD*	0.116	0.049	0.009

NOTE: L = >300 transplants; M = 150–300 transplants; S = <150 transplants; and SD = standard deviation.

This page intentionally left blank.

TABLE B-6 Transplants, Mortality, Waiting Time, and Demographics by OPO Patients During Status 3 or 4, Sorted by OPO Volume, 1995–1999

OPO[a]	*N*	Avg. Wait	Max. Wait	% TX	% Died	% Other[b]	% Died Post-TX	% Male	% B or AB	% Black	Age
5	2,437	464	1,539	6	8	86	0	59	16	3	46
14	1,923	392	1,533	10	7	83	1	56	19	10	45
49	1,790	305	1,510	9	4	87	0	60	19	9	49
47	1,361	204	1,506	23	4	73	1	57	16	3	48
7	1,334	318	1,452	10	4	86	1	59	17	10	45
29	1,269	386	1,440	4	9	87	0	61	16	2	46
59	1,152	352	1,512	15	6	79	1	63	17	4	44
22	983	140	1,011	34	5	60	4	58	14	6	46
39	798	262	1,363	13	4	82	0	61	19	3	50
46	728	442	1,525	3	6	91	1	55	18	18	46
52	714	229	1,484	31	7	63	3	54	13	6	48
40	711	180	955	33	3	64	2	56	18	2	47
41	702	303	1,015	19	4	77	2	60	18	14	46
61	636	152	847	26	5	69	2	59	12	7	47
24	582	302	1,148	16	5	79	1	57	14	12	44
20	558	231	1,105	26	4	70	3	60	12	8	46
42	537	233	1,000	21	7	72	4	53	13	5	38
48	489	318	1,213	22	2	75	1	59	16	4	47
67	474	232	923	24	6	69	4	61	12	3	47
15	455	275	1,126	22	5	73	2	60	18	9	48
50	448	244	1,064	35	6	58	3	55	14	8	46
27	408	151	813	39	4	57	3	56	13	18	44
63	398	322	1,045	34	5	60	4	70	11	2	49
38	393	302	1,125	18	4	79	2	55	13	5	46
44	384	354	1,504	8	7	85	0	60	16	2	49
64	360	198	1,471	58	2	39	3	62	13	2	45

11	358	161	600	39	7	54	3	53	19	8	41
58	317	224	1,014	24	3	73	2	62	19	14	49
17	312	127	546	56	1	43	7	54	13	13	45
37	298	202	1,230	26	5	68	2	60	15	16	47
57	290	270	1,490	38	3	59	2	61	14	10	47
4	258	154	752	39	4	57	7	64	11	4	48
10	231	284	1,344	26	6	68	1	58	14	9	47
35	219	164	892	46	1	53	2	49	10	5	45
45	208	272	1,511	27	1	72	2	58	11	12	36
32	206	255	1,335	33	5	62	3	62	14	5	48
60	197	129	1,021	56	1	43	7	59	18	7	50
23	194	172	629	28	5	66	4	60	16	11	47
34	191	156	1,431	42	7	51	9	61	14	12	45
6	190	145	623	34	6	59	3	69	13	5	50
36	187	194	999	59	3	39	3	54	13	1	43
26	177	283	1,293	32	4	64	3	50	11	2	44
33	165	124	502	64	1	36	10	61	16	1	49
18	159	239	934	31	1	68	4	64	13	4	49
53	127	91	449	70	2	28	7	64	13	6	46
28	126	97	519	63	2	36	5	57	15	7	43
65	103	149	701	20	3	77	1	56	17	3	48
3	101	263	953	19	0	81	1	63	11	4	48
12	96	96	468	47	2	51	0	69	15	0	51
31	89	216	769	45	6	49	3	49	9	0	44
13	48	133	818	54	2	44	8	65	21	2	50
30	36	261	1,109	44	8	47	0	50	22	0	52

[a] The numbers in this column are coded. The number assigned to each OPO does not match the number assigned to OPOs on the UNOS regional map found in Chapter 1 (Figure 1-1).

[b] For example, shifting to another status level, being too sick to receive a transplant, being delisted, receiving a transplant at another OPO, or still waiting.

TABLE B-7 Mixed-Effects Competing Risk Survival Model for Patient Time in Status 3: Maximum Marginal Likelihood Estimates (MMLE), 1998–1999

	MMLE	*SE*	*p*
Transplant vs. Other			
Intercept	–3.593	0.210	0.001
Month	–0.220	0.030	0.001
Age 0–5 vs. adult	1.156	0.154	0.001
Age 6–17 vs. adult	0.844	0.268	0.002
Gender (1 = male)	0.054	0.186	0.769
Race (1 = black)	0.158	0.304	0.603
Blood type (1 = B or O)	–0.477	0.098	0.001
OPO volume (M vs. L)	1.179	0.149	0.001
OPO volume (S vs. L)	0.757	0.228	0.001
Random OPO effect *SD*	1.335	0.162	0.001
Mortality vs. Other			
Intercept	–3.654	0.172	0.001
Month	–0.216	0.041	0.001
Age 0–5 vs. Adult	–2.119	2.099	0.313
Age 6–17 vs. Adult	–1.193	2.000	0.551
Gender (1 = male)	–0.063	0.268	0.814
Race (1 = black)	0.027	0.544	0.960
Blood type (1 = B or O)	–0.017	0.231	0.943
OPO volume (M vs. L)	–0.526	0.300	0.079
OPO volume (S vs. L)	–0.658	0.358	0.066
Random OPO effect *SD*	0.137	0.157	0.191

NOTE: L = >300 transplants; M = 150–300 transplants; S = <150 transplants; and SD = standard deviation.

TABLE B-8 Status of Transplanted Patients by OPO, Percentages (1995–1999)

		Status					
OPO[a]	*N*	1	2	3	4	7	9
49	969	20	59	15	0	0	6
47	943	24	37	29	1	0	9
14	809	32	38	22	0	0	8
22	786	15	37	40	0	0	7
59	769	34	40	20	0	0	6
7	747	26	49	16	0	0	10
5	735	21	54	16	1	0	8
52	532	8	47	40	0	1	4
40	485	8	42	48	0	0	2
39	444	26	45	22	1	0	6
61	444	9	49	34	0	0	8
29	421	15	68	10	0	2	5
20	375	9	49	37	0	0	5
27	370	6	44	43	0	3	4
41	353	12	44	37	0	2	5
42	342	26	35	33	0	3	4
24	327	14	53	27	0	0	7
15	311	12	53	32	0	0	3
17	306	9	27	55	0	1	8
50	299	8	37	49	1	0	6
64	281	6	17	68	6	2	1
48	258	12	44	42	0	0	2
11	247	10	31	55	0	0	4
67	240	8	40	46	0	0	6
63	233	5	33	57	0	0	5
46	226	31	51	9	0	0	8
57	213	14	31	48	0	0	8
37	211	11	49	37	0	0	2
60	200	4	32	53	0	0	12
35	194	15	26	51	1	3	6
4	193	11	33	50	1	0	5
45	191	19	43	28	0	0	9
58	184	10	42	36	1	0	11
38	181	9	45	37	0	4	4
36	162	13	15	65	0	0	7
6	160	8	47	34	4	0	6
10	157	17	38	36	1	0	9
44	152	16	59	20	0	0	5
33	148	9	20	68	0	0	4
23	143	7	48	38	0	0	8
34	143	10	31	55	0	0	3
28	140	14	28	55	0	0	4
32	139	9	40	47	2	2	1
53	125	9	16	69	2	3	2
18	121	14	44	40	0	0	2
26	87	10	23	63	2	0	1
65	80	18	46	26	0	0	10
3	76	4	68	25	0	0	3
12	69	4	29	64	0	0	3
31	53	8	17	70	0	0	6
13	37	8	16	68	0	0	8
30	21	5	14	76	0	0	5

TABLE B-9 Initial Listing Status by OPO, Percentages (1995–1999)

		Status					
OPO[a]	*N*	1	2	3	4	7	9
5	2,647	5	5	54	35	1	0
49	2,434	9	17	64	6	5	0
14	2,322	14	10	64	12	0	0
7	1,832	13	18	56	12	1	0
47	1,775	14	11	52	22	0	0
59	1,572	16	16	56	11	1	0
29	1,559	6	16	71	8	0	0
22	1,244	13	14	71	2	0	0
39	1,042	11	16	53	19	1	0
52	975	7	21	64	7	2	0
46	887	11	11	52	26	0	0
41	872	8	14	77	1	0	0
40	816	5	9	53	33	1	0
61	749	7	7	54	25	8	0
20	700	6	16	70	6	0	0
24	697	7	11	80	1	1	0
42	676	13	13	62	12	0	0
15	588	7	17	74	1	1	0
27	582	5	28	64	3	0	0
48	557	8	6	85	1	0	0
67	553	5	9	59	25	2	0
50	523	4	13	72	10	0	0
11	452	6	19	72	2	1	0
63	451	3	9	86	1	0	0
38	448	6	7	78	9	1	0
17	444	13	19	67	0	1	0
58	443	9	23	61	6	1	0
44	437	6	7	60	26	0	0
37	429	10	21	59	4	6	0
64	422	5	11	73	10	1	0
57	377	10	15	74	1	0	0
10	327	10	21	59	8	1	0
4	321	10	11	71	4	4	0
45	313	13	23	63	0	1	0
35	304	12	17	62	7	2	0
60	270	9	24	67	0	0	0
23	269	9	23	67	1	1	0
6	267	4	26	57	12	1	0
32	263	6	18	65	10	1	0
36	242	10	16	71	0	3	0
34	238	9	13	78	0	0	0
26	212	7	12	78	4	0	0
18	211	9	17	71	0	3	0
33	206	10	13	78	0	0	0
28	165	12	13	67	6	2	0
65	162	9	30	59	0	2	0
53	155	8	13	74	2	4	0
3	145	3	28	68	0	1	0
12	124	8	8	59	2	23	0
31	117	16	9	71	2	2	0
13	61	11	15	74	0	0	0
30	39	3	8	82	5	3	0

TABLE B-10 Mixed-Effects Competing Risk Survival Model for Patient Time in Status 1 as a Function of OPO Size: Maximum Marginal Likelihood Estimates (MMLE), 1998–1999

	MMLE	*SE*	*p*
Transplant vs. Other			
Intercept	–2.071	0.561	0.001
Day	–0.003	0.012	0.82
Size (linear)	0.018	0.243	0.943
Size (quadratic)	–0.005	0.023	0.844
Random OPO effect *SD*	0.404	0.142	0.002
Mortality vs. Other			
Intercept	–4.539	1.349	0.001
Day	0.008	0.027	0.777
Size (linear)	0.234	0.473	0.622
Size (quadratic)	–0.019	0.039	0.627
Random OPO effect *SD*	0.052	0.183	0.388

TABLE B-11 Mixed-Effects Competing Risk Survival Model for Patient Time in Status 2B as a Function of OPO Size: Maximum Marginal Likelihood Estimates (MMLE), 1998–1999

	MMLE	*SE*	*p*
Transplant vs. Other			
Intercept	–2.527	0.432	0.007
Month	–0.105	0.01	0.001
Size (linear)	0.505	0.154	0.001
Size (quadratic)	–0.063	0.013	0.001
Random OPO effect *SD*	0.596	0.05	0.001
Mortality vs. Other			
Intercept	–3.886	0.361	0.001
Month	–0.209	0.027	0.001
Size (linear)	0.328	0.127	0.009
Size (quadratic)	–0.033	0.011	0.004
Random OPO effect *SD*	0.076	0.047	0.054

TABLE B-12 Mixed-Effects Competing Risk Survival Model for Patient Time in Status 3 as a Function of OPO Size: Maximum Marginal Likelihood Estimates (MMLE), 1998–1999

	MMLE	*SE*	*p*
Transplant vs. Other			
Intercept	–4.837	0.604	0.001
Month	–0.233	0.023	0.001
Size (linear)	0.841	0.243	0.001
Size (quadratic)	–0.079	0.021	0.001
Random OPO effect *SD*	1.196	0.105	0.001
Mortality vs. Other			
Intercept	–4.904	0.694	0.001
Month	–0.213	0.029	0.001
Size (linear)	0.28	0.226	0.217
Size (quadratic)	–0.018	0.017	0.313
Random OPO effect *SD*	0.067	0.15	0.327

This page intentionally left blank.

TABLE B-13 Ratios of Transplants to Listings by OPO Sorted by Number of Transplants; Ratios Expressed as a Percentage, 1995–1999

				Percentages Within Status Level			
OPO[a]	Total No. of Transplants	Total No. of Listings	Overall Percentage	Status 1	Status 2	Status 3/4	Population Served (millions)
49	969	2,434	39	7	23	5	9
47	943	1,775	53	12	19	15	7
14	809	2,322	34	11	13	7	9
22	786	1,244	63	9	23	25	5
59	769	1,572	48	16	19	9	6
7	747	1,832	40	10	19	6	9
5	735	2,647	27	5	14	4	9
52	532	975	54	4	25	21	7
40	485	816	59	4	24	28	6
39	444	1,042	42	11	19	9	9
61	444	749	59	5	29	20	3
29	421	1,559	27	4	18	2	9
20	375	700	53	4	26	19	4
27	370	582	63	3	27	27	5
41	353	872	40	4	17	14	9
42	342	676	50	13	17	16	2
24	327	697	46	6	24	12	4
15	311	588	52	6	28	16	4
17	306	444	68	6	18	37	7
50	299	523	57	4	21	28	4
64	281	422	66	3	11	49	3
48	258	557	46	5	20	19	4
11	247	452	54	5	16	30	7
67	240	553	43	3	17	19	7

63	233	451	51	2	17	29	4
46	226	887	25	7	12	2	3
57	213	377	56	7	17	27	3
37	211	429	49	5	24	18	4
60	200	270	74	2	23	39	6
35	194	304	63	9	16	33	3
4	193	321	60	6	19	30	4
45	191	313	61	11	26	17	2
58	184	443	41	4	17	15	4
38	181	448	40	3	18	14	5
36	162	242	66	8	10	43	3
6	160	267	59	4	28	22	4
10	157	327	48	8	18	17	2
44	152	437	34	5	20	6	3
33	148	206	71	6	14	48	3
23	143	269	53	3	25	20	2
34	143	238	60	6	18	33	3
28	140	165	84	11	23	46	5
32	139	263	52	4	21	25	2
53	125	155	80	7	12	57	2
18	121	211	57	8	25	22	3
26	87	212	41	4	9	26	4
65	80	162	49	8	22	12	3
3	76	145	52	2	35	13	2
12	69	124	55	2	16	35	2
31	53	117	45	3	7	31	2
13	37	61	60	4	9	41	2
30	21	39	53	2	7	40	2

TABLE B-14 Number of Transplants (overall and by status) and Number of Listings per Million People Served Sorted by Number of Transplants, 1995–1999

				Total No. of:		No. of Transplants per Million People Served		
OPO[a]	Total No. of Transplants	Total No. of Listings	Pop. Served (millions)	Transplants per Million	Listings per Million	Status 1 Transplants	Status 2 Transplants	Status 3/4 Transplants
49	969	2,434	9	107	270	21	63	16
47	943	1,775	7	134	253	32	49	40
14	809	2,322	9	89	258	28	34	19
22	786	1,244	5	157	248	23	58	62
59	769	1,572	6	128	262	43	51	25
7	747	1,832	9	83	203	21	40	13
5	735	2,647	9	81	294	17	44	13
52	532	975	7	76	139	6	35	30
40	485	816	6	80	136	6	33	38
39	444	1,042	9	49	115	12	22	11
61	444	749	3	148	249	13	72	50
29	421	1,559	9	46	173	7	31	4
20	375	700	4	93	175	8	45	34
27	370	582	5	74	116	4	32	31
41	353	872	9	39	96	4	17	14
42	342	676	2	171	338	44	59	56
24	327	697	4	81	174	11	43	22
15	311	588	4	77	147	9	41	24
17	306	444	7	43	63	3	11	24
50	299	523	4	74	130	5	27	37
64	281	422	3	93	140	5	15	69
48	258	557	4	64	139	7	28	27
11	247	452	7	35	64	3	10	19
67	240	553	7	34	79	2	13	15

63	233	451	4	58	112	2	19	33
46	226	887	3	75	295	23	38	6
57	213	377	3	71	125	9	22	34
37	211	429	4	52	107	5	25	19
60	200	270	6	33	45	1	10	17
35	194	304	3	64	101	9	16	33
4	193	321	4	48	80	5	15	24
45	191	313	2	95	156	18	41	26
58	184	443	4	46	110	4	19	17
38	181	448	5	36	89	3	16	13
36	162	242	3	54	80	7	8	35
6	160	267	4	40	66	3	18	15
10	157	327	2	78	163	13	29	29
44	152	437	3	50	145	8	29	10
33	148	206	3	49	68	4	9	33
23	143	269	2	71	134	5	34	27
34	143	238	3	47	79	4	14	26
28	140	165	5	28	33	3	7	15
32	139	263	2	69	131	6	27	34
53	125	155	2	62	77	5	10	44
18	121	211	3	40	70	5	17	16
26	87	212	4	21	53	2	5	14
65	80	162	3	26	54	4	12	6
3	76	145	2	38	72	1	25	9
12	69	124	2	34	62	1	10	22
31	53	117	2	26	58	2	4	18
13	37	61	2	18	30	1	2	12
30	21	39	2	10	19	0	1	7

C

Current Liver Allocation Policies*

Policy 3.6 Organ Distribution

3.6 Allocation of Livers. Unless otherwise approved according to Policies 3.1.7 (Local and Alternative Local Unit), 3.1.8 (Sharing Arrangement and Sharing Agreement), 3.1.9 (Alternate Point Assignments [Variances]), and Policy 3.4.6 (Application, Review, Dissolution, and Modification Processes for Alternative Organ Distribution or Allocation Systems), the allocation of livers according to the following point system is mandatory first locally, then regionally, and then nationally. Each patient will be assigned a status code corresponding to the degree of medical urgency as described in Policy 3.6.4 below. Each patient also will be assigned points for conditions as described in Policies 3.3.5, 3.6.2, 3.6.3, and 3.6.4.

Livers will be offered for patients with an assigned status of 1 in descending point sequence with the patient having the highest number of points receiving the highest priority before being offered for patients listed in other status categories. Following Status 1, livers will be offered for patients with an assigned status of 2A in descending point sequence with the patient having the highest number of points receiving the highest priority before being offered for patients listed in less urgent statuses.

Following Status 2A, livers will be offered for patients with an assigned status of 2B in descending point sequence with the patient having the highest number of points receiving the highest priority. Following Status 2B, livers will be offered for patients with an assigned status of 3 in descending point sequence with the patient having the highest number of points receiving the highest priority.

---

*United Network for Organ Sharing (UNOS). 1999 Policies. Available at www.unos.org/About/policy_policies3.6.htm (accessed April 16, 1999).

Livers will not be offered to patients with a status of 7. Livers will be allocated in the following sequence:

Local

1. Status 1 patients in descending point order
2. Status 2A patients in descending point order
3. Status 2B patients in descending point order
4. Status 3 patients in descending point order

Regional

1. Status 1 patients in descending point order
2. Status 2A patients in descending point order
3. Status 2B patients in descending point order
4. Status 3 patients in descending point order

National

1. Status 1 patients in descending point order
2. Status 2A patients in descending point order
3. Status 2B patients in descending point order
4. Status 3 patients in descending point order

The liver must be transplanted into the original designee or be released back to the donor center or to the UNOS Organ Center for distribution. The final decision whether to use the organ will remain the prerogative of the transplant surgeon and/or physician responsible for the care of that patient. This will allow physicians and surgeons to exercise judgment about the suitability of the organ being offered for their specific patients; to be faithful to their personal and programmatic philosophy about such controversial matters as the importance of cold ischemia and anatomic anomalies; and to give their best assessment of the prospective recipient's medical condition at the moment. If an organ is declined for a patient, a notation of the reason for the decision not to accept the liver for that patient must be made on the appropriate UNOS form and promptly submitted to UNOS.

BOX C-1 Amended UNOS Policy 3.6—Allocation of Livers (Approved by the UNOS Board of Directors on June 24, 1999 and will be implemented immediately following programming modifications to the UNOS computer system.)

3.6 Allocation of Livers. Unless otherwise approved according to Policies 3.1.7 (Local and Alternative Local Unit), 3.1.8 (Sharing Arrangement and Sharing Agreement), 3.1.9 (Alternate Point Assignments [Variances]), and Policy 3.4.6 (Application, Review, Dissolution, and Modification Processes for Alternative Organ Distribution or Allocation Systems), the allocation of livers according to the following point system is mandatory first locally, then regionally, and then nationally. Each patient will be assigned a status code corresponding to the degree of medical urgency as described in Policy 3.6.4 below. Each patient also will be assigned points for conditions as described in Policies 3.3.5, 3.6.2, 3.6.3, and 3.6.4.

Livers will be offered for patients with an assigned status of 1 in descending point sequence with the patient having the highest number of points receiving the highest priority before being offered for patients listed in other status categories. Following Status 1, livers will be offered for patients with an assigned status of 2A in descending point sequence with the patient having the highest number of points receiving the highest priority before being offered for patients listed in less urgent statuses.

Following Status 2A, livers will be offered for patients with an assigned status of 2B in descending point sequence with the patient having the highest number of points receiving the highest priority. Following Status 2B, livers will be offered for patients with an assigned status of 3 in descending point sequence with the patient having the highest number of points receiving the highest priority. Livers will not be offered to patients with a status of 7. Livers will be allocated in the following sequence:

Local
1. Status 1 patients in descending point order
~~2. Status 2A patients in descending point order~~
~~3. Status 2B patients in descending point order~~
~~4. Status 3 patients in descending point order~~

Regional
~~1~~2. Status 1 patients in descending point order
~~2. Status 2A patients in descending point order~~
~~3. Status 2B patients in descending point order~~
~~4. Status 3 patients in descending point order~~

Local
3. Status 2A patients in descending point order
4. Status 2B patients in descending point order
5. Status 3 patients in descending point order

[*Continued*]

Regional

6. Status 2A patients in descending point order
7. Status 2B patients in descending point order
8. Status 3 patients in descending point order

National

~~1~~ 9. Status 1 patients in descending point order
~~2~~ 10. Status 2A patients in descending point order
~~3~~ 11. Status 2B patients in descending point order
~~4~~ 12. Status 3 patients in descending point order

(NO FURTHER CHANGES TO TEXT OF UNOS POLICY 3.6)

3.6.1 Preliminary Stratification. For every potential liver recipient, the acceptable donor size must be determined by the responsible surgeon. The UNOS Match System will consider only potential liver recipients who are an acceptable size for that particular donor liver.

3.6.2 Blood Type Similarity Points. Except as specified in Policy 3.6.2.1 and 3.6.2.2, transplant candidates with the same ABO type as the liver donor shall receive 10 points. Candidates with compatible but not identical ABO types shall receive 5 points, and candidates with incompatible types shall receive 0 points. Blood type O candidates who will accept a liver from an A_2 blood type donor shall receive 5 points for ABO incompatible matching.

> **3.6.2.1 Blood Type O Liver Allocation**. Blood type O livers shall not be transplanted into Status 2B or 3 candidates who are not a blood type O.
>
> **3.6.2.2 Liver Allocation to Candidates Registered Under Blood Type 'Z'**. The blood type 'Z' designation may be added as a suffix to a candidate's actual blood type, (e.g., 'AZ') only for Status 1 candidates, or Status 2A candidates, who will accept a liver from a donor of any blood type. Liver candidates registered under blood type Z shall receive 0 points for ABO incompatible matching.

3.6.3 Time Waiting. The 'time of waiting' begins when a patient is initially placed on the UNOS Patient Waiting List. Ten points will be accrued by the patient waiting for the longest period for a liver transplant and proportionately fewer points will be accrued by those patients with shorter tenure. For example, if there were 75 persons of O blood type waiting who were of a size compatible with a blood group O donor, the person waiting the longest would accrue 10 points ($75/75 \times 10$). A person whose rank order was 60 would accrue 2 points. ($75 - 60/75 \times 10 = 2$)

3.6.3.1 Statuses 1 and 2A Liver Patients. Time of waiting will be calculated for Status 1 and Status 2A liver patients from the time the patient is listed as a Status 1 or 2A and will only include time listed as a Status 1 or 2A.

3.6.3.2 Waiting Time for Liver Transplant Candidates in an Inactive Status. Patients shall be allowed to accrue an aggregate of 30 days inactive status waiting time. A patient's waiting time accrued during each occurrence of inactivation shall be calculated on a cumulative basis so that once the 30-day aggregate limit is reached no additional waiting time shall accrue on further occurrences of inactivation.

3.6.4 Degree of Medical Urgency. Each patient is assigned a status code which corresponds to how medically urgent it is that the patient receive a transplant.

3.6.4.1 Adult Patient Status. Medical urgency is assigned to an adult liver transplant patient (greater than or equal to 18 years of age) based on the criteria set forth in Table 1 and defined as follows. A patient who does not meet the criteria for a particular status may nevertheless be assigned to such status upon application by his/her transplant physician(s) and justification to the applicable Regional Review Board that the patient is considered, using accepted medical criteria, to have an urgency and potential for benefit comparable to that of other patients in this status as defined below. The justification must include a rationale for incorporating the exceptional case as part of the criteria. A report of the decision of the Regional Review Board and the basis for it shall be forwarded to UNOS for review by the Liver and Intestinal Organ Transplantation and Membership and Professional Standards Committees to determine consistency in application among and within regions and continued appropriateness of the patient status criteria.

Status	Definitions
7	A patient listed as Status 7 is temporarily inactive; however, the patient continues accruing waiting time up to a maximum of 30 days. UNOS staff will confirm the inactive status at the end of 30 days. Patients who are considered to be temporarily unsuitable transplant patients are listed as Status 7, temporarily inactive.
3	A patient listed as Status 3 requires continuous medical care and has a Child-Turcotte-Pugh (CTP) score greater than or equal to 7. Status 3 patients may be followed at home or near the transplant center. Short hospitalizations for intercurrent problems are not considered justifications for a change in status.
2B	A patient listed as Status 2B has a CTP score greater than or equal to 10, or a CTP score greater than or equal to 7 and meets at least one of the following medical criteria: *[Continued]*

(i) Document unresponsive active variceal hemorrhage; Endoscopically confirmed variceal hemorrhage requiring at least two units of red blood cell replacement which continues or recurs after a series of endoscopic sclerotherapy/banding treatments to ablate the varices, or endoscopically confirmed portal hypertensive gastropathy requiring at least two units of red blood cell replacement which continues or recurs. For either variceal or gastropathy hemorrhage, transjugular intrahepatic portosystemic shunt placement (TIPS), or other surgical shunt, must be either contraindicated or failed to control the bleeding.

(ii) Hepatorenal syndrome; The presence of progressive deterioration of renal function in a patient with advanced liver disease requiring hospitalization for management, with no other known etiology of renal insufficiency, and a rising serum creatinine of 1.5 mg/dl. In addition to these major criteria, the patient should meet at least one of the following: a) urine volume < 500 ml/d; b) urine sodium < 10 mEq/ml; or c) urine osmolality > plasma osmolality (U/P ratio > 1.0).

(iii) Spontaneous bacterial peritonitis; The occurrence of a single episode of spontaneous bacterial peritonitis documented by at least one of the following: a) a positive culture of ascitic fluid for bacteria; b) a gram stain of ascitic fluid positive for the presence of bacteria; or c) any polymorphonuclear cells per milliliter, or a total of 500 white blood cells per milliliter.

(iv) Refractory-Ascites/Hepato-Hydrothorax; Severe persistent ascites or hepato-hydrothorax unresponsive to diuretic and salt restriction therapy and requiring either large volume paracenteses of at least 4 liters, or for respiratory distress, more frequently than every 2 weeks with a contraindication or failure of a TIPS procedure to control ascites.

A completed Liver Status 2B Justification Form must be received by UNOS within one working day of a patient's listing as a Status 2B. If a completed Liver Status 2B Justification Form is not received by UNOS within one working day of a patient's listing as a Status 2B, the patient shall be re-assigned to a Status 3. The appropriateness of each Status 2B patient listing shall be re-assessed by the listing transplant center at 6 months from the date the patient is initially listed as a Status 2B and every 6 months thereafter. This reassessment must be based on clinical information (e.g., laboratory test results and diagnosis) that is obtained within the prior 30 days. A completed Liver Status 2B Justification Form must be received by UNOS 6 months from the date the patient is initially listed as a Status 2B and every 6 months thereafter for the duration of the patient's listing as a Status 2B. UNOS shall notify the listing transplant center of the need to reassess a Status 2B patient 30 days prior to the 6-month deadline. If a completed Liver Status 2B Justification Form is not received by UNOS 6 months from the date the patient is initially listed as a Status 2B and every 6 months thereafter, the patient shall be re-assigned to a Status 3.

Status		Definitions
2A		Status 2A provides a transition for currently listed adult patients with chronic liver disease who may have qualified for Status 1, as this category was defined prior to July 4, 1997, and an opportunity to assess the usefulness of such a category when monitored by UNOS Regional Review Boards. An upgrade to Status 2A shall be reviewed by the applicable UNOS Regional Review Board and is intended for the exceptional patient with chronic liver disease who meets the criteria for Status 2B and whose clinical condition acutely deteriorates as defined by the following criteria.
		A patient listed as Status 2A is in the hospital's critical care unit due to chronic liver failure with a life expectancy without a liver transplant of less than 7 days, and with a long-term prognosis with a successful liver transplant equivalent to that of a patient with fulminant liver failure. The patient also has a CTP score greater than or equal to 10 and meets at least one of the following medical criteria:
	(i)	Documented unresponsive active variceal hemorrhage; Endoscopically confirmed variceal hemorrhage requiring at least two units of red blood cell replacement which continues or recurs after a series of endoscopic sclerotherapy/banding treatments to ablate the varices, or endoscopically confirmed portal hypertensive gastropathy requiring at least two units of red blood cell replacement which continues or recurs. For either variceal or gastropathy hemorrhage, transjugular intrahepatic portosystemic shunt placement (TIPS), or other surgical shunt, must be either contraindicated or failed to control the bleeding.
	(ii)	Hepatorenal syndrome; The presence of progressive deterioration of renal function in a patient with advanced liver disease requiring hospitalization for management, with no other known etiology of renal insufficiency, and a rising serum creatinine of 1.5 mg/dl. In addition to these major criteria, the patient should meet at least one of the following: a) urine volume < 500 ml/d; b) urine sodium < 10 mEq/ml; or c) urine osmolality > plasma osmolality (U/P ratio > 1.0).
	(iii)	Refractory Ascites/Hepato-Hydrothorax; Severe persistent ascites or hepato-hydrothorax unresponsive to diuretic and salt restriction therapy and requiring either large volume paracenteses of at least 4 liters, or for respiratory distress, more frequently than every 2 weeks with a contraindication or failure of a TIPS procedure to control ascites.
	(iv)	Stage III or IV encephalopathy unresponsive to medical therapy; A patient shall not be listed as Status 2A if the patient meets at least one of the following medical criteria:

[*Continued*]

(i)	Extrahepatic sepsis unresponsive to antimicrobial therapy;
(ii)	Requirement for high-dose, or 2 or more pressors to maintain adequate blood pressure;
(iii)	Severe irreversible multi-organ system failure.

Patients who are listed as a Status 2A automatically revert back to Status 2B after 7 days unless these patients are relisted as Status 2A by an attending physician. A completed Liver Status 2A Justification Form must be received by UNOS within 24 hours of a patient's original listing as a Status 2A and each relisting as a Status 2A. If a completed Liver Status 2A Justification Form is not received by UNOS within 24 hours of the Status 2A liver candidate registration on the waiting list, the candidate shall be reassigned to a Status 2B. A relisting request to continue a Status 2A listing for the same patient waiting on that specific transplant beyond 14 days accumulated time will result in an on-site review of all local Status 2 liver patient listings.

Status		Definitions
1		A patient greater than or equal to 18 years of age listed as Status 1 has fulminant liver failure with a life expectancy without a liver transplant of less than 7 days. For the purpose of Policy 3.6, fulminant liver failure shall be defined as:
	(i)	Fulminant hepatic failure defined as the onset of hepatic encephalopathy within 8 weeks of the first symptoms of liver disease. The absence of pre-existing liver disease is critical to the diagnosis. While no single clinical observation or laboratory test defines fulminant hepatic failure, the diagnosis is based on the finding of stage II encephalopathy (i.e., drowsiness, inappropriate behavior, incontinence with asterixis) in a patient with severe liver dysfunction. Evidence of severe liver dysfunction may be manifest by some or all of the following symptoms and signs: asterixis (flapping tremor), hyperbilirubinemia (i.e., bilirubin > 15 mg%), marked prolongation of the prothrombin time (i.e., > 20 sec or INR > 2.5), or hypoglycemia.; or
	(ii)	Primary non-function of a transplanted liver within 7 days of implantation; or
	(iii)	Hepatic artery thrombosis in a transplanted liver within 7 days of implantation; or
	(iv)	Acute decompensated Wilson's disease.

Patients who are listed as a Status 1 automatically revert back to Status 2B after 7 days unless these patients are relisted as Status 1 by an attending physician. A patient listed as Status 1 shall be reviewed by the applicable UNOS Regional Review Board. A completed Liver Status 1 Justification Form must be received by UNOS within 24 hours of a patient's original listing as a Status 1 and each relisting as a Status 1. If a completed Liver Status 1 Justification Form is not received by UNOS within 24 hours of the Status 1 liver candidate registration on the waiting list, the candidate shall be reassigned to a Status 2B. A relisting request to continue a Status 1 listing for the same patient waiting on that specific transplant beyond 14 days accumulated time will result in an on-site review of all local Status 2 and 1 liver patient listings.

TABLE C-1 Child-Turcotte-Pugh (CTP) Scoring Systems to Assess Severity of Liver Disease

Points	1	2	
Encephalopathy	None	1–2	3–4
Ascites	Absent	Slight (or controlled by diuretics)	*At least moderate despite diuretic treatment*
Bilirubin (mg/dl)	<2	2–3	>3
Albumin ((g/dl)	<3.5	2.8–3.5	<2.8
Prothrombin time (secs. Prolonged)	<4	4-6	>6
Or (INR)	<1.7	1.7–2.3	>2.3
For primary biliary cirrhosis, primary sclerosing cholangitis, or other cholestatic liver disease: Bilirubin (mg/dl)*	<4	4–10	>10

*For cholestatic liver diseases, these values for bilirubin are to be substituted for the values above.

3.6.4.2 Pediatric Patient Status. Medical urgency is assigned to a pediatric liver transplant patient (less than 18 years of age) based on the criteria defined as follows, including criteria set forth in Appendix 3B. A patient who does not meet the criteria for a particular status may nevertheless be assigned to such status upon application by his/her transplant physician(s) and justification to the applicable Regional Review Board that the patient is considered, using accepted medical criteria, to have an urgency and potential for benefit comparable to that of other patients in this status as defined below. The justification must include a rationale for incorporating the exceptional case as part of the criteria. A report of the decision of the Regional Review Board and the basis for it shall be forwarded to UNOS for review by the Liver and Intestinal Organ Transplantation and Membership and Professional Standards committees to determine consistency in application among and within regions and continued appropriateness of the patient status criteria.

Status		Definitions
7		A pediatric patient listed as Status 7 is temporarily inactive; however, the patient continues accruing waiting time up to a maximum of 30 days. UNOS staff will confirm the inactive status at the end of 30 days. Patients who are considered to be temporarily unsuitable transplant patients are listed as Status 7, temporarily inactive.
3		A pediatric patient listed as Status 3 has met the inclusion criteria to be listed for pediatric liver transplantation as set forth in Appendix 3B, and requires continuous medical care. Status 3 patients may be followed at home or near the transplant center. Short hospitalizations for intercurrent problems are not considered justification for a change in status.
2B		A pediatric patient listed as Status 2B meets at least one of the following medical criteria:
	(i)	Documented, unresponsive upper gastrointestinal bleeding requiring transfusion of at least 10 cc/kg of red blood cells.
	(ii)	Hepatorenal syndrome; The presence of progressive deterioration of renal function in a patient with advanced liver disease requiring hospitalization for management, with no other known etiology of renal insufficiency, and a rising serum creatinine 3 times baseline. In addition to these major criteria, the patient should meet at least one of the following: a) urine volume < 10 ml/kg/d; b) urine sodium < 10 mEq/l; or c) urine osmolality > plasma osmolality (U/P ratio > 1.0).
	(iii)	Spontaneous bacterial peritonitis; The occurrence of a single episode of spontaneous bacterial peritonitis documented by at least one of the following: a) a positive culture of ascitic fluid for bacteria; b) a gram stain of ascitic fluid positive for the presence of bacteria; or c) an ascitic fluid white blood cell count with greater than 300 polymorphonuclear cells per milliliter, or a total of 500 white blood cells per milliliter.
	(iv)	Refractory Ascites/Hepato-Hydrothorax; Severe persistent ascites or hepatohydrothorax defined as any one of the following: unresponsive to diuretic and salt restriction therapy leading to respiratory distress, or requiring supplemental tube feeding, or requiring parenteral nutrition, or requiring paracenteses.
	(v)	Recurrent cholangitis defined as 2 or more episodes in 6 months requiring hospitalization and intravenous antibiotics.
	(vi)	Growth failure, that is < 5th percentile for weight and/or height, or loss of *1.5 standard deviations score of expected growth* (height or weight) based on the National Institute of Health Statistics for pediatric growth curves and requiring initiation of parenteral nutritional support, or nasogastric feedings to supply a minimum of 30 percent of caloric needs.
	(vii)	A patient who meets at least 3 of the 5 following criteria: 1) ascites requiring diuretic therapy 2) bilirubin > 4 mg/dl 3) albumin < 3 g/dl (4) INR > 1.7 (5) malnutrition defined as loss of 1 standard deviation score of expected growth.

A completed Liver Status 2B Justification Form must be received by UNOS within one working day of a pediatric patient's listing as a Status 2B. If a completed Liver Status 2B Justification Form is not received by UNOS within one working day of a patient's listing as a Status 2B, the patient shall be re-assigned to a Status 3. The appropriateness of each Status 2B patient listing shall be re-assessed by the listing transplant center at 6 months from the date the patient is initially listed as a Status 2B and every 6 months thereafter. This reassessment must be based on clinical information (e.g., laboratory test results and diagnosis) that is obtained within the prior 30 days. A completed Liver Status 2B Justification Form must be received by UNOS 6 months from the date the patient is initially listed as a Status 2B and every 6 months thereafter for the duration of the patient's listing as a Status 2B. UNOS shall notify the listing transplant center of the need to reassess a Status 2B patient 30 days prior to the 6-month deadline. If a completed Liver Status 2B Justification Form is not received by UNOS 6 months from the date the patient is initially listed as a Status 2B and every 6 months thereafter, the patient shall be re-assigned to a Status 3.

Status		Definitions
1		A pediatric patient listed as Status 1 is located in the hospital's Intensive Care Unit (ICU) due to acute or chronic liver failure, has a life expectancy without a liver transplant of less than 7 days and meets at least 1 of the following criteria:
	(i)	Fulminant hepatic failure defined as the onset of hepatic encephalopathy within 8 weeks of the first symptoms of liver disease. The absence of pre-existing liver disease is critical to the diagnosis. While no single clinical observation or laboratory test defines fulminant hepatic failure, the diagnosis is based on the finding of stage II encephalopathy (i.e., drowsiness, inappropriate behavior, incontinence with asterixis) in a patient with severe liver dysfunction. Evidence of severe liver dysfunction may be manifest by some or all of the following symptoms and signs: asterixis (flapping tremor), hyperbilirubinemia (i.e., bilirubin > 15 mg%), marked prolongation of the prothrombin time (i.e., > 20 sec or INR > 2.5), or hypoglycemia.
	(ii)	Primary non-function of a transplanted liver within 7 days of implantation.
	(iii)	Hepatic artery thrombosis in a transplanted liver within 7 days of implantation.
	(iv)	Acute decompensated Wilson's disease.
	(v)	On mechanical ventilator.
	(vi)	Upper gastrointestinal bleeding requiring at least 10 cc/kg of red blood cell replacement which continues or recurs despite treatment.

[*Continued*]

(vii) Hepatorenal syndrome; The presence of progressive deterioration of renal function in a patient with advanced liver disease requiring hospitalization for management, with no other known etiology of renal insufficiency, and a rising serum creatinine 3 times baseline. In addition to these major criteria, the patient should meet at least one of the following: a) urine volume < 10 ml/kg/d; b) urine sodium < 10 mEq/l; or c) urine osmolality > plasma osmolality (U/P ratio > 1.0).

(viii) Stage III or IV encephalopathy unresponsive to medical therapy.

(ix) Refractory Ascites/Hepato-Hydrothorax; Severe persistent ascites or hepatohydrothorax, defined as any one of the following: unresponsive to diuretic and salt restriction therapy leading to respiratory distress, or requiring supplemental tube feeding, or requiring parenteral nutrition, or requiring supplemental oxygen, or requiring paracentesis.

(x) Biliary sepsis requiring pressor support of 5 mcg/kg/min of dopamine or greater.

With the exception of hospitalized pediatric liver transplant candidates with Ornithinine Transcarbamylase Deficiency (OTC) or Crigler-Najjar Disease Type I, patients who are listed as a Status 1 automatically revert back to Status 2B after 7 days unless these patients are relisted as Status 1 by an attending physician. A patient listed as Status 1 shall be reviewed by the applicable UNOS Regional Review Board. A completed Liver Status 1 Justification Form must be received by UNOS within 24 hours of a patient's original listing as a Status 1 and each relisting as a Status 1. If a completed Liver Status 1 Justification Form is not received by UNOS within 24 hours of the Status 1 liver candidate registration on the waiting list, the candidate shall be reassigned to a Status 2B. A relisting request to continue a Status 1 listing for the same patient waiting on that specific transplant beyond 14 days accumulated time will result in an on-site review of all local Status 2 and 1 liver patient listings.

3.6.4.3 Pediatric Liver Transplant Candidates with OTC or Crigler-Najjar Disease Type I. A pediatric liver transplant candidate with Ornithine Transcarbamylase Deficiency (OTC) or Crigler-Najjar Disease Type I shall be registered as a Status 2B and may be upgraded to a Status 1 if the patient is hospitalized for an acute exacerbation of his or her disease. The patient shall remain a Status 1 as long as he or she remains hospitalized.

3.6.4.4 Liver Transplant Candidates with Hepatocellular Carcinoma (HCC). A patient with HCC may be registered as a Status 2B if the patient meets all of the following medical criteria:

(i) The patient has known HCC and has undergone a thorough assessment to evaluate the number and size of tumors and to rule out any extrahepatic spread and/or macrovascular involvement (i.e., portal or hepatic veins). A pre-listing biopsy is not mandatory but the lesion must meet established imaging criteria. Histological grade, the presence of encapsulation or histological classification (fibrolamellar versus nonfibrolamellar) are not considered in determining the patient's listing as a Status 2B since a pre-listing biopsy is not required. The assessment of the patient should include ultrasound of the patient's liver, a computerized tomography (CT) or magnetic resonance imaging (MRI) scan of the abdomen and chest, and a bone scan. A re-assessment of the patient must be performed at every 3-month interval that the patient is on the UNOS waiting list.

(ii) The patient has Stage I or Stage II HCC in accordance with the modified Tumor-Node-Metastasis (TNM) classification set forth in the following Table 2, or the patient has an alpha fetoprotein level that is rising on 3 consecutive occasions with an absolute value $\geq$ 500 nanograms even though there is no evidence of a tumor based on imaging studies.

(iii) The patient is not a resection candidate.

A patient with HCC at Stage III or higher may continue to be considered a liver transplant candidate in accordance with each center's own specific policy or philosophy, but the patient must be listed as a Status 3, unless the candidate meets the other criteria specified for Status 2B or 2A in Policy 3.6.4. In addition, a patient with HCC must be reviewed by the applicable UNOS liver regional review board prior to being upgraded to a Status 2B.

TABLE C-2 American Liver Tumor Study Group Modified Tumor-Node-Metastasis (TNM) Staging Classification (1)

Classification	Definition
TX, NX, MX	Not assessed
TO, NO, MO	Not found
T1	1 nodule < 1.9 cm
T2	One nodule 2.0–5.0 cm; two or three nodules, all < 3.0
T3	One nodule > 5.0 cm; two or three nodules, all > 3.0
T4a	Four or more nodules, any size
T4b	T2, T3, or T4a plus gross intrahepatic portal or hepatic vein involvement as indicated by CT, MRI, or ultrasound
N1	Regional (portal hepatic) nodes, involved
M1	Metastatic disease, including extrahepatic portal or hepatic vein involvement
Stage I	T1
Stage II	T2
Stage III	T3
Stage IV	A1 T4a
Stage IV	A2 T4b
Stage IV	B Any N1, any M1

Reference:

1. American Liver Tumor Study Group—A Randomized Prospective Multi-Institutional Trial of Orthotopic Liver Transplantation or Partial Hepatic Resection with or without Adjuvant Chemotherapy for Hepatocellular Carcinoma. Investigators Booklet and Protocol. 1998.

3.6.4.4.1 Pediatric Liver Transplant Candidates with Hepatoblastoma. A pediatric patient with non-metastatic hepatoblastoma who is otherwise a suitable candidate for liver transplantation may be registered as a Status 2B on the UNOS Patient Waiting List.

3.6.4.5 Status Verification for Potential Liver Recipients. As a condition for liver acceptance, it is the responsibility of the accepting surgeon to verify the status of the candidate for whom the liver is offered. If it is determined that the actual status of the candidate is lower than the UNOS waiting list status by which the offer was made, then the procuring OPO shall be notified and the points for the candidate in question shall be re-calculated after the candidate's waiting list status has been appropriately downgraded.

3.6.5 Center Contact and Acceptance. Livers shall be offered in descending computer print-out order but the offering calls may be made concurrently (e.g., 5 liver teams may be called and given donor information provided that each team is told its priority number for the liver offer). Policy 3.4.1 (Time Limit for Acceptance) assures that each team will know within one hour whether or not another center with a patient who has higher points has accepted or rejected the offer.

3.6.6 Removal of Liver Transplant Candidates from Liver Waiting Lists When Transplanted or Deceased. If a liver transplant candidate on the UNOS Patient Waiting List has received a transplant from a cadaveric or living donor, or has died while awaiting a transplant, the listing center, or centers if the patient is multiple-listed, shall immediately remove that patient from all liver waiting lists and shall notify UNOS within 24 hours of the event. If the liver recipient is again added to a liver waiting list, waiting time shall begin as of the date and time the patient is relisted.

3.6.7 UNOS Organ Center Assistance with Liver Allocation. It is recommended that the UNOS Organ Center be notified when a liver donor is identified and provided all clinical information that is necessary to offer the liver to potential recipients on the UNOS Patient Waiting List. Upon request by the OPO, the Organ Center shall attempt to locate a liver recipient on the UNOS Patient Waiting List or identify backup recipients for the liver.

3.6.8 Local Conflicts. Regarding allocation of livers, locally unresolvable inequities or conflicts that arise from prevailing OPO policies may be submitted by any interested local member for review and adjudication to the UNOS Liver and Intestinal Organ Transplantation Committee and Board of Directors.

3.6.9 Minimum Information for Liver Offers.
Essential Information Category. When the Host OPO or donor center provides the following donor information, with the exception of pending serologies, to a recipient center, the recipient center must respond to the offer within one hour pursuant to UNOS Policy 3.4.1 (Time Limit for Acceptance); however, this requirement does not preclude the Host OPO from notifying a recipient center prior to this information being available:

(i) Donor name and UNOS I.D. number, age, sex, race, height, and weight;
(ii) ABO type;
(iii) Cause of brain death/diagnosis;
(iv) History of treatment in hospital including current medications, vasopressors, and hydration;
(v) Current history of hypotensive episodes, urine output, and oliguria;
(vi) Indications of sepsis;

(vii) Social and drug activity histories;
(viii) Vital signs including blood pressure, heart rate, and temperature;
(ix) Other laboratory tests within the past 12 hours including:
(1) Bilirubin
(2) SGOT/AST
(3) PT
(4) BUN
(5) Electrolytes
(6) WBC
(7) HH
(8) Creatinine;
(9) Arterial blood gas results;
(10) Pre- or post-transfusion serologies for HIV, hepatitis, CMV, HTLV, and VDRL/RPR.

3.6.10 Allocation of Livers for Other Methods of Hepatic Support. A liver shall not be utilized for other methods of hepatic support prior to being offered first for transplantation. Prior to being utilized for other methods of hepatic support, the liver shall be offered by the UNOS Organ Center in descending point order to all Status 1 candidates, Status 2A candidates, and ABO-compatible Status 2B candidates in the Host OPO's region followed by Status 1 candidates, Status 2A candidates, and ABO-compatible Status 2B candidates in all other regions. If the liver is not accepted for transplantation within 6 hours of attempted placement by the Organ Center, the Organ Center shall offer the liver to Status 1 and Status 2A candidates for whom the liver will be considered for other methods of hepatic support. Livers allocated for other methods of hepatic support shall be offered first locally, then regionally, and then nationally in descending point order to transplant candidates designated for other methods of hepatic support.

3.6.11 Allocation of Livers for Segmental Transplantation. A transplant center that accepts a liver for segmental transplantation may allocate the remaining segment to any medically appropriate candidate on the UNOS Patient Waiting List. If the segment is not allocated for transplantation, it should be offered for other methods of hepatic support as stated in Policy 3.6.10.

D

The "Final Rule"

DEPARTMENT OF HEALTH AND HUMAN SERVICES
42 CFR Part 121
Organ Procurement and Transplantation Network; Final Rule
(63 Federal Register 16295, at 16332, April 2, 1998)

PART 121—ORGAN PROCUREMENT AND TRANSPLANTATION NETWORK

Sec.
121.1 Applicability.
121.2 Definitions.
121.3 The OPTN.
121.4 OPTN Policies; Secretarial review and appeals.
121.5 Listing requirements.
121.6 Organ procurement.
121.7 Identification of organ recipient.
121.8 Allocation of organs.
121.9 Designated transplant program requirements.
121.10 Reviews, evaluation, and enforcement.
121.11 Record maintenance and reporting requirements.
121.12 Preemption.

Authority: Sections 215, 371–376 of the Public Health Service Act (42 U.S.C. 216, 273–274d); Sections 1102, 1106, 1138 and 1872 of the Social Security Act (42 U.S.C. 1302, 1306, 1320b-8 and 1395ii).

§Sec. 121.1 Applicability.

(a) The provisions of this part apply to the operation of the Organ Procurement and Transplantation Network (OPTN) and to the Scientific Registry.
(b) In accordance with Section 1138 of the Social Security Act, hospitals in which organ transplants are performed and which participate in the programs under titles XVIII or XIX of that Act, and organ procurement organizations designated under Section 1138(b)(1)(F) of the Social Security Act, are subject to the requirements of this part.

§Sec. 121.2 Definitions.

As used in this part—Act means the Public Health Service Act, as amended. Designated transplant program means a transplant program that has been found to meet the requirements of Sec. 121.9.

Family member means a family member of a transplant candidate, transplant recipient, or organ donor.

National list means the OPTN computer-based list of transplant candidates nationwide.

OPTN computer match program means a set of computer-based instructions which compares data on a cadaveric organ donor with data on transplant candidates on the national list and ranks the candidates according to OPTN policies to determine the priority for allocating the donor organ(s).

Organ means a human kidney, liver, heart, lung, or pancreas, and for purposes of the Scientific Registry, the term also includes bone marrow.

Organ donor means a human being who is the source of an organ for transplantation into another human being.

Organ procurement organization or OPO means an entity so designated by the Secretary under Section 1138(b) of the Social Security Act. Organ procurement and transplantation network or OPTN means the network established pursuant to Section 372 of the Act.

Potential transplant recipient or potential recipient means a transplant candidate who has been ranked by the OPTN computer match program as the person to whom an organ from a specific cadaveric organ donor is to be offered.

Scientific Registry means the registry of information on transplant recipients established pursuant to Section 373 of the Act.

Secretary means the Secretary of Health and Human Services and any official of the Department of Health and Human Services to whom the authority involved has been delegated.

Transplant candidate means an individual who has been identified as medically suited to benefit from an organ transplant and has been placed on the national list by the individual's transplant program.

Transplant hospital means a hospital in which organ transplants are performed.

Transplant physician means a physician who provides non-surgical care and treatment to transplant patients before and after transplant.

Transplant program means a component within a transplant hospital which provides transplantation of a particular type of organ. Transplant recipient means a person who has received an organ transplant. Transplant surgeon means a physician who provides surgical care and treatment to transplant recipients.

§Sec. 121.3 The OPTN.

(a) Composition of the Board. (1) The OPTN shall establish a Board of Directors of whatever size the OPTN determines appropriate, provided that it includes at least the following members: (i) Six members representing the following categories (two members from each category):

(A) Transplant coordinators;

(B) Organ procurement organizations;

(C) Histocompatibility experts;

(ii) Eight individuals representing transplant candidates, transplant recipients, organ donors, and family members;

(iii) Ten members from the following categories (two members each):

(A) Transplant surgeons;

(B) Transplant physicians;

(C) Transplant hospitals;

(D) Voluntary health associations; and

(E) Other experts from related fields including medical examiners, hospital administration, or donor hospital personnel in such fields as trauma, emergency medical services, critical care, neurology, or neurosurgery; and

(iv) Six members from the general public from fields such as behavioral science, computer science, economics, ethics, health care financing, law, policy analysis, sociology, statistics, or theology. These members need not have technical expertise in organ donation or allocation.

(2) None of the members who are transplant recipients, transplant candidates, organ donors, family members, or general public members under paragraph (a)(1) of this section shall be employees of, or have a similar relationship with, the categories of members listed in paragraph (a)(1)(i) or paragraph (a)(1)(iii) or the OPTN.

(3) The Board of Directors shall include:

(i) Individuals representing the diversity of the population of transplant candidates and recipients served by the OPTN, including, to the extent practicable, minority and gender representation reflecting the population of potential transplant candidates served by the OPTN;

(ii) No more than 50 percent transplant surgeons or transplant physicians; and

(iii) At least 25 percent transplant candidates, transplant recipients, organ donors, and family members.

(4) Individuals on the Board shall be elected for a two-year term.

(b) Duties of the OPTN Board of Directors. (1) Executive Committee. The Board of Directors shall elect an Executive Committee from the membership of the Board. The Executive Committee shall include at least one member who is a transplant candidate, transplant recipient, organ donor, or family member; one general public member, one OPO representative, and not more than 50 percent transplant surgeons and transplant physicians.

(2) Executive Director. The Board of Directors shall appoint an Executive Director of the OPTN. The Executive Director may be reappointed upon the Board's determination that the responsibilities of this position have been accomplished successfully.

(3) Committees. The Board of Directors shall establish such other committees as are necessary to perform the duties of the OPTN. Committees established by the Board of Directors shall include:

(i) Representation by transplant coordinators, organ procurement organizations, and transplant hospitals, and at least one transplant candidate, transplant recipient, organ donor, or family member; and

(ii) to the extent practicable, minority and gender representation reflecting the diversity of the population of potential transplant candidates served by the OPTN.

(4) The Board of Directors shall develop and propose policies for the equitable allocation of organs, as described in Sec. 121.8.

(c) Membership of the OPTN. (1) The OPTN shall admit and retain as members the following:

(i) All organ procurement organizations;

(ii) Transplant hospitals participating in the Medicare or Medicaid programs; and

(iii) Other organizations, institutions, and individuals that have an interest in the fields of organ donation or transplantation.

(2) To apply for membership in the OPTN:

(i) An OPO shall provide to the OPTN the name and address of the OPO, and the latest year of designation under section 1138(b) of the Social Security Act;

(ii) A transplant hospital shall provide to the OPTN the name and address of the hospital, a list of its transplant programs by type of organ; and

(iii) Any other organization, institution, or individual eligible under paragraph (c)(1)(iii) of this section shall demonstrate to the OPTN an interest in the fields of organ donation or transplantation.

(3) The OPTN shall accept or reject as members entities or individuals described in paragraph (c)(1)(iii) of this section within 90 days.

(4) Applicants rejected for membership in the OPTN may appeal to the Secretary. Appeals shall be submitted in writing within 30 days of rejection of the application. The Secretary may:

(i) Deny the appeal; or

(ii) Direct the OPTN to take action consistent with the Secretary's response to the appeal.

(d) Corporate Status of the OPTN. (1) The OPTN shall be a private, not-for-profit entity.

(2) The requirements of this section do not apply to any parent, sponsoring, or affiliated organization of the OPTN, or to any activities of the contracting organization that are not integral to the operation of the OPTN. Such an organization is free to establish its own corporate procedures.

(3) No OPTN member is required to become a member of any organization that is a parent, sponsor, contractor, or affiliated organization of the OPTN, to comply with the by-laws of any such organization, or to assume any corporate duties or obligations of any such organization.

(e) Effective date. The organization designated by the Secretary as the OPTN shall have six months from July 1, 1998, or six months from its initial designation as the OPTN, whichever is later, to meet the board composition requirements of paragraph (a) of this section. The organization designated by the Secretary as the OPTN shall have six months from July 1, 1998, or six months from initial designation as the OPTN, whichever is later, to meet any other requirements of this section, except that the Secretary may extend such period for good cause.

§Sec. 121.4 OPTN policies: Secretarial review and appeals.

(a) The OPTN Board of Directors shall be responsible for developing, with the advice of the OPTN membership and other interested parties, policies within the mission of the OPTN as set forth in section 372 of the Act and the Secretary's contract for the operation of the OPTN, including:

(1) Policies for the equitable allocation of cadaveric organs in accordance with Sec. 121.8;

(2) Policies, consistent with recommendations of the Centers for Disease Control and Prevention, for the testing of organ donors and follow-up of transplant recipients to prevent the spread of infectious diseases;

(3) Policies that reduce inequities resulting from socioeconomic status, including, but not limited to:

(i) Ensuring that patients in need of a transplant are listed without regard to ability to pay or source of payment;

(ii) Procedures for transplant hospitals to make reasonable efforts to make available from their own resources, or obtain from other sources, financial resources for patients unable to pay such that these patients have an opportunity to obtain a transplant and necessary follow-up care;

(iii) Recommendations to private and public payers and service providers on ways to improve coverage of organ transplantation and necessary follow-up care; and

(iv) Reform of allocation policies based on assessment of their cumulative effect on socioeconomic inequities;

(4) Policies regarding the training and experience of transplant surgeons and transplant physicians in designated transplant programs as required by Sec. 121.9;

(5) Policies for nominating officers and members of the Board of Directors; and

(6) Policies on such other matters as the Secretary directs.

(b) The Board of Directors shall:

(1) Provide opportunity for the OPTN membership and other interested parties to comment on proposed policies and shall take into account the comments received in developing and adopting policies for implementation by the OPTN; and

(2) Provide, at least 30 days prior to their proposed implementation, proposed policies to the Secretary, who may provide comments and/or objections within a reasonable time, or may publish the policies in the Federal Register to obtain comments from the public. The Board of Directors shall indicate which of the proposed policies it recommends be enforceable under Sec. 121.10. If the Secretary seeks public comments, these comments will be considered and may affect subsequent response to the OPTN. The OPTN shall take into account any comments the Secretary may provide. If the Secretary objects to a policy, the OPTN may be directed to revise the policy consistent with the Secretary's direction. If the OPTN does not revise the policy in a timely manner or if the Secretary otherwise disagrees with its content, the Secretary may take such other action as the Secretary determines appropriate.

(c) The OPTN Board of Directors shall provide the membership and the Secretary with copies of the policies as they are adopted, and make them available to the public upon request. The Secretary will publish lists of these documents in the Federal Register, indicating which ones are subject to the special compliance requirements and potential sanctions of section 1138 of the Social Security Act. The OPTN shall also continuously maintain OPTN policies for public access on the Internet, including current and proposed policies.

(d) The OPTN, or its members, or other individuals, or entities objecting to policies developed by the OPTN or the Secretary may submit appeals to the Secretary in writing. Any such appeal shall include a statement of the basis for the appeal. The Secretary will seek the comments of the OPTN on the issues raised in the appeal of an OPTN-developed policy. Policies remain in effect during the appeal. The Secretary may:

(1) Deny the appeal;

(2) Direct the OPTN to revise the policies consistent with the Secretary's response to the appeal, or

(3) Take such other action as the Secretary determines appropriate.

(e) The OPTN shall implement policies and:

(1) Provide information to OPTN members about these policies and the rationale for them.

(2) Update policies developed in accordance with this section to accommodate scientific and technological advances.

§Sec. 121.5 Listing requirements.

(a) A transplant hospital which is an OPTN member may list individuals only for a designated transplant program.

(b) Transplant hospitals shall assure that individuals are placed on the national list as soon as they are determined to be candidates for transplantation. The OPTN shall advise transplant hospitals of the information needed for such listing.

(c) An OPTN member shall pay a registration fee to the OPTN for each transplant candidate it places on the national list. The amount of such fee shall be determined by the OPTN with the approval of the Secretary. No less often than annually, and whether or not a change is proposed, the OPTN shall submit to the Secretary a statement of its proposed registration fee, together with such supporting information as the Secretary finds necessary to determine the reasonableness or adequacy of the fee schedule and projected revenues. This submission is due at least three months before the beginning of the OPTN's fiscal year. The Secretary will approve, modify, or disapprove the amount of the fee within a reasonable time of receiving the OPTN's submission.

§Sec. 121.6 Organ procurement.

The suitability of organs donated for transplantation shall be determined as follows:

(a) Tests. An OPTN member procuring an organ shall assure that laboratory tests and clinical examinations of potential organ donors are performed to determine any contraindications for donor acceptance, in accordance with policies established by the OPTN.

(b) HIV. Organs from individuals known to be infected with human immunodeficiency virus shall not be procured for transplantation.

(c) Acceptance criteria. Transplant programs shall establish criteria for organ acceptance, and shall provide such criteria to the OPTN and the OPOs with which they are affiliated.

§Sec. 121.7 Identification of organ recipient.

(a) List of potential transplant recipients. (1) An OPTN member procuring an organ shall operate the OPTN computer match program within such time as the OPTN may prescribe to identify and rank potential recipients for each cadaveric organ procured.

(2) The rank order of potential recipients shall be determined for each cadaveric organ using the organ-specific allocation criteria established in accordance with Sec. 121.8.

(3) When a donor or donor organ does not meet a transplant program's donor acceptance criteria, as established under Sec. 121.6(c), transplant candidates of that program shall not be ranked among potential recipients of that organ and shall not appear on a roster of potential recipients of that organ.

(b) Offer of organ for potential recipients. (1) Organs shall be offered for potential recipients in accordance with policies developed under Sec. 121.8 and implemented under Sec. 121.4.

(2) Organs may be offered only to potential recipients listed with transplant programs having designated transplant programs of the same type as the organ procured.

(3) An organ offer is made when all information necessary to determine whether to transplant the organ into the potential recipient has been given to the transplant hospital.

(4) A transplant program shall either accept or refuse the offered organ for the designated potential recipient within such time as the OPTN may prescribe. A transplant program shall document and provide to the OPO and to the OPTN the reasons for refusal and shall maintain this document for one year.

(c) Transportation of organ to potential recipient. (1) Transportation. The OPTN member that procures a donated organ shall arrange for transportation of the organ to the transplant hospital.

(2) Documentation. The OPTN member that is transporting an organ shall assure that it is accompanied by written documentation of activities conducted to determine the suitability of the organ donor and shall maintain this document for one year.

(3) Packaging. The OPTN member that is transporting an organ shall assure that it is packaged in a manner that is designed to maintain the viability of the organ.

(d) Receipt of an organ. Upon receipt of an organ, the transplant hospital responsible for the potential recipient's care shall determine whether to proceed with the transplant. In the event that an organ is not transplanted into the potential recipient, the OPO which has a written agreement with the transplant hospital must offer the organ for another potential recipient in accordance with paragraph (b) of this section.

(e) Wastage. Nothing in this section shall prohibit a transplant program from transplanting an organ into any medically suitable candidate if to do otherwise would result in the organ not being used for transplantation. The transplant program shall notify the OPTN and the OPO which made the organ offer of the circumstances justifying each such action within such time as the OPTN may prescribe.

§Sec. 121.8 Allocation of organs.

(a) Policy development. The Board of Directors established under Sec. 121.3 shall develop, in accordance with the policy development process under Sec. 121.4, organ-specific policies (including combinations of organs, such as for heart-lung transplants) for the equitable allocation of cadaveric organs among potential recipients. Such policies shall meet the requirements in paragraphs (a)(1), (2), (3), (4), and (5) of this section. Such policies shall be reviewed periodically and revised as appropriate.

(1) Minimum listing criteria for including transplant candidates on the national list shall be standardized and, to the extent possible, shall contain explicit thresholds for listing a patient and be expressed through objective and measurable medical criteria.

(2) Transplant candidates shall be grouped by status categories ordered from most to least medically urgent, with a sufficient number of categories to avoid grouping together persons with substantially different medical urgency. Criteria for status designations shall contain explicit thresholds for differentiat-

ing among patients and shall be expressed, to the extent possible, through objective and measurable medical criteria.

(3) Organ allocation policies and procedures shall be in accordance with sound medical judgment and shall be designed and implemented: (i) To allocate organs among transplant candidates in order of decreasing medical urgency status, with waiting time in status used to break ties within status groups. Neither place of residence nor place of listing shall be a major determinant of access to a transplant. For each status category, inter-transplant program variance in the performance indicator waiting time in status shall be as small as can reasonably be achieved, consistent with paragraph (a)(3)(ii) of this section. Priority shall be given to reducing the waiting time variance in the most medically urgent status categories before reducing the waiting time variance in less urgent status categories, if equivalent reductions cannot be achieved in all status categories; and

(ii) To avoid futile transplantation, to avoid wasting organs, and to promote efficient management of organ placement.

(4) The OPTN shall:

(i) Develop mechanisms to promote and review compliance with each of these goals;

(ii) Develop performance indicators to facilitate assessment of how well current and proposed policies will accomplish these goals;

(iii) Use performance indicators, including indicators described in paragraph (a)(4)(iv) of this section, to establish baseline data on how closely the results of current policies approach these goals and to establish the projected amount of improvement to result from proposed policies; and

(iv) Timely report data to the Secretary on performance by organ and status category, including program-specific data, OPO-specific data, data by program size, and data aggregated by organ procurement area, OPTN region, the nation as a whole, and such other geographic areas as the Secretary may designate. Such data shall include inter-transplant program variation in waiting time in status, total life years pre- and post-transplant, patient and graft survival rates following transplantation, patients misclassified by status, and number of patients who die waiting for a transplant. Such data shall cover such intervals of time, and be presented using confidence intervals or other measures of variance, as appropriate to avoid spurious results or erroneous interpretation due to small numbers of patients covered.

(5) Transition. (i) General. When the OPTN revises organ allocation policies under this section, it shall consider whether to adopt transition procedures that would treat people on the national list and awaiting transplantation prior to the adoption or effective date of the revised policies no less favorably than they would have been treated under the previous policies. The transition procedures shall be transmitted to the Secretary for review together with the revised allocation policies.

(ii) Special rule for initial revision of liver allocation policies. When the OPTN transmits to the Secretary its initial revision of the liver allocation policies, as directed by paragraph (c)(2) of this section, it shall include transition procedures that, to the extent feasible, treat each individual on the national list and awaiting transplantation on April 2, 1998, no less favorably than he or she would have been treated had the revised liver allocation policies not become effective. These transition procedures may be limited in duration or applied only to individuals with greater than average medical urgency if this would significantly improve administration of the list or if such limitations would be applied only after accommodating a substantial preponderance of those disadvantaged by the change in the policies.

(b) Secretarial review of policies and performance indicators. The OPTN's transmittal to the Secretary of proposed allocation policies and performance indicators shall include such supporting material, including the results of model-based computer simulations, as the Secretary may require to assess the likely effects of policy changes and as are necessary to demonstrate that the proposed policies comply with the performance indicators and transition procedures of paragraph (a) of this section.

(c) Deadlines for initial reviews. (1) The OPTN shall conduct an initial review of existing allocation policies and, except as provided in paragraph (c)(2) of this section, no later than July 1, 1999, transmit initial revised policies to meet the requirements of Sec. 121.8 (a), together with supporting documentation to the Secretary for review in accordance with Sec. 121.4.

(2) No later than August 31, 1998, the OPTN shall transmit revised policies and supporting documentation for liver allocation to meet the requirements of Sec. 121.8 (a) to the Secretary for review in accordance with Sec. 121.4. The OPTN may transmit these materials without seeking further public comment under Sec. 121.4(b) or (c).

(d) Variances. The OPTN may develop experimental policies that test methods of improving allocation. All such experimental policies shall be accompanied by a research design and include data collection and analysis plans. Such variances shall be time-limited. Entities or individuals objecting to variances may appeal to the Secretary under the procedures of Sec. 121.4.

(e) Directed donation. Nothing in this section shall prohibit the allocation of an organ to a recipient named by those authorized to make the donation.

§Sec. 121.9 Designated transplant program requirements.

(a) To receive organs for transplantation, a transplant program in a hospital that is a member of the OPTN shall abide by these rules and shall:

(1) Be a transplant program approved by the Secretary for reimbursement under Medicare and Medicaid; or

(2) Be an organ transplant program which has adequate resources to provide transplant services to its patients and agrees promptly to notify the OPTN and patients awaiting transplants if it becomes inactive and which:

(i) Has letters of agreement or contracts with an OPO;

(ii) Has on site a transplant surgeon qualified in accordance with policies developed under Sec. 121.4;

(iii) Has on site a transplant physician qualified in accordance with policies developed under Sec. 121.4;

(iv) Has available operating and recovery room resources, intensive care resources and surgical beds, and transplant program personnel;

(v) Shows evidence of collaborative involvement with experts in the fields of radiology, infectious disease, pathology, immunology, anesthesiology, physical therapy and rehabilitation medicine, histocompatibility, and immunogenetics and, as appropriate, hepatology, pediatrics, nephrology with dialysis capability, and pulmonary medicine with respiratory therapy support;

(vi) Has immediate access to microbiology, clinical chemistry, histocompatibility testing, radiology, and blood banking services, as well as the capacity to monitor treatment with immunosuppressive drugs; and

(vii) Makes available psychiatric and social support services for transplant candidates, transplant recipients and their families; or

(3) Be a transplant program in a Department of Veterans Affairs hospital which is a Dean's Committee hospital which shares a common university-based transplant team of a transplant program which meets the requirements of Sec. 121.9(a) (1) or (2).

(b) To apply to be a designated transplant program, transplant programs shall provide to the OPTN such documents as the OPTN may require which show that they meet the requirements of Sec. 121.9(a) (1), (2), or (3).

(c) The OPTN shall, within 90 days, accept or reject applications to be a designated transplant program.

(d) Applicants rejected for designation may appeal to the Secretary. Appeals shall be submitted in writing within 30 days of rejection of the application. The Secretary may:

(1) Deny the appeal; or

(2) Direct the OPTN to take action consistent with the Secretary's response to the appeal.

§Sec. 121.10 Reviews, evaluation, and enforcement.

(a) Review and evaluation by the Secretary. The Secretary or her/his designee may perform any reviews and evaluations of member OPOs and transplant programs which the Secretary deems necessary to carry out her/his responsibilities under the Public Health Service Act and the Social Security Act.

(b) Review and evaluation by the OPTN. (1) The OPTN shall design appropriate plans and procedures, including survey instruments, a peer review process, and data systems, for purposes of:

(i) Reviewing applications submitted under Sec. 121.3(c) for membership in the OPTN;

(ii) Reviewing applications submitted under Sec. 121.9(b) to be a designated transplant program; and

(iii) Conducting ongoing and periodic reviews and evaluations of each member OPO and transplant hospital for compliance with these rules and OPTN policies.

(2) Upon the approval of the Secretary, the OPTN shall furnish review plans and procedures, including survey instruments and a description of data systems, to each member OPO and transplant hospital. The OPTN shall furnish any revisions of these documents to member OPOs and hospitals, after approval by the Secretary, prior to their implementation.

(3) At the request of the Secretary, the OPTN shall conduct special reviews of OPOs and transplant programs, where the Secretary has reason to believe that such entities may not be in compliance with these rules or OPTN policies or may be acting in a manner which poses a risk to the health of patients or to public safety. The OPTN shall conduct these reviews in accordance with such schedules as the Secretary specifies and shall make periodic reports to the Secretary of progress on such reviews and on other reviews conducted under the requirements of this paragraph.

(4) The OPTN shall notify the Secretary in a manner prescribed by the Secretary within 3 days of all committee and Board of Directors meetings in which transplant hospital and OPO compliance with these regulations or OPTN policies is considered.

(c) Enforcement of OPTN rules. (1) OPTN recommendations. The Board of Directors shall advise the Secretary of the results of any reviews and evaluations conducted under paragraph (b)(1)(iii) or paragraph (b)(3) of this section which, in the opinion of the Board, indicate noncompliance with these rules or OPTN policies, or indicate a risk to the health of patients or to the public safety, and shall provide any recommendations for appropriate action by the Secretary. Appropriate action may include removal of designation as a transplant program under Sec. 121.9, termination of a transplant hospital's participation in Medicare or Medicaid, termination of a transplant hospital's reimbursement under Medicare and Medicaid, or termination of an OPO's reimbursement under Medicare and Medicaid, if the noncompliance is with a policy designated by the Secretary as covered by section 1138 of the Social Security Act.

(2) Secretary's action on recommendations. Upon the Secretary's review of the Board of Directors' recommendations, the Secretary may:

(i) Request further information from the Board of Directors or the alleged violator, or both;

(ii) Decline to accept the recommendation;

(iii) Accept the recommendation, and notify the alleged violator of the Secretary's decision; or

(iv) Take such other action as the Secretary deems necessary.

§Sec. 121.11 Record maintenance and reporting requirements.

(a) Record maintenance. Records shall be maintained and made available subject to OPTN policies and applicable limitations based on personal privacy as follows:

(1) The OPTN and the Scientific Registry, as appropriate, shall:

(i) Maintain and operate an automated system for managing information about transplant candidates, transplant recipients, and organ donors, including a computerized national list of individuals waiting for transplants;

(ii) Maintain records of all transplant candidates, all organ donors, and all transplant recipients;

(iii) Operate, maintain, receive, publish, and transmit such records and information electronically, to the extent feasible, except when hard copy is requested; and

(iv) In making information available, provide manuals, forms, flow charts, operating instructions, or other explanatory materials as necessary to understand, interpret, and use the information accurately and efficiently.

(2) Organ procurement organizations and transplant programs. (i) Maintenance of records. All OPOs and transplant programs shall maintain such records pertaining to each potential donor identified, each organ retrieved, each recipient transplanted, and such other transplantation-related matters as the Secretary deems necessary to carry out her/his responsibilities under the Act. The OPO or transplant program shall maintain these records for seven years. (ii) Access to facilities and records. OPOs and transplant hospitals shall permit the Secretary and the Comptroller General, or their designees, to inspect facilities and records pertaining to any aspect of services performed related to organ donation and transplantation.

(b) Reporting requirements. (1) The OPTN and the Scientific Registry, as appropriate, shall:

(i) In addition to special reports which the Secretary may require, submit to the Secretary a report not less than once every fiscal year on a schedule prescribed by the Secretary. The report shall include the following information in a form prescribed by the Secretary:

(A) Information that the Secretary prescribes as necessary to assess the effectiveness of the Nation's organ donation, procurement, and transplantation system;

(B) Information that the Secretary deems necessary for the report to Congress required by Section 376 of the Act; and,

(C) Any other information that the Secretary prescribes.

(ii) Provide to the Scientific Registry data on transplant candidates and recipients, and other information that the Secretary deems appropriate. The information shall be provided in the form and on the schedule prescribed by the Secretary;

(iii) Provide to the Secretary any data that the Secretary requests;

(iv) Make available to the public timely and accurate program-specific information on the performance of transplant programs. This shall include free dissemination over the Internet, and shall be presented, explained, and organized as necessary to understand, interpret, and use the information accurately and efficiently. These data shall be updated no less frequently than every six months and shall include three-month, one-year, three-year and five-year graft and patient survival rates, both actual and statistically expected, and shall be presented no more than six months later than the period to which they apply. Data presented shall include confidence intervals or other measures that provide information on the extent to which chance may influence transplant program-specific results. Such data shall also include such other cost or performance information as the Secretary may specify, including but not limited to transplant program-specific information on waiting time within medical status, organ wastage, and refusal of organ offers. These data shall also be presented no more than six months later than the period to which they apply;

(v) Respond to reasonable requests from the public for data needed for bona fide research or analysis purposes, to the extent that the OPTN's or Scientific Registry's resources permit, or as directed by the Secretary. The OPTN or the Scientific Registry may impose reasonable charges for the separable costs of responding to such requests. Patient-identified data may be made available to bona fide researchers upon a showing that the research design requires such data for matching or other purposes, and that appropriate confidentiality protections, including destruction of patient identifiers upon completion of matching, will be followed. All requests shall be processed expeditiously, with data normally made available within 30 days from the date of request;

(vi) Respond to reasonable requests from the public for data needed to assess the performance of the OPTN or Scientific Registry, to assess individual transplant programs, or for other purposes. The OPTN or Scientific Registry may impose charges for the separable costs of responding to such requests. An estimate of such charges shall be provided to the requester before processing the request. All requests should be processed expeditiously, with data normally made available within 30 days from the date of request; and

(vii) Provide data to an OPTN member, without charge, that has been assembled, stored, or transformed from data originally supplied by that member.

(2) An organ procurement organization or transplant hospital shall, as specified from time to time by the Secretary, submit to the OPTN, to the Scientific Registry, as appropriate, and to the Secretary information regarding transplantation candidates, transplant recipients, donors of organs, transplant program performance, and other information that the Secretary deems appropriate. Such information shall be in the form required and shall be submitted in accordance with the schedule prescribed. No restrictions on subsequent redisclosure may be imposed by any organ procurement organization or transplant hospital.

(c) Public access to data. The Secretary may release to the public information collected under this section when the Secretary determines that the public interest will be served by such release. The information which may be released includes, but is not limited to, information on the comparative costs and patient outcomes at each transplant program affiliated with the OPTN, transplant program personnel, information regarding instances in which transplant programs refuse offers of organs to their patients, information regarding characteristics of individual transplant programs, information regarding waiting time at individual transplant programs, and such other data as the Secretary determines will provide information to patients, their families, and their physicians that will assist them in making decisions regarding transplantation.

§Sec. 121.12 Preemption.

No State or local governing entity shall establish or continue in effect any law, rule, regulation, or other requirement that would restrict in any way the ability of any transplant hospital, OPO, or other party to comply with organ allocation policies of the OPTN or other policies of the OPTN that have been approved by the Secretary under this part.

[FR Doc. 98-8191 Filed 3-26-98; 8:45 am]

E

Committee and Staff Biographies

COMMITTEE BIOGRAPHIES

Edward E. Penhoet, Ph.D. (*Chair*), is dean of the School of Public Health at the University of California, Berkeley, where he is also professor of health policy and administration and professor of molecular and cell biology. Prior to his appointment as dean in 1998, Dr. Penhoet was president and chief executive officer of Chiron Corporation in Emeryville, California. He also taught at the University of California, Berkeley, from 1971 to 1998. Dr. Penhoet received his Ph.D. in biochemistry from the University of Washington in 1968 and was a National Institutes of Health (NIH) postdoctoral fellow at the University of California, San Diego. Dr. Penhoet is active in state and national service organizations including the California Healthcare Institute and the California Governor's Biotechnology Council. At the National Research Council, he serves on the Commission on Life Sciences, the Committee on National Needs for Biomedical and Behavioral Scientists, and the Committee of Undergraduate Science Education. He was a member of the NIH Economic Roundtable on Biomedical Research and was on the board of the National Foundation for Biomedical Research. In 1994, he chaired the NIH Forum on Sponsored Research Agreements. He has also served as a member of the National Science Foundation National Visiting Committee. His awards include the Dreyfus Foundation Teacher-Scholar Award; the 1991 Distinguished Service Award from the University of California, Berkeley; and the Northern California Entrepreneur of the Year Award, which is presented by Ernst & Young, *Inc.* Magazine, and the Harvard Business School.

Naihua Duan, Ph.D., is with the Statistical Group at the RAND Corporation in Santa Monica, California. Dr. Duan holds a Ph.D. in statistics from Stanford University, an M.A. in mathematical statistics from Columbia University, and a B.S. in mathematics from National Taiwan University. His research interests include nonparametric and semiparametric regression methods, sample design, hierarchical models, health care policy, environmental exposure assessment, and intergenerational relationships, and he has published extensively in these areas. He is a member of the Service Research Review Committee and the Behavioral Sciences Workgroup of the National Advisory Mental Health Council at the National Institute of Mental Health. He is also serving as a consultant to the Institute of Medicine Committee on Measuring the Health Status of Persian Gulf Veterans and was a member of the National Academy of Sciences Committee on Advances in Assessing Human Exposure to Airborne Pollutants. He is associate editor of the *Journal of Exposure Assessment and Environmental Epidemiology* and past associate editor of the *Journal of the American Statistical Association and Statistical Sinica.* His honors include the Distinguished Achievement Award from the American Statistical Association Section on Statistics and the Environment in 1994, and he is an elected fellow of the American Statistical Association (1992) and the Institute of Mathematical Statistics (1991). Resigned from committee May 6, 1999 due to a potential conflict of interest.

Nancy Dubler, LL.B., is director of the Division of Bioethics, Department of Epidemiology and Social Medicine, Montefiore Medical Center, and professor of bioethics at the Albert Einstein College of Medicine. She received her B.A. from Barnard College and her LL.B. from Harvard Law School. Ms. Dubler founded the Bioethics Consultation Service at Montefiore Medical Center in 1978 as a support for analysis of difficult cases presenting ethical issues in the health care setting. She lectures extensively and is the author of numerous articles and books on termination of care, home care and long-term care, geriatrics, prison and jail health care, and AIDS. She is co-director of the Certificate Program in Bioethics and the Medical Humanities, conducted jointly by Montefiore Medical Center and the Albert Einstein College of Medicine with the Hartford Institute of Geriatric Nursing at New York University. Her most recent books are *Ethics On Call: Taking Charge of Life and Death Choices in Today's Health Care System*, published by Vintage in 1993, and *Mediating Bioethical Disputes*, published by the United Hospital Fund in New York City in 1994. She consults often with federal agencies, national working groups, and bioethics centers and served as co-chair of the Bioethics Working Group at the National Health Care Reform Task Force.

Charles K. Francis, M.D., is president of the Charles R. Drew University of Medicine and Science, a private academic institution located in south central Los Angeles. Prior to his present position, he was professor of clinical medicine, College of Physicians and Surgeons of Columbia University, and chair, Department of Medicine at the Harlem Hospital Center, New York, New York. Dr. Francis is a native of Newark, New Jersey. He is a graduate of Dartmouth College and received his medical degree from Jefferson Memorial College in Philadelphia. Following his internship at Philadelphia General Hospital, he served as a general medical officer in the U.S. Air Force. He received his training in internal medicine and cardiology at the Boston City Hospital, Massachusetts General Hospital, and Harvard Medical School. He was assistant professor of medicine at the Charles R. Drew Postgraduate Medical School (as it was then known) and the University of Southern California Medical School, and chief of cardiology at the Martin Luther King, Jr., General Hospital. Dr. Francis has served as assistant professor of medicine at the University of Connecticut School of Medicine and was chief of cardiology at the Mount Sinai Hospital in Hartford, Connecticut. He was associate professor of medicine at the Yale University School of Medicine and director of the Cardiac Catheterization Laboratory at Yale-New Haven Hospital. In addition to his interest in health services and medical effectiveness research, he has contributed to literature in the areas of coronary artery disease in African Americans, thrombolysis in myocardial infarction, hypertensive heart disease, and access to medical care and the advancement of health care for minorities. Dr. Francis serves on the Board of Governors of the Warren Magnuson Clinical Center at NIH and served on the National Advisory Council of the National Heart, Lung and Blood Institute (NHLBI) as co-chair of the NHLBI Working Group on Coronary Artery Disease in Blacks. Dr. Francis is chair of the Council on Clinical Cardiology of the American Heart Association, serves on the Board of Regents of the American College of Physicians and the Board of Trustees of the New York Academy of Medicine, and is a member of the Institute of Medicine of the National Academy of Sciences. He is the recipient of the Louis B. Russell Memorial Award presented by the American Heart Association and the Daniel D. Savage, M.D., Memorial Award presented by the Association of Black Cardiologists.

Robert Gibbons, Ph.D., holds joint appointments in the Department of Biometry, School of Public Health, and the Department of Psychiatry, College of Medicine, at the University of Illinois at Chicago. He received his doctorate in statistics and psychometrics from the University of Chicago in 1981. In 1985 he received a Young Scientist Award from the Office of Naval Research, which funded his statistical research in the areas of the analysis of multivariate binary data and the analysis of longitudinal data. Dr. Gibbons has also received additional grant support from NIH and the John D. and Catherine T. MacArthur Foundation. He currently has a Research Scientist Award from the National Institutes of Health that provides full-time support for statistical research. Applications of Dr. Gibbons' work are widespread in the general areas of mental health and environmental sciences. Dr. Gibbons has authored more than 100 peer-reviewed scientific papers and two books. He is working on a book entitled *Statistical Methods for Detection and Quantification of Environmental Contamination*, which will be published by John Wiley & Sons. He served on the Institute of Medicine Committee on Halcion: An Assessment of Data Adequacy and Confidence.

Barbara Gill, R.N., M.N., has been a clinical nurse specialist with Abilene Cardiothoracic and Vascular Surgery since 1992, where her primary focus is on clinical assessment, care planning, case management, and education. Before that she was a fellow with the Annenberg Washington Program, where she served as primary investigator, adviser, and program facilitator in public policy studies of communications issues in critical medical decisions. Study topics included transplantation, patient self-determination, and professional education relating to health care public policy. As director of education for the Partnership for Organ Donation, she established and directed a multicity, multihospital education program. Ms. Gill received a master's of nursing from the University of Kansas in 1981. She holds a faculty appointment at the San Angelo State University and has taught at the School of Nursing at the University of Kansas and the School of Nursing at the University of Missouri. She has published widely in the areas of cardiac patient care and transplantation and serves on the editorial boards of *Critical Care Nurse, Heart & Lung*, and the *Journal of Acute and Critical Care.* Ms. Gill is a member of the Board of Directors of the Certification Corporation at the American Association of Critical Care Nurses, the Sigma Theta Tau National Nursing Honorary Society, and the American Nurses Association.

Eva Guinan, M.D., is a pediatric oncologist and associate professor of pediatrics at Harvard Medical School, where she earned her M.D. in 1980. She is board certified in pediatrics with a subspecialty in pediatric hematology–oncology and serves as director of the Bone Marrow Transplant Service at Children's Hospital in Boston. Dr. Guinan's research interests, supported by funding from the National Institutes of Health, include acquired and congenital marrow failure syndromes, clinical application of hematopoietic factors, and novel immunologic approaches to alternative donor allogeneic bone marrow transplantation. She has published extensively in these areas and serves on the editorial board of *Pediatric Transplantation.* Dr. Guinan is a member of the American Society of Hematology, the Pediatric Oncology Group, the Society for Pediatric Research, and the American Society of Bone Marrow Transplantation.

Maureen Henderson, M.D., D.P.H., is professor emeritus of epidemiology and medicine at the University of Washington. Dr. Henderson received both her M.B.B.S. and her D.P.H. degrees from the School of Medicine, University of Durham, England. She has served as professor of epidemiology and professor of medicine at the University of Washington; founder and head of the Cancer Prevention Research Program at the Fred Hutchinson Cancer Research Center; director for community liaison at the Fred Hutchinson Cancer Research Center; associate vice president for health sciences at the University of Washington; chair of the Department of Social and Preventive Medicine at the University of Maryland School of Medicine; and associate director of the Regional Medical Program, Epidemiology and Statistics Center, at the Johns Hopkins University. Dr. Henderson has been a member of numerous national and international boards, including the National Cancer Advisory Board, and is a member of the Institute of Medicine of the National Academy of Sciences.

Suzanne T. Ildstad, M.D., is director of the Institute for Cellular Therapeutics and professor of surgery, Department of Surgery, at the University of Louisville. Dr. Ildstad received her medical degree from the Mayo Medical School in Rochester, Minnesota, followed by a residency in general surgery at Massachusetts General Hospital in Boston. After completing a medical staff fellowship in immunology at the NIH, where she, with Dr. David Sachs, established the model for mixed hematopoietic stem cell chimerism, and a pediatric surgery–transplant surgery fellowship in Cincinnati, Dr. Ildstad joined the faculty at the University of Pittsburgh. She is the director of the Institute for Cellular Therapeutics and a professor in the Department of Surgery at the University of Louisville in Louisville, Kentucky. Her research on mixed chimerism to induce tolerance to organ allografts and treat nonmalignant diseases such as sickle cell anemia and autoimmune disorders is currently being applied clinically in six Food and Drug Administration (FDA) approved Phase I trials. She is actively involved in numerous professional associations and has been the recipient of numerous awards and honors. Dr. Ildstad holds several patents related to her research in expanding bone marrow transplantation to treat nonmalignant diseases by optimizing the risk–benefit ratio through graft engineering and partial conditioning. She is the founding scientist of Chimeric Therapies, Inc., a biotechnology company focused on bone marrow graft engineering, and she serves on the board of directors of the company. Dr. Ildstad has been a member of the Institute of Medicine since 1997 and is serving as correspondent for the Committee on Human Rights.

Patricia A. King, J.D., is professor of law at Georgetown University Law Center. Ms. King received her B.A. from Wheaton College and her J.D. from Harvard Law School. She is the Carmack Waterhouse Professor of Law, Medicine, Ethics and Public Policy at Georgetown University Law Center. She is also an adjunct professor in the Department of Health Policy and Management, School of Hygiene and Public Health, at Johns Hopkins University. She is the coauthor of *Cases and Materials on Law, Science, and Medicine* and an area editor of the *Encyclopedia of Bioethics*. She is a member of the American Law Institute and the Institute of Medicine, a fellow of the Hastings Center, and a senior research scholar at the Kennedy Institute of Ethics. Her work in the field of bioethics has included service as co-chair for policy of the Embryo Research Panel, National Institutes of Health; the U.S. Department of Health, Education, and Welfare Recombinant DNA Advisory Committee; the President's Commission for the Study of Ethical Problems in Medicine and Biomedical and Behavioral Research; the National Commission for the Protection of Human Subjects of Biomedical and Behavioral Research; and the Ethics, Legal and Social Issues Working Group of the Human Genome Project. She is active with medical and health professional organizations and serves on the Board of Advisors of the

American Board of Internal Medicine and on the Institute of Medicine Council. She is also a member of the boards of the National Partnership for Women and Families and the Hospice Foundation. She is a trustee of Wheaton College. Her professional experience before joining the Georgetown University Law Center was primarily in the civil rights field; she was the deputy director of the Office of Civil Rights at the U.S. Department of Health, Education, and Welfare and special assistant to the chairman of the Equal Employment Opportunity Commission. She also served as a deputy assistant attorney general in the Civil Division of the U.S. Department of Justice.

Manuel Martinez-Maldonado, M.D., is professor of medicine and vice provost for research at the Oregon Health Sciences University in Portland. He is a board-certified nephrologist. He received his training at the University of Texas Southwestern Medical School in Dallas. He has held professorships at Baylor College of Medicine, the University of Puerto Rico, and Emory School of Medicine. He has also taught at Harvard and Vanderbilt. He has served on numerous NIH committees, most recently on the Board of Scientific Counselors of the NHLBI. His research interests include prevention, detection, and treatment of renal diseases, the use of renal replacement technology in developing countries, the effect of nutrition on kidney function and disturbances in body fluid composition, and the effects of hypertension on kidney function. He was elected to the Institute of Medicine in 1987 and most recently served on the Committee on Health and Human Rights.

George E. McLain, M.D., is assistant chief of the Anesthesia Department and medical director of the Surgery Centers at Martin Memorial Hospital in Stuart, Florida. Dr. McLain received his medical degree from Northwestern University in 1973 and completed his internship and residency in anesthesia at Wilford Hall Medical Center at Lackland Air Force Base. He then served at Wilford Hall until 1980 as coordinator of resident education, primary cardiac anesthesiologist, and assistant chief of the Department of Anesthesia. Dr. McLain also completed a fellowship at the University of Arizona College of Medicine in 1997. He is board certified in anesthesiology and holds memberships in the Florida Society of Anesthesiology, the American Medical Association, the Florida Medical Association, and the American Society of Anesthesiologists.

David Meltzer, M.D., Ph.D., is an assistant professor in the Department of Medicine and an associated faculty member of the Harris School of Public Policy Studies and the Department of Economics at the University of Chicago. Dr. Meltzer received his M.D. and Ph.D. in economics from the University of Chicago in 1993. He completed his residency in internal medicine at Brigham and Women's Hospital in Boston. He graduated from Yale University in 1986 with distinction in economics and in molecular biophysics and biochemistry. Dr. Meltzer serves on the faculty of the Robert Wood Johnson Clinical Scholars Program, the Graduate Program in Health Administration and Policy, the Population Research Center, and the Center on Aging. His research explores problems in health economics and public policy. His recent work has focused on the theoretical foundations of medical cost-effectiveness analysis, including issues such as accounting for future costs due to the extension of life and the empirical validity of quality-of-life assessment, which he has examined in the context of diabetes and prostate cancer. Other work concerns the effects of physician experience and of managed care on the cost and quality of patient care and the educational process in teaching hospitals, the role of mortality decline in the economic growth and demographic transition of developing countries, and the effects of FDA regulation on innovation in the pharmaceutical industry. Dr. Meltzer is the recipient of numerous awards, including an NIH Medical Scientist Training Program Fellowship, a National Science Foundation Graduate Fellowship in Economics, the University of Chicago Searle Fellowship, the Lee Lusted Prize and Outstanding Paper by a Young Investigator Award from the Society for Medical Decision Making, the Health Care Research Award of the National Institute for Health Care Management, the Robert Wood Johnson Generalist Physician Award, and an Olin Foundation Faculty Fellowship. He is also a faculty research fellow for the National Bureau of Economic Research and recently served on a panel that examined the future of Medicare for the National Academy of Social Insurance.

Joseph E. Murray, M.D., is professor of surgery, emeritus, at Harvard Medical School. He is a pioneer in the transplantation of organs. After extensive laboratory studies at Harvard Medical School's Surgical Research Laboratory, Dr. Murray carried out the first successful human kidney transplantation between identical twins in 1954. He also achieved the first successful kidney transplant between fraternal twins in 1959, and performed the first successful allotransplantation under immunosuppressive chemotherapy, the model for organ transplantation. Dr. Murray was awarded the Nobel Prize in Physiology or Medicine in 1990 for his pioneering work in solid organ transplantation. Dr. Murray is a member of the Institute of Medicine. Previously he was a member of the National Research Council Office on Public Understanding of Science Advisory Committee and committees of the Commission on Life Sciences. Dr. Murray's expertise and research interests are general surgery, plastic surgery, and transplantation surgery.

Dorothy Nelkin holds a university professorship at New York University, where she is professor of sociology and affiliated professor in the School of Law. She was formerly at Cornell University. Her research focuses on controversial areas of science, technology, and medicine as a means to understand their social and political implications and the relationship of science to the public. This work includes studies of antiscience movements, and the impact of technology, science policy, and media communications on science and risk. She has recently written a book on the uses of the diagnostic test emerging from research in genetics and on hereditary themes in popular culture. She is presently working on a study of the value of body tissue in the biotechnology age. Ms. Nelkin is a member of the National Academy of Sciences' Institute of Medicine. She has served on the Board of Directors of the American Association for the Advancement of Science and the National Academy of Sciences Committee on a National Strategy for AIDS. She has been a Guggenheim fellow and a visiting scholar at the Russell Sage Foundation.

Mitchell W. Spellman, M.D., Ph.D., is director of Academic Alliances and International Exchange Programs at Harvard Medical International. Dr. Spellman is also professor of surgery, emeritus, and dean for medical services, emeritus, at Harvard Medical School and is honorary senior surgeon at Beth Israel Hospital. He was formerly professor of surgery at Charles R. Drew Postgraduate Medical School and professor of surgery at the School of Medicine, University of California, Los Angeles. He received his M.D. from Howard University and his Ph.D. from the University of Minnesota. Dr. Spellman has served on numerous boards of directors, including those of the National Medical Association Foundation, the Duke University Medical Center, and the Kaiser Foundation Health Plan, and on the Board of the Massachusetts Institute of Technology Corporation. Some of his memberships in professional and academic societies include the American Surgical Association, American College of Cardiology, American College of Surgeons, and the Institute of Medicine of the National Academy of Sciences. In recognition of his contributions to the field, Dr. Spellman has been the recipient of numerous awards and honors.

IOM PROJECT STAFF

Andrew Pope, Ph.D., is director of the Division of Health Sciences Policy at the Institute of Medicine and served as study director for the Organ Procurement and Transplantation Policy study. With expertise in physiology, toxicology, and epidemiology, his primary interests focus on environmental and occupational influences on human health. Dr. Pope's previous research activities focused on the biochemical, neuroendocrine, and reproductive effects of various environmental substances on food-producing animals. During his tenure at the National Academy of Sciences and since 1989 at the Institute of Medicine, Dr. Pope has directed and edited numerous reports on environmental and occupational issues; topics include injury control, disability prevention, biologic markers, neurotoxicology, indoor allergens, and the inclusion of environmental and occupational health content in medical and nursing school curricula. Most recently, Dr. Pope directed the fast-track study on NIH priority-setting processes, and a review of fluid resuscitation practices in combat casualties.

Christine Domzal, Ph.D., was a senior project officer in the IOM's Division of Health Sciences Policy. She received her doctorate in applied social psychology from George Washington University, with an emphasis in research methods, program evaluation, and data analysis. With prior experience in a consulting firm, Dr. Domzal has directed projects under management support contracts with federal clients including the U.S. Department of Education and the U.S. Department of Defense (Health Affairs). Her projects included analysis of data from a longitudinal study of Army officer careers, long-range and strategic planning, quality management in the military health system, and disability statistics. She has also worked as a research analyst at the General Accounting Office and the National Science Foundation and as a legislative assistant in the U.S. Senate. Dr. Domzal is a member of the American Evaluation Association and the Washington Statistical Society. She resigned from the IOM staff on May 7, 1999.

Sarah Pitluck, M.S., is a research assistant for the Organ Procurement and Transplantation study. She is also a research assistant for the IOM Roundtable on Environmental Health Sciences, Research, and Medicine. She received her undergraduate degree in political science at Washington University in St. Louis, Missouri, before completing her master's degree in public policy and public administration at the London School of Economics and Political Science. Sarah's master's thesis addresses the sources of divergent policies toward screening for prostate cancer in the United States and United Kingdom.

Alden Chang is a project assistant in the Division of Health Sciences Policy. He has been with the IOM since February 1999 and is also working on the Committee to Assess Occupational Safety and Health Training Needs. Alden earned his bachelor's degree in International Relations from The George Washington University, Washington, D.C.

Glen Shapiro was a research assistant in the Division of Health Sciences Policy for the Organ Procurement and Transplantation study. He also provided support for the Committee on Fluid Resuscitation for Combat Casualties and the Committee on Environmental Justice. Glen earned his bachelor's degree in Russian language and literature at Wesleyan University, Middletown, Connecticut. He resigned from the IOM to attend medical school on June 4, 1999.

Stephanie Smith was a research associate in the IOM Division of Health Sciences Policy, working for the Committee on Organ Procurement and Transplantation Policy. She returned to IOM while pursuing her M.S. in health–fitness management at American University and performing independent research on bone mineral density in postmenopausal women. While previously working at the IOM for three years, she supported the Board on International Health and the Division of Health Promotion and Disease Prevention. Her undergraduate degree is in international relations and Spanish. She resigned from the IOM staff on June 1, 1999.

Thelma L. Cox is a project assistant in the Division of Health Sciences Policy. During her seven years at the Institute of Medicine (IOM), she has also provided assistance to the Division of Health Care Services and the Division of Biobehavioral Sciences and Mental Disorders. Ms. Cox has worked on several IOM reports, including *Designing a Strategy for Quality Review and Assurance in Medicare*; *Evaluating the Artificial Heart Program of the National Heart, Lung, and Blood Institute*; *Federal Regulation of Methadone Treatment; Legal and Ethical Issues Relating to the Inclusion of Women in Clinical Studies*; and *Review of the Fialuridine (FIAU/FIAC) Clinical Trials*. She has received the National Research Council Recognition Award and the IOM Staff Achievement Award.

Carlos Gabriel is the financial associate for the Division of Health Sciences Policy. Carlos graduated from California State University at Los Angeles with a degree in Mathematics and a minor in Business. He briefly taught mathematics at the high school level and has many years of experience in the field of finance and analysis, having worked in this capacity for a large real estate development company, banks, insurance companies, and in the audit department of Price Waterhouse prior to joining the Academy. He has been working for The National Academies as a financial associate since 1989.

Index

A

B

C

D

E

F

L

M

N

O

P

Q

R